THE ADVENTURES

OF A

ROVING DIPLOMATIST.

BY

HENRY WIKOFF,

AUTHOR OF "MY COURTSHIP AND ITS CONSEQUENCES."

King.—What do you call the play?
Hamlet.—The mousetrap.
HAMLET, *Act* III. *Scene* 2.

NEW YORK:
W. P. FETRIDGE & CO., PUBLISHERS,
HARPERS' BUILDINGS—FRANKLIN SQUARE.

1857.

PRINTED BY
E. N. GROSSMAN,
82 Beekman-st.

TO

HENRY LORD BROUGHAM,

HUMANI GENERIS DECUS,

This Volume

IS RESPECTFULLY INSCRIBED,

BY HIS HUMBLE FRIEND,

THE AUTHOR.

INTRODUCTION.

THIS book is of so personal a nature as to require some explanation, if not an excuse. It is easy to make the first, and it is hoped the last will prove as acceptable. In a volume published nearly two years since, "My Courtship and its Consequences," I related, with extreme candor, the remarkable vicissitudes that befell me in pursuit of a wife; but no portion of this singular narrative appeared to excite more surprise than the strange fact that I was immured fifteen months in a Genoese prison for no other offense than obtaining a stolen interview with the object of my *penchant.* I made it apparent enough that this unjustifiable outrage was perpetrated through the active instrumentality of the British consul at Genoa; but the American public was at a loss to know what insidious motive could urge such a person to so extraordinary an interference, and next, how so humble an official could wield such power over a court of law, even though it existed in Italy. The clue to this mystery was in my hands at the time, but I considered it indiscreet to make, then, the revelations contained in the present volume. The misrepresentations launched against me *en masse* in the English press, and naturally copied into our own, had so prejudiced the public mind against me, that I thought it first necessary to convince all impartial persons that I was wholly innocent of any legal or moral offense at Genoa that could justify the unprovoked persecution I suffered there. This object has been fully achieved by the flattering success that attended the story of my wooing already alluded to, and which has been received with implicit belief by the reading public, since no one of the many who figured in its details has ventured to gainsay a single assertion, or even to quibble over a single line.

Thus entirely relieved of the cloud of suspicions that cunning calumny had thrown over me, and fortified by the conviction, now generally entertained, that I was caught in the meshes of some artful conspiracy, I presume to appeal once more to public confidence while I seek to disclose the occult purpose that led to my imprisonment at Genoa, as well as the secret aim of all the odious attempts made to traduce me in England and elsewhere. It will then be seen that the lady who has hitherto been regarded as my fair persecutor was, in fact, only a screen and a pretext; and that the British consul, who has been supposed her champion, was, in truth, merely the instrument for effecting the covert designs of another party; and finally, that the party in question was no other and no less than the British Minister for Foreign Affairs, Lord Viscount Palmerston.

Such a statement as this may seem, at first sight, incredible. What could Lord Palmerston have to do by any concatenation of events with my former *fiancée*, Miss Gamble, or with the British consul, Brown, and my love-adventure at Genoa in 1851? It is just the solution of this romantic imbroglio at which this volume aims; and it is my hope, that the reader who wandered through the intricate mazes of my "Courtship," and who may from curiosity or interest pick up this sequel, will discover in its pages ample proofs that my misfortune at Genoa is less due to the thoughtlessness of a woman than to the craft of a callous politician. At all events, the tale, in all its phases, will only tend to confirm the fact that in this nether world of ours the wildest romance is often found fantastically blended with the gravest incidents of reality.

What I have said may serve as some explanation of the present publication, and my excuse for it is short and simple. It is true I felt the most poignant reluctance to make public the secret relations I once held with a leading minister of the British government, not only from a deep sense of propriety, but from the respect I have always entertained for Lord Palmerston, in spite of his harsh behavior to me. Still, it was necessary that the public imputation on my veracity by the British consul at Genoa, who declared that I never had any connection with the English government, should be as publicly removed; and furthermore, I considered that some atonement was due for all the disrepute and suffering so wantonly heaped on me. Up to this moment Lord Palmerston has, for his own reasons, constantly thought fit to decline giving me his co-operation to obtain either the one or the other. I submit, then, as incontestable, not only my right, but the propriety of my laying this second vindication before the world, for this is one of those cases that not unfrequently occur, where law and equity afford no remedy, but where the ends of justice are satisfied by the sympathy and support of the public.

I trust it will be admitted that in defending myself I have shown sufficient forbearance toward others, and that I have not sought to enhance the interest of my book, at the expense of my self-respect, by any ostentatious parade of important disclosures, or even by an unreserved revelation of matters which I did not deem necessary to my justification.

In the course of my narrative I have found it necessary to enter into a somewhat careful record of events in France during an epoch of extreme interest, beginning with the presidency of the Prince Louis Napoleon, and ending with the *coup d'etat* which elevated him to the throne. This portion of my book I beg to recommend to the attentive perusal of the reading public, and I venture to hope that after the most searching investigation and the keenest critical analysis, it will be finally pronounced an impartial and faithful sketch of the rise and fall of the late French Republic. The cause of truth, as well as their own interests, demand that the people of the United States should form a correct and independent opinion of European events, and it is hardly less than a misfortune for us that we are in the habit of taking all our views of transatlantic affairs from the English press. It is in the nature of things that the journalists of England should form conclusions corresponding to their own point of view, and which are necessarily more or less shaped and colored by personal prejudice and national interest. The public of this country are, consequently, often led astray by adopting too confidingly the judgments of England upon the facts of European history, and more especially upon the affairs of France. I do not hesitate to accuse the English press of frequently misrepresenting both men and things in France, to serve party purposes or to pamper national illusions.

Under these circumstances, is it not the manifest duty of American journalism to investigate facts for themselves, and, guided solely by their own intelligence, to draw such deductions as are conformable to truth and logic? It should be remembered that the safety of the oligarchy and the duration of parliamentary government in England, depend on the deliberate distortion of events both in France and the

United States. This may serve to explain those singular and startling oscillations of the leading English journal, the London *Times*, which at one period denounces the French emperor as a tyrant, and at the next lavishes upon him the most eloquent panegyric. The *Times* is obliged to steer its difficult course between the necessity of supporting its own national organization, and the expediency of not assailing the institutions of its formidable neighbor, France. Happily, there is no reason under heaven why the press of this country should seek to throw dust in the eyes of the people, or any why they should not assert their independence of English journalism by declaring their own unbiased sentiments when reliable information is offered them. The statements of an American upon matters that have passed under his personal observation may be received without suspicion, and are entitled to consideration. It may be thought by some that my former acquaintance with the Emperor of France may have induced me to color his best acts too highly, or to throw an artful *mirage* over his more doubtful ones. The most emphatic assertions to the contrary would avail nothing, and all I ask, therefore, is a calm, thorough, and impartial examination of my unpretending narrative of recent events in France. I challenge the utmost scrutiny, and I await without apprehension the verdict of public opinion. Let it always be borne in mind that to France we are indebted, to say nothing of revolutionary obligations, for two of the ablest books that have ever appeared on our country. The institutions and material resources of the United States have received at the hands of M. de Tocqueville and M. Michel Chevalier, an elucidation and a record not more remarkable for fidelity than the friendly spirit that inspired them. It is, therefore, doubly incumbent on every American, when writing of France, not to pronounce a judgment upon her institutions or men based upon the English or American standard of right and wrong, but rather to look dispassionately at both, in order to discover if the first are not in conformity with historical antecedents, and the last the mere passive instruments of some overruling necessity. In this clear, philosophical light let the history of the French Republic of 1848 be regarded, and it is not to be doubted that the American opinion of its prominent actors will differ widely from that which may be entertained in other countries.

HENRY WIKOFF.

NEW YORK, November 22, 1856.

CONTENTS.

CHAPTER IV.

A DINNER AT THE ELYSÉE.

CHAPTER V.

THE LAST REVOLT.

CHAPTER VI.

A LITERARY ADVENTURE.

CHAPTER VII.

THE VISCOUNT PALMERSTON.

CHAPTER VIII.

A VISIT TO THE FOREIGN OFFICE.

CHAPTER IX.

A DIPLOMATIC TRIUMPH.

CHAPTER X.

THE GAUNTLET RAISED.

CHAPTER XI.

A MISUNDERSTANDING.

CHAPTER XII.

A TRIP TO LILLE.

CHAPTER XIII.

A REPRIEVE.

CHAPTER XIV.

THE DIE CAST.

CHAPTER XV.

THE DENOUEMENT.

CHAPTER XVI.

A PRETEXT.

CHAPTER XVII.

FOREIGN OFFICE VERSUS THE UNITED STATES.

CHAPTER THE LAST.

THE LEX TALIONIS.

APPENDIX.

THE ADVENTURES

OF A

ROVING DIPLOMATIST.

THE ADVENTURES

OF A

ROVING DIPLOMATIST.

CHAPTER I.

A RETROSPECT.

I embarked in February, 1849, in the good steamer Herman, bound from New York to Southampton, on my way to France, my fourteenth passage across the Atlantic. This fact must sufficiently attest the interest with which I had regarded the progress of affairs in Europe for many years past, as well as the opportunities that must have been afforded for familiarising myself with the real meaning of events, and the true motives of those who had instigated or profitted by them. I remembered no instance when I had set off on a visit to Europe with my feelings so keenly stirred as on the present occasion, and certainly the political hurricane that had swept over Europe in 1848 had left such startling proofs of its intensity and ravages as must have aroused the dullest mind. How much more, then, was my curiosity stimulated, who had so often contemplated the men and scenes that now lie buried under the Alpine avalanche that had so suddenly descended, and who was accustomed to mix so often in the society of those who were either the victims of these disasters, or the more fortunate participators in that which had succeeded. There was nothing on shipboard to divert my attention, and my mind found constant aliment, therefore, the entire voyage in contrasting the condition of France as I left it in the spring of '47, having passed the winter there, with all the incredible changes that had since transpired, and which, urged by an insatiable curiosity, I was on my road to contemplate.

Louis Philippe was, *then*, King of the French. His royal brow, so often shadowed over by threatening perils and perplexing fear of change, beamed, at last, with a sense of complete security. His smile was radiant, his confidence unbounded. He believed his dynasty permanently established.

M. Guizot was, *then*, Prime Minister. His majority, in the Chamber of Deputies, was so strong, that he treated the Opposition with contempt. When they declared that a suffrage of less than 200,000 for a population of thirty-five millions was a mockery, the arrogant Minister replied, "It is enough," and turned his back upon them. Thus, the King swayed his Minister; the Minister ruled the Chamber; and the Chamber dictated to France. This was the political situation, and the structure was skilfully constructed, and seemed firm enough.

The literary world was then in a state of violent fermentation. The "Girondists" was just published. Lamartine, its author, selecting the most striking epoch of the first revolution, had depicted its fierce commotions with thrilling power. The ex-page of Charles X. announced himself the apologist of Robespierre, and extenuated the terrible excesses of the Reign of Terror. The aristocratic world was horrified, but the people were not indifferent to this startling transformation.

The journals were, *then*, discussing electoral reform. The organs of Government derided boldly any increase of the franchise, whilst the Opposition prints contended modestly that the national mind was not fairly represented. Such an extravagant idea as universal suffrage never entered the brain of any serious person.

The financial world, *then*, was absorbed in all the vicissitudes of railway speculation, and Rothschild wielded the golden wand that had once broken in the grasp of the scheming John Law.

The fashionable world was never gayer than in the winter of '47.

The middle classes were busy in the pursuit of gain, and satisfied with the results.

The masses were occupied, industrious, and calm. Were they as content as silent; no one knew or cared. This was the aspect of things in April of '47. France seemed tranquil, prosperous, and happy.

I was not deceived, though, by the blue sky overhead, for I had scanned the whole horizon round, and knew there were portentous clouds gathering. My short sojourn in Paris in the winter of '47 was given to frequent interviews with the leading intellects of France, *les grands esprits*, both actors and thinkers. I passed from one to the other, discussing France and her destiny. Their elocution was brilliant, their views striking, but their conclusions universally differed, for each started from his own point of view. I thought it idle to analyse how far self-interest, or partriotism, or conviction, may have swayed their opinions, but one distinct impression I bore away with me, viz., that all the leading men of France, with a single exception, seemed plunged in a sea of doubt, both of themselves and their doctrines. None knew the present, none thought of the past, none penetrated the future. They seemed to me like so many gamesters at *rouge et noir*, each playing his stake with more or less composure, but all blindly uncertain of the results.

I breakfasted often at this epoch with Louis Blanc, and peering into his intelligent face, sought to fathom the mysteries of Socialism. He talked most eloquently, but when I desired to examine the machinery of his system, he hesitated. His theory was not yet in governmental shape.

I dropped in occasionally on M. Marrast, Editor of the *National*, the democratic journal.

"If the monarchy falls," I asked, "what then?"

"The Republic," he exclaimed!

"What kind of Republic?"

"*Cela depend*" (that depends), and he explained no further. I saw the contemplated French Republic was in a nebulous state.

I observed on one occasion to M. de Lamartine, "Your book is making a deep sensation."

"I am glad of it," he returned, "for my publisher gave me a large sum. Here, take the prospectus with you for your friends."

Strange that the illustrious author thought only of the pecuniary success of his book, little dreaming, likely, of the blow he had given the monarchy.

I went to the house of M. Thiers, one evening, with his friend, the Prince de la Moskowa. M. Thiers was the chief *accoucheur* of Louis Philippe's dynasty, but was supplanted, at last, by his rival Guizot. I inferred his discontent, and ventured to touch a new chord. I spoke to him opportunely of the Prince Louis Napoleon. He listened. I continued my remarks, when, at length, he said, "How old is he?" A word from such a man is a volume. I divined his thought, to wit, that the Prince was young enough to wait till he had Bonapartized France more deeply with his magnificent history of the Consulate and the Empire.

I discussed one morning with the brilliant chivalric Berryer the chances of the old monarchy.

"Will it ever return?" I queried.

"Why not," he said; "it returned once, and may it not again?"

Many more remarkable men I had the good fortune to meet at the moment I speak of, but each, as I have shown, was sailing in a bark of his own and to a different and uncertain haven. The interview that affected me most was that, which, after great difficulty, I obtained with the illustrious Chateaubriand. He was broken down in health and confined to his bed-room, where for a couple of hours daily he was propped up in a chair. His family alone were admitted, and I was the last stranger that ever approached him. He sat, as I entered, with his venerable head drooping on his breast, plunged apparently in stupor. I conversed in a low tone with his nephew, the Marquis de ———. Our conversation gradually wandered on to politics, when the nephew talked of the restoration some day of his legitimate King. Chateaubriand shook his head slowly but spoke not. After a pause we went on, commenting on the career of the existing Monarchy, and in the course of a little time the Patriarch with difficulty raised his head, his eye gazing on vacancy. "*Cela ira comme tout le reste. L'avenir est au peuple.*" (That will pass like all the rest. The future belongs to the people.) His voice was sepulchral, and the words seemed to struggle up from his heart. His head sank downward again, and soon after I withdrew. How solemn and emphatic this renunciation of all his efforts, of all his hopes. Chateaubriand gave Christianity back to France, but his last breath closed it against that Royal race to whom his ancestors for centuries had faithfully clung.

I spoke of a single exception, amongst all the great intellects I encountered, that seemed to have come to a clear and positive conclusion. I sat one day at an open casement with an old man, whose thin grey locks fluttered in the gentle breeze of spring. His face overflowed with benevolence; the fire of genius sparkled in his eye. This was the Abbé Lammenais, first a Priest of Rome, and last a fervent Democrat, and the writer whose burning words had seared deepest the popular heart of France. His tones were calm and deep like his conviction.

"Then, the Monarchy of July," I said as I rose.

"Dead."

"Its elder brother '—

"Dead."

"May they not revisit France ?"

"Like spectres—only to vanish."

"The Bonapartes"—

"Yes, in their turn."

"The Republic"—

"Inevitable."

"Will it stand ?"

"It matters not."

"Wherefore ?" His eye wandered over the plains to a distant point.

"Because in its arms only can France, the world, find rest."

I have thus glanced briefly at the smiling surface of French Society in '47, and as hurriedly pointed at the powerful under-currents that were percolating beneath.

I passed from Paris at the time in question, on my return home, through London. I found there the Prince Louis Napoleon, curious to know my recent impressions of men and things in France. It was at three different epochs, what contrasts! I had met this remarkable man. First, in 1840, I sat opposite to him at the hospitable table of his uncle, the good King Joseph, in London. He was then only known to the world as the youthful insurgent of Italy, the unfortunate conspirator of Strasburg, and the proscribed citizen of Switzerland. His career excited interest, his aspirations to the Imperial sceptre challenged curiosity. Short of stature, of symmetrical form, graceful address, distinguished appearance, a lofty bearing that was rather military than haughty—these were features easily discerned. His countenance was an enigma that defied penetration. Neither passion, nor emotion, nor thought had left any trace. The brow was calm. The eyes had an inverted look, as though steadily fixed on some inward thought. No outward indication gave token of the inner man. Impassibility wrapped him round like a mantle. Was it only a disguise, and what was concealed beneath? I was foiled, but fascinated by the mystery that enveloped him, and from that hour I put a singular faith in his star. The Prince lived in splendour, was fêted and followed, and no one suspected the scheme then maturing in his mind.

Next, in 1845, I obtained, with much effort, access to his prison at Ham. Five years of captivity, defeat, ingratitude, desertion, all had done their worst, but in his dungeon, as in the saloons of London, he was still master of himself, and superior to fate. His mind clear, his spirit firm, his hopes the same. I left him again as I left him before—a believer in his destiny. I remember well the ridicule that assailed my predictions in Paris and elsewhere in 1845, but what I thought I wrote, and the Prisoner for life thus endorsed the prophecy he had inspired.

Ham, le 11 Octobre, 1845.

MONSIEUR—

Je vous renvoie les deux premiéres feuilles de votre manuscrit el je vous en remercie sincérement. Il est impossible de mettre plus de tact, de bon gout, et d'esprit que vous en avez fait dans votre relation de votre voyage à Ham. Il n'y a pas un mot à changer.

* * * * *

N'oubliez pas lorsque vous irez en Angleterre de me donner une adresse pour vous écrire et recevez de nouveau l'assurance de mes sentimens d'estime et d'amitié.

NAPOLEON LOUIS.

[TRANSLATION.]

Ham, the 11th October, 1845.

SIR—

I return to you the first two sheets of your manuscript, and I thank you sincerely. It is impossible to display more tact, good taste, and talent than you have done in the recital of your trip to Ham. There is not a word to change.

* * * * *

Do not forget when you leave for England to send to me an address where to write to you, and receive anew the assurances of my sentiments of esteem and friendship.

NAPOLEON LOUIS.

It was no fanaticism in the Prince, nor a fantasy of mine, for I believed, and the captive of Ham well knew, that in the heart of the French peasant lay smouldering the memory of the first Napoleon, a soldier of the people, and that one day the masses would summon a second Napoleon to their head.

Last, in 1847, I encountered the Prince again, who was once more a denizen of London. Neither exhilarated by freedom, nor depressed by *ennui*, he wore the same imperturbable air that had captivated me at first, and that astonished me at last. He lived tranquilly:

books—some chosen friends—simple amusements—this was the small orbit in which he moved, and appeared to know no world beyond. His moderate language, gentle gesture, mild regard; his slow movement, kind disposition, who could reconcile with these a boundless ambition, reckless courage, fiery ardour, an inflexible will, a commanding intellect, and yet stranger than all the rest, these singular contradictions, these powerful elements, were all covered over by a thick panoply which the superficial thought apathy, but which the keenest could not penetrate. So deeply buried within himself, his character was a problem none might hope to solve, and all could differently interpret. His opinions, his reflections, his intentions, who knew them? His theories, his politics, his schemes, what were they?

It was a curious study to contrast this imposing reserve, this marvellous self-control, with the overflowing intelligence and animated character of his younger cousin Napoleon (son of Jerome), living with him in London at the last named date. One day I accompanied the Princes to a hunt, and whilst driving to the rendezvous the conversation turned on war—what a theme for the heirs of the Imperial Dynasty! The young Napoleon was eloquent, historical, convincing; the Prince Louis was brief, precise but grave, as such a subject demanded. He neither discussed nor reasoned, but occasionally intervened between his cousin and myself with a sententious remark that had the effect of a judicial *resumé*. War, he admitted, might be a necessity; but it was impossible to foresee whether he would accept or resist it. My surprise was all the greater at what followed. Leaving the domains of reason for that of fact, the Princes mounted their horses, and, once in action, their characters seemed exchanged. The Prince Louis was daring, impetuous, and audacious; his cousin, on the contrary, was prudent, careful, and calculating. The one dashed headlong after his object, the other sought it with less risk.

In bidding the Prince Louis adieu, I referred to the past. "I am resigned," was his reply. I glanced at the future without a promise. He smiled serenely, whilst he spoke. "*J'attends les evénemens*" (I am waiting events), were his significant words. He seemed not to doubt that they would come to his aid; but who could then imagine them so near?

It was with recollections like these, and with all the random musings they suggested, that made my Atlantic trip seem a short and easy one. When I reflected that in the brief interval that had transpired since the incidents I have just related, a moral earthquake had swept over Europe, and that the monarch I had left with the sceptre so firm in his gripe was now fugitive and forlorn, and that the man whom some thought mad, and all a dreamer, was the sovereign elect of France, I felt almost disposed to doubt my reason, and was really bewildered at such stupendous changes in the fortunes of men and the fate of nations. I had read of them and pondered over them, and marvelled, but till I could witness them I felt as though my incredulity would never cease.

CHAP. II.

FRANCE REPUBLICANIZED.

I had no sooner landed at Southampton than I hurried across the Channel, impatient to see the fresh traces of the strange transformation that had occurred. The old port of Havre, with its granite quays, its stone houses, and rampart of hills behind, looked as solid and immovable in its republican youth as in the monarchical years they had defied. The familiar tricolour fluttered from tower and mast-head as gaily as of yore; unconscious that the eloquence of Lamartine had ever saved it from suppression. I looked about for some token of change. "Liberty, Equality, Fraternity," the symbol of the new order of things, soon met my eyes in every direction; but the only interpretation I encountered of these fine words was in the shape of passports, gens d'armes, and police. Why, these were the attributes of the Monarchy I had left, and seemed incongruous and out of place at present. To be sure, I remarked the passport bore the stamp of "The French Republic." This sounded well, but it was a passport still, whilst the gentry aforesaid had only changed their uniforms, and not their occupation. The motive of this, I suspected, was that some hungry contractors had suddenly professed Republicanism for the sake of a job. A change of costume for such a corps as the police, or the army, or navy of France, is an affair of millions; but buying up Republicans at such a rate is costly work.

In the railway to Paris I expected to hear the Republic extolled and Monarchy derided, but everybody eschewed politics, to my surprise. Now and then an allusion would be dropped, but the variety of comical grimaces that ensued soon led me to perceive that opinions vastly differed upon what was, had been, or might be. One topic, however, was discussed with great relish—the rise in stocks and the return in value of property of all descriptions since the election of the President of the Republic. The effects of a revolution in an old community like France may be highly dramatic for foreigners, but I found it had made sad havoc with the interests of all classes. The Funds had fallen from 117 to 56, and real property was unsaleable for months, but the Constitution adopted, and the President chosen for four years—there was an end of the political chaos that had prevailed, and property ran up again rapidly.

I found Paris in March '49 as gay and busy as I had left it 18 months ago. The shops were frequented, the theatre, crowded, the cafes and hotels were in no want of business. The population flowed and ebbed through the brilliant Bouvelards and its tributaries with the same easy and smiling unconcern that distinguishes the Parisians from all others. No marks of devastation met the eye. Who could have believed that in my brief absence a Dynasty had been overturned, a Republic proclaimed, a civil war quenched in blood, and a new political organisation established. These amazing feats had been performed, and yet the French were apparently as engrossed by their ordinary avocations as though nothing had occurred. This I soon found was only the surface of things, for the minds and feelings of men were by no means in the same placid condition. Everybody talked of recent events in a whisper and with 'bated breath, as though an escape had been made from some vague and dreadful catastrophe. So rapid, and various, and portentous had been events, that the minds of all were thrown into a state of confusion that rendered any distinct opinion impossible. No one hardly knew whether to regret the past, be content with the present, or satisfied with the future. The more I sounded, the more palpable was the profound moral disorder into which all conditions and classes had been cast. A nation, no more than a stage-coach, cannot be suddenly overturned, and set up again without its occupants finding themselves in a very mixed state of mind and body, hardly knowing whether to cry out or rejoice.

The lower classes of France seemed quite elated with their performances. They had dethroned a King, turned out his successors, the Republican Cavaignac and party and set up a Bonaparte. They regarded this as a pretty fair specimen of their dexterous celerity in the short time employed, and they were inclined to resume order, and work with more relish.

The middle classes scratched their heads, looked unutterable things, but said nothing. They did not care to have it known they never meant to upset Louis Philippe, much less to start a Republic, or, least of all, to raise up a Bonaparte, whom they enthusiastically voted for to escape something worse. They considered they had made fools of themselves, jeopardized their interests, but hoped to get out of the scrape without avowing it.

The upper classes were divided in sentiment. The Legitimists, or followers of the old Monarchy, were in ecstacy at the downfall of the Orleanist Dynasty. They patted the Republic on the back at having removed their hated rival. They embraced the new Bonaparte as a reaction towards Monarchy, and the mirth on their happy faces showed how fervently they believed "a good time was coming" at last. The poor Orleanists were in a woful plight, hardly knowing whether to curse others or themselves. They were in the last state of desperation, on their backs and in the gutter, groaning inwardly, unheeded, and forgotten.

That small portion of society dating from the first Empire, and which had been snubbed in turn by the elder branch and the younger, by Louis 18th and by Louis Phillippe, now came out of their hiding places, brushed up their old souvenirs, and dared to avow themselves Bonapartists.

What perplexed me most was to find a Republic in France but no Republicans. I have given a faithful sketch of the National mind in its three great phases, but save the small knot of politicians sitting on the left of the National Assembly then deliberating in Paris, I could discover no Republicans. This was a curious and interesting state of things, I saw, and every one felt it, that they had only stopped at a station, as it were, and that a journey fraught with mystery was still before them. If I had neither political theories or sympathies to stimulate my attention, my interest in the fate of a great people, and in the career of an extraordinary man was too deep and absolving not to strain every faculty of my mind in watching the progress of events towards some unknown but inevitable *dénouement*.

Soon after my arrival I paid a visit to the Prince Napoleon, then residing at the Hopital des Invalides,* of which his Father, the ex-King Jerome, was just named Governor. When I saw the Prince last in London he was forbid by the laws of France to enter its territory, and now his family were in possession of the Government. The Prince gave me a cordial reception. In his present exalted position I found him as affable and unstudied in his manner and conversation as when in exile. He received me in his *robe de chambre*, handed me a cigar, and began chatting in his usual ready and off-hand way. The intelligence of the Prince was striking;

* An Asylum for disabled soldiers, founded by Louis XIV.

his acquirements for so young a man were remarkable. His mind was quick, discerning, and exact. He measured a subject at a glance, and formed a conclusion with singular correctness. His views were always large and profound, and expressed with that *netteté* and point which reminded one of the first Emperor, whom he marvellously resembled in other respects. The same pallid complexion, penetrating glance, expansive brow; the same form of head, with its short, dark hair; perfect parity of feature, and that abrupt, rapid movement which in the Uncle betrayed his ardent character and electric flash of thought. I commented in the course of my remarks on the strange events that had occurred since last I saw the Prince, and he discussed them without reserve, and with an appreciation both impartial and sagacious. He enumerated the errors of the fallen dynasty, and whilst his opinions of the future were neither extravagant nor theoretical, he displayed great zeal for the popular cause, and decided aversion to any reactionary movement. After awhile he suddenly asked me—

"*Mais, avez vous vu Louis ?*"—["Have you seen Louis ?"]

I was really startled to hear the Head of the State so familiarly treated, forgetting for an instant that it was his cousin addressing me.

"No, your Highness," I replied, "I have been only a few days in Paris, and I feel, besides, that my acquaintance with the Prince naturally ends with his elevation to his present august position."

"Believe me, the President will be happy to see you," returned the Prince Napoleon. Go to the ball to-night at the Elysée, and you will meet him there."

"But I have no invitation."

"That's easily remedied ;" and ringing the bell, he ordered an invitation to be sent to my hotel.

As I wended my way home I wondered how far the sentiments of the Prince Napoleon were shared by the President of the Republic. They were in daily contact, and their relations were intimate and cordial.

The ripe intellect, varied experience, and lofty position of the President must inspire his cousin with due respect, while I was aware that the Prince Napoleon had always been an object of lively solicitude and affection to his august relative. But I saw that the progressive views of the Prince Napoleon, however sound or acceptable they might be in the President's eyes, were not such as could be easily or hastily carried out in Government, hampered, as was the Executive power, by the most jealous restrictions. I felt pretty sure that if the counsels of the Prince Napoleon were adopted, the President would soon be involved in a hot collision with the Legislative body, and the consequences might be fatal to one or the other. If the President, however, refused advice, I thought it not unlikely that the Prince Napoleon would throw himself into the ranks of the Opposition, not out of hostility to the President, but from a conviction that the interests of both required it. I feared an estrangement would then ensue, but still I believed that their mutual affection would survive political dissensions.

Strange to say, neither the Prince Napoleon, nor any one else, seemed to know the views or purposes of the President. The marvellous transition in his fortunes, the possession of power, the enthusiasm of the nation, were as impotent as his previous disasters to work any change on his mind or character. The inscrutable man he was, he still remained, and this strange reserve was so new to the French that it awed whilst it perplexed them. Of the Prince Louis Napoleon the masses knew nothing, save his name and his misfortunes; but the reading public of France and elsewhere entertained profound doubts both of his capacity and judgment, whilst the adroit politicians of the day were in high glee at the prospect of handling so pliant a tool as they took him to be. His canvass had been ardently sustained by the Monarchical parties, because they considered his election would pave the way to a restoration of Monarchy. The Legitimists, with Berryer at their head, gladly hoped he would be the precursor of Henry V. The Orleanists, under the guidance of Thiers and Môlé, meant to prop him up till the Count de Paris, grandson of Louis Philippe, was old enough to assume his rôle in a limited Monarchy. The Republicans had opposed his election, simply because he was the nephew of an Emperor, and they feared his tendencies to Royalty.

What his opinions or views really were no one took the trouble to inquire, for no one gave him the credit of any. At the moment I speak of, near three months had elapsed since his election, and the same notion generally prevailed of his utter incompetency to shape or carry out any policy of his own. A ludicrous struggle as to whom he should belong was going on between the Legitimists and Orleanists, who frequented his table and crowded his levées. The haughty Duchesses of the Faubourg St. Germain revived their faded recollections of Court intrigue, and stimulated by the auguries of their oracle, Berryer, they employed every act of seduction to win the seemingly flexible President over to their purposes. No doubt they were ready to pledge him, for his aid in restoring Henry V., a good place at Court and a splendid revenue.

The leaders of the Orleanists were more practical men, and employed other means. Messieurs Thiers and Molé, sure of their Parliamentary tactics, promised in their turn to increase his actual allowance, in consideration of his obedience to their suggestions.

To all these temptations the President lent a ready ear, but made no reply, which was attributed naturally to his hesitation as to whose offers he would finally accept. The Orleanists made a bold and adroit effort at the very outset, not only to monopolize the President, but, better still, to get rid of the Republic at the same time. The anecdote I shall relate in proof of this I have from the *best* authority.

The very day after the installation of the President into office, in December, 1848, a grand review of the National Guard, and of all the Troops in Paris, was ordered, to furnish the new President an opportunity of showing himself in public for the first time. The enthusiasm for the heir of the "Emperor" was at that instant deep and universal. The upper class for the reason assigned, the middle class at the prospect of order, the lower class from pure love of the name, were each and all sincere and ardent in their rejoicing at Louis Napoleon's elevation. An astute politician, like M. Thiers, perceived at a glance how easy it was to transform the newly-fledged President into a ready-made Emperor. He thought to accomplish it at once. General Changarnier was, then, commanding the Army of Paris, and was both an Orleanist and a partisan of M. Thiers. This political metamorphosis was simple enough, for General Changarnier had only to give the hint, and both the Army and the National Guard would have readily raised the cry of "Vive l'Empereur." Republican opposition would have availed little. The morning of the review the President, the Prince Napoleon, and General Changarnier were together in one of the saloons of the Palais d'Elysée, waiting till the Troops got into line before mounting their horses. It was at that moment General Changarnier suggested to the President how easy a thing it was to exchange his Republican toga for the Imperial mantle, and that if he would speak the word he was fully prepared to effect this splendid change in his toilette. The President paced the room in silence. as if busied in rumination, whilst General Changarnier continued to urge on him the expediency of an act so facile and so desirable, At this solemn moment the President remained, as usual, calm and collected, whilst General Changarnier was feverish and agitated. The Prince Napoleon stood by a passive spectator. Suddenly word was brought that all was ready, and Louis Napoleon mounted his horse without uttering a word of reply. General Changarnier did not venture to act without his authority, and the Imperial project of M. Thiers fell, therefore, to the ground. The motive of the President's silence is left to speculation. Did he secretly approve the plan, but wished General Changarnier to accept the sole responsibility, or *did he doubt the good faith of the proposition, suspecting it to be only a snare to ruin him*, or did he consider the step premature and disloyal? His reflections at that critical instant have never been disclosed.

The rivalry of the two Royalist factions to outstrip each other in their separate objects was ardent enough at this time, but they were equally disposed to unite should the Président prove refractory or manifest the hardihood of acting on his own authority. A curious instance of this occurred soon after his election. The President was aware that the documents connected with his expedition to Boulogne, in 1840, had been preserved in the archives of the State, by order of Louis Philippe, and it was only natural that in his present exalted position he should wish such vestiges of the past to be consigned to oblivion. He had not been in office many days when he sent a request to his Minister of Interior, Léon de Malleville, to remit to him the documents in question. To his great surprise the Minister hesitated to comply. The President insisted, however, when the presumptuous Minister brought the matter before the National Assembly, and declared his purpose of throwing up his portfolio rather than submit to this illegal abuse of the Executive power. He resigned accordingly, and a great hubbub was the result.

All this was only an ingenious trick of the politicians of all the factions, headed by Messieurs Thiers and Môlé, to reduce the President at once to subjection, so that he might not venture thereafter to interfere with them. The power assigned to the Executive by the Republican Constitution of M. Marrast and Co. was vague enough, and it was equally the interest of the politicians of all shades to convert the President into a mere fiction of State, similar to the English Monarch, so that all authority might be wielded by themselves, at the head of a Parliamentary majority, as in England. To accomplish this the paltry occasion of the President sending for the documents I have alluded to was laid hold of, and the object was to manage the thing in such a way in the Assembly and the Press as to put the President in the wrong before the public, and so turn opinion against him. M. Thiers displayed his usual dexterity in getting his camp-follower, M. de Malleville, to resign, and such a tempest in a tea-pot was raised, that in France, England, and the United States, the public, who only saw the outside of the dispute, considered the politicians in the right, and were more confirmed than ever in their previous unfavourable impressions of the Prince Louis Napoleon.

The President detected at once the Parliamentary juggle, and deeming it unwise to alarm the public mind by so early a collision between himself and the Assembly, he prudently withdrew his demand, and gracefully submitted to his would-be masters. The exultation of the Parliamentary leaders was extreme, and they mistook the tact and good sense of the President for weakness and incapacity. The Republican party was in majority at this time in the Assembly, but they readily followed the Royalists in this decisive effort to put down the President.

The state of things, when I arrived in Paris in March, was seemingly pleasant enough. In the Assembly the Royalists and Republicans were contending for the mastery; the former superior in Parliamentary tactics, the latter greater in numbers. Out of doors the two Royalist factions, as I have described, were struggling for the exclusive possession of the President, who assumed the complacent demeanour of Captain Macheath—

"How happy could I be with either,
Were t'other dear charmer away."

The Republican party, all this while, avoided contact with the President, and frequented his fêtes in limited numbers. They were mortified at the defeat of their candidate, General Cavaignac, and looked upon his successful rival with consequent dislike.

CHAPTER III.

THE PRESIDENT'S BALL.

The invitation to his cousin's ball, which the Prince Napoleon had so graciously procured for me, as before stated, duly reached me, and I drove, at nine o'clock the same evening, to the Palace of the Elysée. This was the residence assigned by the Assembly to the President, and it was singular enough that the career of Prince Louis Napoleon should begin in the very abode where that of his illustrious uncle finished. It was here that Napoleon, after the battle of Waterloo, resided previous to his quitting Paris, and from the fact of his not returning to the Palace of the Tuilleries it seemed as though he recognized the loss of his right longer to inhabit it. Whether it was from jealousy or fear of expense that the Republican Assembly selected the smaller Palace of the Elysée for the President's use, instead of the Tuilleries, the gorgeous abode of the old Kings of France, I do not know, but any potentate, Republican, or otherwise, might well be satisfied with so delightful a habitation as that of the Elysée. The reception rooms are numerous, lofty, and elegant, but had they been double their size they would only have conveniently accommodated the throng that crammed them to excess on the night I refer to. Until a portion of the company had gone, locomotion was well-nigh out of the question. This singular affluence of guests proved that invitations had been liberally distributed, and showed the disposition of the President to conciliate all classes and ranks at starting. The amazing variety of condition and strange mixture of position that harmoniously blended together at the *fêtes* of the President of the Republic at this precise period, was the best illustration of the singular confusion of opinion and social disorganisation that followed the political tempest of 1848.

The President displayed admirable sagacity in not prematurely seeking to restore the broken-down barriers and artificial distinctions that had formerly prevailed, and he exhibited equal tact in recognizing the interregnum existing by scattering broad-cast the invitations to his levees and balls.

To judge only from the appearance and manners of the guests, a stranger might have supposed them exclusively drawn from the highest ranks only, for in no nation of Europe does that easy self-possession, characteristic of good society, so universally distinguish all classes as in France. This is a relic of the olden time, for the *Grand Seigneur* of the middle ages, however privileged and powerful, was still familiar and natural in his relations with his inferiors, and from this it comes that in point of social equality France takes precedence of all other countries. My frequent visits to Paris, however, had accustomed my eye to the nicer shades of its different grades of society, and I could discern on every side indications of the extraordinary jumble then prevailing. Every shade of politics, Legitimists, Orleanists, Bonapartists, with a sprinkling of Republicans; every branch of the Army and Navy; every learned profession, Priests, Lawyers, and Physicians; every elevated industry, financiers, and manufacturers; the world of letters; the representatives of art, painters, sculptors, and architects; every strata of society, from the loftiest rank and fashion down to the unknown parvenu and obscure nondescript, were chatting, staring, dancing, promenading, eating, and drinking, in the glittering saloons of Louis Napoleon on the occasion I am now speaking of.

Not long after my *entrée* I spied the short, round figure of M. Thiers. He was standing by a chimney-piece, his hands behind him, a favourite attitude, peering through his spectacles, with an air of quiet importance, at the motley throng before him. Occasionally he would make a brief remark to a friend in his usual abrupt, curt way. I contemplated him a moment, and could almost divine his reflections. He considered himself at that moment the master spirit of France, and his manner seemed to say—"This is all very well for the nonce, but I will put things to rights in my own good time." Turning round I remarked the fine form of the courtly Berryer, promenading with the Princess Mathilde, daughter of the Ex-King Jerome, and cousin of the President. The beauty, grace, and intelligence of this lovely Princess gave additional interest to her romantic history, and as she moved along, the cynosure of all-admiring eyes, the brilliant leader of the Legitimists seemed fully conscious of the honor conferred on him. Whilst others were discussing the appearance of these distinguished persons, the Imperial bearing of one, the oratorical genius of the other, I was alone occupied with the fact that the chief adviser of Henry V. in France was paying assiduous court to the near relative of the President of the Republic.

At every instant my attention was drawn to some celebrity of the past or the present. I was surprised to find the illustrious Lamartine amongst the guests of the Elysée. I remembered, only a few months previously, when the star of Louis Napoleon began to twinkle in the distant horizon, that Lamartine, startled at the omen, strode to the Tribune, and denounced, with vehement eloquence, the very name of Bonaparte, accusing Napoleon the Great of sacrificing France to a selfish ambition. Yet here he was playing the satellite to the luminary he had vainly essayed to extinguish. His inconsistency occasioned me no wonder, for amid the rapid transition of events in a revolutionary epoch a politician must either yield to circumstances or be overwhelmed. There stood Lamartine near a door, his tall, erect person towering above the group of greedy listeners about him. There is an expression in his countenance, a something in his bearing, a dignity of sentiment, an elevation of soul, that impress all who approach him. I regarded him with deep interest. Since I saw him in '47 he had been the hero of a drama as thrilling and bloody as history records. It was he who launched the Revolution of '48, when he answered the supplications of the Duchess of Orleans with the signal words, "It is too late," and bid her depart. It was he, in the front of the Hotel de Ville, who quelled, by his magic eloquence, the fierce frenzy of the mob, and saved France from the bloody terrors of the red flag, by declaring it was "the tricolor that had made the tour of Europe at the head of her victorious legions." It was he who dared resist revolutionary fanaticism in the fiery councils of the Provisional Government, and when demanded by a madman, who placed a pistol against his head, "What prevented him from blowing out his brains," saved his life, and turned the tide of history, by calmly answering, "Your conscience." Still, after such efforts and such success, he was forced to resign the helm of State, that demands not only courage and eloquence but skill to guide it. I scanned his face. Was he content after so much fame achieved in so many different fields to give up the pomp and glory of the world? Poet, orator, historian, statesman, with France for his tribune, and the world for his audience. I approached him with deference, and he welcomed me kindly. His manner was more serious than formerly, less impetuous, like a man who felt his work was done. I spoke of *les grands evénemens* [the great events] that had transpired. I sought to solve a doubt that compromised his wisdom, or his fealty to the people.

"The Provisional Government," I remarked, "swayed for three months the sovereignty of France, and how was it, permit me to ask, M. de Lamartine, that the abuses of the past were not destroyed, and the Revolution satisfied?"

"Because," gravely replied the man of '48, "I felt that to France alone belonged the initiative. Until the National Assembly met I struggled only to stay the arm of the Provisional Government." And so ruined the Republic, was my inward reflection, and bowing low, I fell back into the crowd.

I stood a moment gazing curiously at a man that few knew and none noticed. Short and slender in person, with a slight stocp, very unassuming in his manner, there was nothing, save the keen, restless glance of his dark eye that could attract for an instant the attention of the observer. Who could have thought that this was the only man in France who possessed the secret of secrets, who knew the hidden purpose of the Brutus of the epoch, playing the shallow to entrap the profound; that this was the only man who had access, at mysterious hours, to the President, was always listened to, and frequently consulted? In short, that this was the Vicomte de Persigny. When the Prince Louis Napoleon lived in London, '39 and '40, this gentleman was one of his suite. He did not figure in the Expedition to Boulogne, nor was he with the Prince on his return to London in '46. No sooner did the Prince come to Paris in '48 than M. de Persigny was found at his side, secretly but actively occupied with his canvass for the Presidency. He exhibited great tact in moderating the excessive zeal of embryo Bonapartists, nor would he allow a public meeting to be held in behalf of the Prince Louis till the proper moment arrived. That his intelligence and address must be rare indeed is evident from his sharing the confidence of a Prince playing so intricate a game as the President of the Republic.

I exchanged a word, *en passant*, with Horace Vernet, who was dressed in military uniform, whilst his breast had the appearance of a target at which the orders and stars of all the Courts of Europe had been fired. This illustrious painter of battle pieces is really a Colonel in the National Guard, but so strong is his sympathy with the Military subjects he so marvellously illustrates, that he believes himself destined some day to head a campaign, if not to become a Marshal of France. I once had the good luck to see this great artist at work. He was painting the battle of Isly, and no one was present save the celebrated Isabey and myself. The picture was of immense dimensions, and Vernet stood on a ladder painting, which he descended rapidly every few minutes, and running off some twenty yards, eyed the effect, talking volubly all the time. His finest touches were given with astonishing celerity, and Isabey was constantly thrown into ecstacies of admiration. To see Vernet paint, whilst Isabey criticised, was a treat not to be met with every day.

At last I encountered the person I was in search of, Mr. Rush, our Minister in France, whom I had not met since my arrival. Long before I came to England I had read with delight the interesting book of Mr. Rush on his long sojourn at the Court of St. James's, and since 1836 I had enjoyed his acquaintance. Mr. Rush was sent to France just previous to the Revolution of '48, and it was fortunate at so critical a moment we had an Envoy of so much judgment and experience. He was the first to recognize the new Republic, but not till he saw it firmly on its legs, and England followed his example.

I anticipated great advantage in discussing the condition of Europe at such a juncture with a diplomatist of so much sagacity and moderation. Mr. Rush was of our early school of statesmen now fast disappearing. To learning and high breeding was united a respect for routine and a decided conservative tendency that imparted dignity and stability to our new institutions, but which has been forced to yield to the inordinate progression of ideas and rapid march of events so characteristic of the age. I canvassed the opinions of Mr. Rush on the "situation" with much interest. The reaction, he thought, had set in, and the *statu quo* would finally be restored. I ventured, however, to express my belief that whether the Republic survived or no, the electoral body of France would never be reduced to what it was under Louis Philippe.

"But, have you seen the President?" inquired Mr. Rush.

"I was just. looking for you to be presented to him," was my answer.

"Indeed!" exclaimed the Minister. "Do you think such ceremony necessary with the Prnce, whom you know so well?"

"I knew the Prince Louis Napoleon, it is true, but I have never been presented to the President of the Republic."

"Come along; then," exclaimed Mr. Rush, whose scruples of etiquette were gratified by my reserve, "he'll welcome you kindly, for he has frequently inquired after you."

Launching ourselves into one of the currents of the overflowing crowd, we set off in quest of our illustrious host, remarking the while on the variegated aspect of his guests, where the showy costumes of official and military functionaries contrasted oddly with a broad back-ground of black cloth—a rare sight in the palaces of European Princes. We had made the tour of several apartments before we spied the President through a dense mass of heads that enclosed him round like a body guard. Before we could reach him I had a good opportunity for observation. He was dressed in a General's uniform, which became him exceedingly. Though not tall, Prince Louis is erect and well formed. His new dignity had in no wise changed his manner, which was graceful, affable, but dignified. He was moving slowly along, smiling and bowing to the eager crowd, and occasionally addressing a remark to some one he recognized. By dint of effort Mr. Rush managed to reach him, whilst I stood a pace in the rear till I was announced. I remarked that the mention of my name brought an expression of surprise to the façe of the President, who was till that moment unaware of my being in Paris. I advanced, and he shook me cordially by the hand. His manner was as pleasant as in the olden time, though his conversation in the presence of so many gazers was necessarily more formal. The President finished by saying he hoped to see me soon again, when I fell back to join Mr. Rush, who was standing near. I remarked that the British Ambassador, Lord Normanby, was at the side of the President, and listened attentively to what passed during my short audience. He continued accompanying the President about the rooms during the evening, somewhat in the manner of a chamberlain. I supposed this to have some political meaning, and was likely meant to indicate, if not any sympathy for the Republic or its President, at least the desire of the English Government to remain on the best terms with both. It certainly afforded food for curious reflection that the self-same oligarchy that had wasted so much blood and treasure in assailing the first French Republic, and in aiding to overthrow the first Napoleon, should now avow their mistaken policy by anxiously seeking to conciliate the second Republic and the second Napoleon. This is only one of the many proofs that history affords of the utter impotency of all the force or art of Governments to turn the tide of human destiny.

CHAP. IV.

A DINNER AT THE ELYSEE.

In March, 1849, the public eye was bent with suspicious scrutiny on the Constituent Assembly in permanent session at Paris. This body was the product of the universal suffrage of France, immediately after the Revolution of 1848, and it was, therefore, the reflex of the popular sentiment at that moment. The majority was Republican, the minority Monarchical, and the former is, therefore, accountable for what occurred during their tenure of power. From the beginning the Republican politicians committed a fatal error, for instead of occupying themselves with the interests of their constituents, the masses, they directed their attention solely to the best means of prolonging their political preponderance. None of them were sagacious enough to see that the only mode of preserving their popularity was to effect those reforms that up to this time the people had failed to obtain from the Monarchy. Soon after they met in May it was so apparent that they meant to touch as little as possible the organisation of France as the Monarchy had left it, that a portion of the Parisian populace, at the instigation of Louis Blanc, made a demonstration against them, and only a month later nearly the whole populace of Paris rose in arms to overthrow them. A Republican chief, General Cavaignac, undertook successfully to defend the Assembly, and was rewarded by being made the temporary head of the State, with the title of "Chief of the Executive power." The Assembly then commenced the business for which it was especially elected, the structure of a new Constitution;

that was duly carried by the majority, but they avoided submitting it to the approval of the French people. I will reserve my remarks on this instrument for another place. What the people of France finally thought of the Constitution and the Assembly that voted it, may be gathered from the overwhelming rejection of the representative of both, General Cavaignac, when he came forward as the opponent of Louis Napoleon Bonaparte for the Presidency of the Republic. On that occasion the upper, middle, and lower classes, united to mark their condemnation of the Republican politicians, who had proved themselves either incapable or false.

The Assembly remained in session after the election of the President, but for want of equal Parliamentary ability the Republicans fell in a measure under the sway of the Monarchists. This body was to dissolve, by the terms of the Constitution, on the election of a new Legislature in May, 1849, and at the time I am speaking of, the month of March, the Republican majority was sinking lower still in public estimation by unseemly brawls with the Monarchists on the subject of their party interests, entirely forgetting the popular cause they were sent to promote. The President of the Assembly was M. Marrast, ex-editor of the *National*, already spoken of, and the number of brilliant entertainments he gave had procured him the *sobriquet* of the "petit Marquis." From the profound dissatisfaction of the public, high and low, it was considered certain that at the forthcoming election the Monarchists would obtain the majority, and Messrs. Thiers, Mô1é, and Berryer, were in high spirits at the prospect. At this delicate juncture, the President was, perhaps, the only man in France that understood his own position and the state of the public mind. The politicians of both parties and of all shades were entirely engrossed with their party or personal interests. The President saw their error, and wisely resolved to avoid identifying himself with any of them, but to remain in a perfectly neutral position. The Republicans could not accuse him of being against them, whilst the Monarchists believed he was secretly with them, which led M. Thiers to hope, with his aid, to get back the Orleanists, whilst M. Berryer calculated equally on him to restore Henry V. The French people, meanwhile, had their gaze fixed on President Bonaparte, and were content to wait, as they knew by the Constitution of M. Marrast, he had no power to serve them if he wished.

This was the complicated state of things when I received, one day, soon after the ball I have spoken of, an invitation from the President to dine with him at the palace of the Elysée, already mentioned. I was surprised and flattered at this prompt mark of his friendly remembrance, but I did not allow my self-love to overrate it. I attributed it at once to that good taste and kind feeling so characteristic of the Prince Louis Napoleon, and not to any desire to renew his former relations with me, which in his present exalted position it would have been presumptuous to expect. I felt very curious indeed to know something of his state of mind on the amazing revolution in his fortunes since I saw him last in May, 1847, an exile in London. I remembered still his parting phrase, "*j'attends les evénemens*" (I am waiting events), which indicated that if his hopes were inflexible, he felt it useless to wrestle longer with Fate. I was still more eager to ascertain his political views, and to divine his future policy, but I did not for a moment deceive myself, nor underrate the Prince. I felt sure his tact was quite adequate to the occasion, and that, whilst avoiding his old familiarity, which might embolden me too much, he could still show he was not unmindful of the fact that I was the only one, not interested in the result, who cherished a profound belief in his final success, when all else pronounced it a shallow delusion. In the dreary solitude of Ham, after five years of imprisonment, and forgotten by the world, the visit of even so humble a person as myself was cheering to him, as I afterwards learnt, not only as an act of personal devotion, but as a proof his fortunes could not be utterly desperate, since a foreigner, and without a motive, still persisted unshaken in his faith.

I drove at a few minutes before the hour named on the day in question to the Elysée, and on entering the saloon I found several members of the President's household assembled. I recognized amongst them his faithful friend and physician, Dr. Conneau, who through every vicissitude had remained true to his trust. No one could have divined in the mild countenance and quiet but genial demeanour of Dr. Conneau, that his sagacity, firmness, and courage, had, in many trying emergencies, rendered services far more precious than any his professional skill had ever been called on to afford, and it is not to be wondered at that he held so high a place in the affectionate esteem of his august patron. I fell into pleasant chat with my former acquaintance, expecting every moment to see the President enter the room, as I supposed the dinner was only to be, in common parlance, a family party. I was of a sudden surprised to hear the ushers announce "Monsieur Thiers," who passed through into an adjoining saloon of grander dimensions. Immediately after M. Môlé was annouuced; then M. Berryer; M. Montalembert; General Changarnier, and others of little less celebrity. It turned out that it was a grand dinner of state that the President was giving, and I found myself not a little elated at coming so unexpectedly into contact not only with the most illustrious names of the day, but the very men who aspired to shape the future destinies of France.

I strolled along into the principal saloon, where I found the company was gathering to await the coming of the President, and I ensconced myself in a quiet corner, talking the while with an Aide-de-Camp in waiting. On the opposite side of the room small groups of two or three were collected about the political oracles I have mentioned, who were conversing in under tones, but with considerable animation. As my glance fell in turn on the distinguished persons before me, it was natural my mind should revert rapidly to the singular features of their different careers.

There was M. Thiers, with the star of the Legion of Honour on his breast. Of humble extraction, he came to Paris at the age of 24, and began life in a garret. Employed on a newspaper, his literary talent raised him at once. Finding public opinion running against the priest-ridden government of Charles X., he wrote a democratic history of the first revolution, and so hastened the second, when he became a Minister of Louis Philippe. Finally discarded by the King, and foreseeing his downfall, he began Bonapartising France by a dazzling history of the Consulate and Empire, and Louis Napoleon came sooner than he expected or wished. Writer, orator, statesman; brilliant, profound, and unscrupulous, M. Thiers is an antagonist any ruler might fear. Is the President a match for this political Titan? The result will show.

Count Môlé is listening to him. The Count, though of ancient lineage, owed his title, and everything to the first Napoleon, whose fortunes he never abandoned. He was more than once Prime Minister to Louis Philippe. High respectability more than great talent is the secret of his distinction.

M. Berryer is near him: the first advocate of France, and the political champion of a hopeless cause. Splendid talents, lofty character, chivalric nature. He defended the Prince Louis Napoleon in '40 before the Chamber of Peers.

The Count Montalembert stands apart, proud and cynical in manner and disposition. An orator, devoted to Church influence, he would revive the middle ages if he could.

General Changarnier, cold and haughty, promenades about as though impatient for the *entrée* of the President. This soldier of Fortune rose rapidly in the African campaigns, under Louis Philippe, and if as successful in politics as in strategy, he will play a prominent part hereafter.

My mind was pleasantly engaged with these retrospects for some little time, when the company having all arrived, the President was duly announced, and a moment after entered the saloon. His guests bowed low and remained silent. To my astonishment, and still more to that of his distinguished *convives*, he advanced directly towards me, and shaking my hand, with a friendly word or two passed over to receive the salutations of his company. I was at no loss to understand this delicate attention of the Prince, whose eye happened to fall on me, standing almost alone, on the side opposite to the remarkable persons I have mentioned. He knew me to be the humblest of his guests, and intended, by an act of condescension, to put me at my ease, and to show his consideration for an old partizan. I went on talking with the Aide-de-Camp near me. Presently the President approached me again—

"You don't know Count Mólé, I think," he said. "Come with me, I wish to present you to him."

Bowing, I followed him across the room, amid the evident surprise of the company, who looked on me as some illustrious unknown, little dreaming that I was a Yankee and a democrat.

"Count Mólé," said the Prince, "I wish to make you acquainted with an old friend of mine who has twice crossed the Atlantic to pay me a visit."

Of course I was received by the Count with the greatest cordiality, but if the Prince had stated I had twice come from the moon, his puzzled guests could hardly have been more perplexed to know really who and what I was.

One of the latent traits of the President, that I had occasionally seen, was a sly love of humour—and I half suspected that he was playing on the curiosity of the jealous politicians around by treating me with so much partiality.

"*Le diner est servi,*" said the master of ceremonies in a loud voice, and the President led the way alone to the banquet-room, his guests following in groups. Each person's place was designated as usual. The Count Môlé was put on the right of the President, who sat in the centre of the table, according to French custom. I found myself on the right of Count Môlé. M. Thiers was on the left of the President, with M. Berryer for his neighbour. General Changarnier was *vis-a-vis* to the President. Nothing could exceed the ease, affability, and self-possession of the Prince. No affectation in his manner, no effort in his conversation, he maintained the superiority of his position with natural but imposing dignity.

The situation of the President was a novel one—a stranger to France, and but newly acquainted with her greatest Statesmen, it demanded a rare combination of qualities, mental and moral, to acquire the ascendency he had clearly obtained. Conversation at table went on in an under-tone. The President quietly ate his dinner, occasionally dropping a comment upon some remark he chose to overhear. I fell into easy chat with Count Môlé, who, fancying that I was deep in the confidence of the President, gave unreserved expression to his opinions on the strange events of the past, and the prospects just dawning. His astonishment was almost ludicrous when I proclaimed in reply the strong democratic notions that possessed me. I stated my belief that the time had come when something more than Parliamentary discussion was necessary to meet the desire of France for material progress, and that unless the Prince and his advisers gave heed to the national conviction, that, perhaps, the gulf of revolution was not finally closed. The ex-Minister of Louis Philippe really seemed not to comprehend me, for so absorbed was he in Parliamentary intrigues, and so embedded in routine, that plain common-sense sounded like the jargon of an unknown land. He stared at me for a moment, and then concluding that I was only employing *finesse* to conceal my real opinions, went on with his repast. The President, I could see, was not unconscious of what was going on, and, I fancied, was trying to conceal his amusement at the unexpected collision of a staunch Monarchist of the old school, like the Count Môlé, with an American democrat, who looked at facts as they were, and at things as they ought to be.

About the middle of the banquet M. Thiers raised his voice, and gave strong utterance to his indignation against the intolerable licentiousness of the Press, which respected neither place nor person. He called attention to one of the morning papers that had outraged decency in its coarse vituperation of the President. The note was caught up till every one at table had joined in the chorus of anathema against peccant journalism. When the tide of sympathetic horror had fairly exhausted itself, every eye was turned upon the President, whose feelings, it was hoped, might be touched, and above all, whose opinion on this vital point it was thus artfully sought to extract. The silence was profound. The President seemed to reflect, when draining his glass of the few drops it contained, he remarked—

"Every one, of course, has his own point of view. I can comprehend your dissatisfaction at the licence of the Press, and your anger at their violent attacks upon myself; but, Messieurs, shall I own the truth?" Every head converged towards the President.

"I read these diatribes," he continued, "each morning at breakfast, and I assure you they afford me so much amusement, that I am kept in good humour for the rest of the day." It was with an effort that I suppressed my mirth at the blank disappointment I detected in every face around me. The dinner ended without further incident, and the President leading the way, as before, the company returned to the drawing-rooms.

I joined M. Berryer, whom I had not met since my arrival, and after chatting awhile, playfully remarked on my satisfaction at seeing him in the palace of a Republican President. He smiled significantly, whilst he added that—

"In times like these a luckless politician was hardly responsible for what he said or did."

During our dinner Mr. Brett, so well known for his telegraphic enterprise, had obtained the permission of the Prince to run a wire through the various saloons of the palace, in order to exhibit to him some striking improvements, jointly invented by himself and an American associate. As the preparations were going on, I happened to be standing near the President, when M. de Montalembert came up, and with that cynicism so characteristic of the man, remarked, in a sneering tone—

"*Qu'est que vaut tout cela?*"—(what is all that worth?) pointing to the telegraph. I shall never forget the genuine look of astonishment of the President.

"What is all that worth!" he repeated mechanically, "*mais c'est la civilization*" (why, it is civilization), he added.

"*Oh, le beau mót?*" (Oh, the fine phrase) returned M. de

Montalembert in real disdain. The President said no more, but turning, talked with Mr. Brett.

When all was ready, the President was solicited to make the first experiment, and he wrote a single line to the effect "that M. Berryer dined at the Elysée on day of March, 1849," which was duly printed on slips, and passed round amongst the guests. The simple use of M. Berryer's name, who was accidentally standing by when the President was called on for a phrase, threw all the politicians present, I could observe, into deep rumination. What could it mean! was a mystery that likely cost them whole days of perplexity. The wires were soon taken down, and the company began rapidly to disperse.

On going, I advanced to thank the President for the honor of his invitation, and to express the interest that meeting so many remarkable men had afforded me. In return, the Prince was kind enough to avow his satisfaction at some publications of mine, during the summer of '48, wherein I declared my conviction of his being called to the head of France so positively that the French Minister at Washington, M. Poussin, pronounced me *un fou.*

"As often happens," remarked the Prince, playfully, "I dare say you are not a little surprised to find all your predictions at last so completely verified."

"However that may be," I replied, "I assure your Highness that it is fortunate for me as well as for France that you were elected."

"How so?" enquired the President.

"Simply because I foretold your success with such unqualified confidence, that I should have been a lost prophet if the event had turned out otherwise."

Bidding the Prince good night, I wended my way home, fully occupied with my reflections. I have detailed the incidents of my first dinner at the Elysée with some minuteness, with a view to convey a more vivid impression of the actual state of things at this interesting epoch.

CHAPTER V.

THE LAST REVOLT.

A violent political agitation pervaded France in April, 1849. A decisive struggle for the supremacy was shortly to ensue between the Monarchical and Republican parties. The former, emboldened by past successes, worked with a hearty good will, whilst the latter, discouraged by conscious short-comings, carried on the contest with deep forebodings of the result. All the machinery that modern ingenuity has invented to arouse public feeling and guide opinion was brought into active requisition. That tremendous organ, the press, was powerfully and skilfully employed by both sides to promote their interests, and the first intellects and most practised pens of either party did their utmost to secure the victory. The streets of Paris were placarded with highly seasoned appeals to the "electors of the Seine," whilst public meetings were nightly called to listen to the inflammatory harangues of chosen orators and aspiring candidates. To an American all this political hubbub, with its familiar demonstrations, was both novel and exciting, and he was tempted at times to believe he was in the midst of the usual commotion of an ardent Presidential canvass at home. The subjects discussed, however, soon scattered these illusions, for instead of practical measures of local or national benefit, instead of debating the expediency of reform or the abolition of abuse, nothing was expatiated on by one party but the necessity of "Order," whilst the other enlarged on the manifold blessings of "Liberty." Such themes as these sounded strangely in an American ear, and showed at once that France was in an exceptional state, not going through the operation of some organic function, but rather involved in a struggle for political existence. The speakers at these meetings were always fluent and often eloquent. In oratory and conversation the French surpass all nations in readiness and facility, which, in part, may be ascribed to their language, more highly perfected than any in Europe, but still more so, to their ambition to shine in the art of conveying their ideas with *éclat*. The lower classes especially express themselves with an ease and propriety nowhere else seen. The conduct of the audience at these popular assemblies was singularly calm and decorous, in marked contrast to that boisterous animation which pervades such places in the United States and England; there was a gravity and dignity quite at variance with the general notions of the French character. How much of these results may be ascribed to the presence of the police I don't know; but at every public gathering at this epoch the Government thought it necessary to see that order was preserved. It may be thought that this was a gross interference with that freedom of discussion, which is the essence of a popular Government; but opinions were so divided, and passions so inflamed, at this juncture in France, that the first duty of the Government was, at any cost, to prevent brawls that might swell into insurrection and civil war. The President raised no obstacle to the expression of opular feeling; but he made it distinctly known, through his *Prefet* of Police, whose placards covered France, that he would uphold, inviolate, the public peace at every sacrifice. His resolute language had due effect on the demagogues of all parties, and the community at large breathed freer as the chances of new revolutions diminished.

I witnessed a curious spectacle at one of the political reunions I attended at this time. It was generally announced that the Prince Napoleon was to preside and would address the meeting. This was only another of the daily incongruities that presented themselves on every side, and afforded lively interest to an impartial looker-on. In England it is common enough for the nobility and even princes of the blood to make public speeches, though it may seem strange in the eyes of a continental monarch to see a nobleman, or royal scion, hand over his opinions for approval or condemnation to the classes socially and politically below them; but it was a far different sight to behold the nephew of an Emperor, the son of a King, and the cousin of the head of the State, lay aside title and pretension and come down into the arena of public discussion, meeting on terms of perfect equality the intellectual athletæ of whatever class or position that chose to pit themselves against him. In England a Prince enjoys *prestige*, and her aristocracy possess privilege and power such as to imbue the lower classes with a servile respect, so that the twaddle of a Lord is often better greeted than the sense of an untitled man; but France at this moment was *en pleine republique ;* social and political equality was rigidly enforced, and no superiority but that of real capacity was recognised. Under such circumstances M. Napoleon Bonaparte did not shrink from taking the chair at a gathering of Republicans and Socialists of the lower orders, who would show him no quarter if found inadequate to the occasion. It was in the outskirts of Paris, in the midst of the operative population, that the meeting was to come off, and the place selected, though of vast dimensions, was crammed to suffocation long before the hour appointed. Nothing could be more orderly and well-behaved, though it was evident the audience consisted solely of the labouring class. The curiosity to see the Prince was intense, and when he entered the whole mass rose up in silence to contemplate him. He took his place on a platform, with a table before him, with an easy self-possession that had its effect, for the French are more sensitive to manner than other people. The first sensation was that of wonder at the striking resemblance of young Napoleon to his immortal uncle. "*C'est étonnant, mais il lui ressemble comme deux pois,*" was the general exclamation. [" It is astonishing, but he is as like *him* as two peas."]

As soon as silence was restored the Prince rose and began his address. His manner was graceful, his elocution fluent, his matter well-assorted, and expressed with a perspicuity and force that the oldest orator might have envied. As he went flowing on without hesitation or effort, uttering the soundest opinions in the concisest language, the surprise and admiration of his auditors broke out in exclamations that showed they had anticipated a different result. *Mais il a de l'esprit, beaucoup même—il fera son chemin celui la.* [" Why, he has talent, great talent, even—he will make his way, that one there."] The moment the Prince saw that he had obtained complete ascendancy over his hearers, he carried out the purpose that probably induced him to appear in such a place. He declared himself a friend to equal rights, and therefore a Republican, but he derided as impracticable and deceptive the shallow theories circulating under the name of Socialism. He attacked the dogmas of Louis Blanc with so much decision, and explained their hollowness with so much precision and point, as to carry conviction home to the rude but vigilant minds that caught up every word. He spoke an hour at least, and sat down amid universal enthusiasm. A Socialist got up to reply, and the audience refused to hear him, but the Prince obtained him a hearing; his oratory, however, was so inferior to that just listened to that he was compelled at last to sit down amid general marks of impatience. I am satisfied that the temperate but resolute assault of M. Napoleon Bonaparte on the spurious doctrines of Socialism, on this occasion, had a deep and rectifying effect. It is only necessary to make the people in France or elsewhere understand, as the Prince so clearly did, that "common property" only means common robbery, to stamp Socialism as the code of the idle and desperate, the refuse of society.

The elections passed over in all parts of France without the least infraction of order, and the results threw the Republican party into dismay. Lamartine, the apostle of the Revolution of '48, who was then elected by acclamation in every quarter of the country, was now silently discarded by every constituency, and consigned to private life—a prey, no doubt, to the bitterest reflections. Many people pointed at this as only another instance of the fickleness of the masses, but I marvelled at it as a new proof of their vigilance and discernment. Both Lamartine and the Revolution had wofully disappointed the just expectations of the French people, and they seized the first occasion to make their indignation known. The Monarchists obtained the majority in the new "Legislative Assembly," and were intoxicated at their unexpected triumph. Instead of interpreting the rebuke administered to the Republicans as an evidence of popular acumen, they set it down either to their frivolity, or their love of Monarchy. M. Thiers, like poor Lamartine, has lived to learn his error, and to expiate it.

No sooner did the New Assembly meet, than, believing that the country had really come back to its first love, the Monarchists, under the direction of Thiers, Môlé and Co., began zealously to imitate the mistakes of their Republican predecessors; and instead of legislating instantly for the good of the country, they began at once to take the whole political power of the State, Executive as well as

Legislative into their own hands, meaning, at a convenient moment, to restore the fallen Monarchy. The Republican party they considered as prostrate, and as for the President, Louis Napoleon, why, in their view, he was a mere nullity. If he lent himself, as expected, to the intrigues of the Monarchists, a good pension would be secured him when the legitimate King was restored; if he ventured to oppose them he would find his way to a dungeon in Vincennes. M. Thiers and his political staff never troubled themselves about Louis Napoleon, whose silent impassability, in their eyes, passed for dullness and weakness. His opposition to the experience, eloquence, and *savoir faire* of the leaders of the Monarchists, was laughed to scorn. The Monarchists, too, had the majority in the Assembly, and were justified in saying the country was with them. Would the President dare, then, to withhold his signature to any laws they chose to make?

Whilst the Monarchists were absorded in their intrigues Louis Napoleon was, doubtless, studying the new phase of things. He knew exactly what France wanted, and he was, apparently, the only politician that did. The Republicans had played the fool, and were dismissed. Would the Monarchists imitate them, and share the same fate? Keenly and eagerly must he have watched their course, for his career depended on it. His *rôle* was becoming delicate and difficult. The first year of his Presidency he had only to stand aside, a calm spectator of the contest between the Republican and Monarchical parties. The latter was victorious, and he alone foresaw the deadly combat likely to ensue between them and himself. The thing was clear enough. If the Monarchists were true to the country, his time was short; but if, as always, despising the interests of the masses, they employed power only to aggrandize themselves, then it remained for him, after what fashion he pleased, to give the country a chance to choose between them. For the present he had nothing to do but stand on the defensive, and let M. Thiers and the other leaders of the Monarchists play out their game.

It may be supposed that when the Republican party found themselves repudiated by the people, and in a minority in the Assembly, where only a year ago their sway was supreme, their mortification knew no bounds. The leaders in the Assembly would have consented, with the usual pliancy of politicians, to submit to circumstances with the best grace possible; not so, however, that influential class of demagogues out of doors who were in close connection with the riotous and disorderly always abounding in a great metropolis, and whose influence arose from their skill in organizing street conspiracies. I have encountered not a few of these gentry in France, and in talent and courage they surpass those of all other countries, whilst in disinterestedness they are no worse than their betters. The street-leaders of the French Republicans and Socialists naturally expected, when they succeeded, to get their share of place and power. "To the victor belongs the spoils" is an ancient motto. The Revolution of '48 did wonders for many a gentleman of the back slums who crept from dark holes and corners into numberless snug places with small salaries attached. It may have been their original intention to abolish, when they obtained the power, all these "vile sinecures" which they had so often denounced, and to carry Socialism into effect for the benefit of the mob if not for themselves. But it is well known that circumstances alter opinions, and perhaps they foresaw that, if faithful to their professions, they swept away abuses, the people might be the better off—but that they assuredly would not be. This must have cost them a little perplexity, but as the problem was hard to solve, they concluded to leave well alone, and instead of demolishing Bureaucracy, they appropriated its salaries, leaving their dupes in the street to console themselves with the high-sounding decree that "they had deserved well of the country," and of mankind in general.

The election of May, '49, must have been a thunderbolt for the Republican chiefs, high and low, and whether they suspected the people to be sharper than they thought, or believed, like the Royalists, that they didn't know their own minds, it was still clear that something must be done to preserve the pleasant retreats they had secured. It was settled by the demagogues of the Faubourg that a demonstration in the streets would be the best thing, as it would frighten the Royalists and awe the Government into making a compromise, and allowing them to keep what they had got in the scramble of February, '48. This was not at all acceptable to the more experienced leaders of the party in the Assembly, for they perceived that the populace of Paris, like the masses of the country, were cured of their illusions, and that any attempt at revolution, even in sham, would recoil upon the heads of its authors. The foremost man of the ultra Republican party in the Assembly was Ledru Rollin. A lawyer by profession, he distinguished himself by his oratory and popular professions in the Chamber of Deputies, under Louis Philippe. He was less conspicuous than Lamartine and others in the Revolution of '48, for he was, then, less known; but as these had all vanished from the scene, Ledru Rollin was the recognised head of the Red Republicans in May, '49.

Without questioning his zeal for his principles, there is no denying that Ledru Rollin had all along displayed a degree of prudence that did credit to his shrewdness. He was always ready to speak for his cause, and no one could do it better; but he had all a politician's aversion to dying for it. From all the street battles that had occurred during the previous year, whatever he may have had to do with the intrigues that led to them, he had kept himself clear: and to avoid figuring as an actor in the massacre of June, '48, he betook himself to the best position possible for contemplating it as a spectator. The very spot has been pointed out to me by the Count de Niewkerke, on the leads of the Louvre, where he lay in concealment till the dreadful tragedy was over in the streets below. I am far from seeking to insinuate aught against the courage of Ledru Rollin—there is no Frenchman without it—but I aim simply to show what shifts he was put to only to escape being mixed up with events that would have sent him to prison or to exile. Consequently, when the proposition reached him in June, '49, to raise the barricades once more, he replied by a flat refusal to take any part in it. Nothing could be more sensible; but a man who plays at revolution must be prepared for the freaks of revolutionists. It was one of the most daring of these who stepped forward at this crisis and told Ledru Rollin that his turn had come, and that he must choose either to put himself at the head of the intended movement, or have his brains blown out.

"This," said the speaker, "has been decided *au comité*, and I am delegated to receive your answer." He drew a pistol from his pocket as he spoke, and his resolution was known to be equal to the act. Ledru Rollin, like a man of sense, chose the least of two evils, and preferred the chances of exile to the certainty of dying by the hand of a fellow Republican. Neither roofs nor cellars afforded refuge this time, for he was surrounded by men not to be trifled with.

Preparations were then rapidly made for a final attempt to overthrow the Government, and to plunge France again into the foaming vortex of revolution. The motives of these misguided men must be apparent enough. The most of them only sought their own gain at the sacrifice of the country. Some of them were furious at the Revolution of '48 falling into the hands of Lamartine, whom they considered an aristocrat in disguise; but what they meant to do, if they got the power, besides cutting people's heads off, and appropriating their property, was a perfect mystery to themselves. If the leaders of the proposed revolt had either been honest or intelligent, they would not have resorted to violence whilst universal suffrage was the law of the land. What could be more illogical or absurd? They were rebelling against their own doctrines and proving their ignorance of true Republicanism in seeking to overthrow what the will of the people had created. They were stung, no doubt, that in '49 the people gave the majority to the Monarchists, which in '48 was bestowed on the Republicans. If this reaction arose from their own proved incapacity or bad faith, they should have hid themselves in sackcloth and ashes. If, however, they considered the nation too precipitate in rejecting them, their only course was to appeal to it through their orators and journals. It would have defied the ingenuity of both, and they knew it, to explain why, instead of diminishing taxation, the revolutionary Government had shamefully increased it. This single act convinced the country they were Republicans only in name, and as they felt it useless to sophisticate, they proposed forcing themselves on the nation whether they would or no. Such insane conduct as this served only to elate the Monarchical party, who saw it would strengthen them and bring more disgrace on the Republican name. The President of the Republic kept his eye upon all that passed, and without troubling his mind about the notions or sentiments of individuals or parties, quietly made up his mind to perform fearlessly the duty allotted to him and to preserve order against whoever assailed it.

It became every day more and more evident that the Republicans were getting ready for a desperate effort, which the moderate men, such as Cavaignac and Dufaure, would have prevented if they could. The ultra journals of the party teemed daily with furious invectives against the Government and the Monarchists of the Assembly. Prudhomme, the Socialist, in a journal which he edited, made the most grotesque efforts to excite sedition and to acquire notoriety. He declared, in a phrase that he thought would immortalize him, that "Property was robbery," *(la proprieté, c'est le vol)*, and pointed in proof of it to the condition of society in Europe and America. If he had limited his tirades against property to that portion of it which he could show was the result of unjust laws, well and good; but was that a reason why property acquired by intelligence and industry in spite of such laws should be confiscated? This conceited Socialist proposed to raze society to its foundations, for the pleasant occupation of reconstructing the world politically and morally anew. after patent plans of his own, whose efficacy he cried up with all the fervour of a charlatan, and all the insincerity of a demagogue. This wholesale reformer carried his impious audacity to the point of scoffing at all religion, and of denying the existence of the Deity—*le Dieu, c'est moi* (God, that's myself!), was another of his odious phrases. The greater the disgust of sensible people the greater the delight of M. Prudhomme, for notoriety, at any cost, was food for his vanity, and he revelled in that acquired by ridiculous means, from his inability to obtain it in any other way. The days of Anarchisis Clootz are gone by, and France, as well as the rest of the world, is advanced too far into the 19th century to listen seriously to the shallow ravings of idiots like Prudhomme,

As June wore on the din of discord rose higher. Menaces loud and deep resounded in the Republican camp, and one day in the Assembly, Ledru Rollin, after an intemperate speech, launched the threat of an appeal to arms. Signs of apprehension began to pervade Paris, and all classes dreaded some fearful catastrophe. I was assured by one of the Red Republicans that the houses of the rich were all marked for plunder; and I was earnestly advised to provide myself with a red cap and a dirty blouse as a protection against the fury of the mob. It was impossible to know how far disaffection spread, or what were the resources of the *emeutiers*, but deep uneasiness prevailed from the conviction that their intentions were bloody, and that their struggle would be desperate, as it would be the last.

At this moment of feverish suspense a new terror suddenly appeared in the shape of a ravaging pestilence. The cholera, after a fitful prelude of some days, broke out with appalling violence, and nothing was heard on every side but sounds of fear and woe. One would have thought that even the fury of murderous revolt would have yielded before such a piteous spectacle of universal distress, and have dropped from its parricidal hand the red brand of discord; but, on the contrary, it seized on this moment as the most opportune to effect its sinister purposes.

It was on the 13th of June, when the mortality was so great that the dead were carried off uncoffined in waggon-loads and thrown into pits, that the rumour spread through the streets of Paris that the barricades were erecting in the Faubourg St. Antoine. The tidings then came that Ledru Rollin, with sundry colleagues, had installed themselves in one of the public buildings (the School of Arts and Trades), and had constituted themselves into a Provisional Government. Every shop was closed throughout the metropolis, and every door and avenue bolted and barred in dread anticipation of the conflict. The streets were stripped of population, and their deserted and silent aspect at mid-day had an ominous and unnatural appearance. The news began to circulate that the insurrection was on march and was coming down the Boulevardes on its way to the Assembly. People wondered not to hear the rappel beating in the streets as usual, not to see the troops in motion, and parties of horse flying about to add to the general alarm. They trembled lest the Government, in dismay, would allow, as had so often happened, the revolt to get the upper hand. Down came the Revolutionists in great numbers, shouting for "*Liberty!*" "*Equality!*" and "*Fraternity!*" and really believing the day was their own, from the absence of any signs of resistance. They were just crossing the broad avenue of the Rue de la Paix when they were unexpectedly assailed by a powerful force of cavalry, with General Changarnier at their head, that dashed with fiery impetuosity through their midst, cutting them in two, and throwing them into such dire confusion, as to leave no resource but flight. In five minutes the Insurrection, which had been ushered in with so much *fracas*, and had weighed so heavily for weeks on the public mind, was at an end without firing a gun or killing a man. The President, serene amid pestilence and rebellion, had coolly planned a military *coup de main* worthy the genius of his uncle. I witnessed its execution, and the feverish, absorbing eagerness for the result which till now enchained me, suddenly gave place to feelings of unchecked merriment at this unlooked-for and grotesque *dénouement* of the Red Republican programme.

Meanwhile, the Provisional Government, with Ledru Rollin for its reluctant chief, were hard at work up town—*risum teneatis*—turning out Decrees of all sorts and sizes, totally unmindful that the Irish recipe for cooking a fish is quite as applicable to Revolutions, and that both must be caught and secured before they can be appropriated to use. The grave deliberations of these devoted patriots were unceremoniously disturbed by some ill-mannered policemen, who rushed into their Council Chamber, and bid them surrender, as the building was already in possession of the Troops. This was just such an occasion as the Romans of old would have chosen for dying on their swords, martyrs to their cause, but such heroism is out of fashion now-a-days, and the Provisional Government, scarcely an hour old, put an end to its existence by precipitately leaping right and left out of the windows that were, happily, not far from the ground, a precaution that may have been taken. The next heard of them was their safe arrival in England or Switzerland, glad enough of their escape, but as ready to serve their country, and pocket the profits, as ever. This was the inglorious end of Red Republicanism in France, which, from the breaking out of the Revolution in February, '48, had made several fierce attempts to obtain the ascendancy, that were, happily, frustrated.

CHAPTER VI.

A LITERARY ADVENTURE.

The Red Republicans and Socialists, the party of violence, was, as I have shown, finally suppressed, and France was now left in the hands of Parliamentary tacticians. Henceforth, art, not blows; intrigues, not barricades; argument, not cannon-shot, were to decide on the destinies of the country. It is important to take a cursory glance at the position of the pieces in the political game of chess now to begin. Let us look at the Assembly for a moment. On the right, *la droite*, sat the Monarchists in majority, whose votes, therefore, gave law to the land, but, unluckily for themselves, they were divided into two factions. The Orleanists, with M. Thiers, wished for a king and parliamentary institutions; that is a King Log to *reign*, with a legislative body to govern him and the country. This would have made M. Thiers, or whoever was leader of the legislative majority, a king *de facto*, as in England, where the Prime Minister is Absolute. The Legitimists, with M. Berryer, aimed at the old style of monarchy, a king both to reign and govern with as little interference as possible from those modern inventions, legislative bodies. These two branches of Monarchists, with different creeds, could work harmoniously against any third party that threatened their interests, but it was evident when they got rid of all opposition they must fight between themselves for the supremacy.

On the left of the Assembly, *la gauche*, sat the Republicans, shorn of their ultra members, now in exile or in prison. They were in the minority, and downcast from the conviction of having played their *rôle* badly. General Cavaignac was their recognised lleader.

In the centre, *le centre*, sat a number of respectable gentlemen, such as M. Dufaure, &c., who eschewed the Monarchists, doubting if they would get up again, and who shyed the Republicans, as they seemed going down. They were in the best position for jumping down on the strongest side when it was discovered. I may add, that the cousin of the President, Napoleon Bonaparte, was a member of the Assembly, and sat among the Republicans, at which the Monarchists sneered visibly. As he was neither an Orleanist nor a Legitimist, he could not appear amongst them. To have taken his place in the centre would show he was against the Republic, the form of government existing, which was not the case, and so he naturally sat on the left. This was the condition of the Assembly in the autumn of '49.

The President of the Republic, as I have shewn, had hitherto kept aloof from the contests of the Monarchists and the Republicans from reasons as prudent as patriotic. He perceived that neither sought the good of the nation, but merely their own advantage. The time, however, had come when isolation was no longer possible. The Constitution divided the powers of the State between the Executive and the Legislative—that is, between the President and the Assembly. This was well enough ; but the error of its Republican framers was not to define distinctly the attributes of each. This was designed, no doubt, to prevent the Executive doing anything without the concurrence of the Legislature; but why, then, leave him any initiative whatever ?

The President had the command of the Army and Navy, as well as all the vast patronage of the State. The Assembly had the control of the Finances, and could, further, pass laws every hour of the day to illegalize what the Executive did. The Constitution was, therefore, so badly planned as to render harmony between these two co-ordinate powers very unlikely, and even impossible, if they entertained different views. The duration of the Republic was, therefore, a matter of accident. The Monarchists at this epoch had no misgivings as to the future. Taking the President to be nothing else than a doll in their hands, a rivalry was springing up between the Orleanists and Legitimists to obtain his adhesion to their separate projects.

It was rumoured that M. Thiers was planning a marriage between the President and the Duchess of Orleans, in order to get back the fallen dynasty with Parliamentary institutions. M. Berryer, it was supposed, was seeking to effect a pleasant arrangement between the President and the Count de Chambord, in the hope to set the old dynasty on its legs again. The Republicans eyed these manœuvres with considerable relish, knowing they would regain their ascendancy if the Monarchical majority broke in twain. All these schemes and illusions were suddenly scattered for ever by a blast as sweeping as unexpected. A thunder-bolt in mid-winter could not have been more startling. All the leaders of party were petrified, like Don Bartolo in the opera, and stood gazing on vacancy, motionless and dumb.

A letter appeared one day in the papers from the President to his Aide-de-Camp, Colonel Ney, wherein enough was said to prove he was not the pliant, timid, incapable tool the politicians of France had taken him to be; but that he had a mind of his own, and meant to show it. The moment had arrived, as I said, for the President to manifest himself. He saw there was nothing in common between him and the selfish politicians that agitated the country. Orleanists, Legitimists, Republicans, and Socialists, they were all alike. A stable Government, wise Legislation, the developement of the country, the good of the masses—these things never entered the heads of one of them. They sought power merely for emolument, for their personal benefit, not for the national welfare. I will not assert the President was more disinterested or patriotic than the others, but it is evident he was more sagacious. He believed the French people both intelligent and resolute, and attributed the downfall of preceding Governments to the obstinacy or blindness of Statesmen in ignoring so plain a fact. A politician now-a-days who derides the common sense of the masses builds his projects on sand, There was no choice for the President but to truckle to the leaders of the Assembly, or to champion the cause of the nation. It was a fearful decision to make. His career, his name, his head, were in the scale. Arrayed against him was the entire Assembly, Monarchists and Republicans. Each was willing to use him as a stepping-stone; but all were ready to bury their antipathies, and to make a mockery of their principles to overthrow him if he should attempt to rescue the country out of their hands.

The position of the President was singular and interesting; without a party or followers; his very Ministers deserting him at every crisis; his best friends vacillating and alarmed; his conviction in the wisdom of his policy and the discernment of the people must have been profound indeed to encourage him to stand up against all the chiefs of all the parties of France, with all their experience, ability, and renown. His designs, however, were unknown. Did he mean to overthrow the Republic? Did he aspire to set up the Empire? No one knew. He appealed to the hopes of none, and risked the opposition of all. I remember no parallel in history. His Uncle had devoted friends at the head of the Army. Cromwell was the agent of a pervading fanaticism. Augustus openly aimed at Empire. The President Bonaparte, with no interest in the Army, no hold on the nation, his purpose unspoken, modestly made known, as already stated in his letter to Edgar Ney, that he would not bow down his head to the idols of the Assembly, either Monarchical or Republican.

The first shock of astonishment over, measures were decided on to put an end to this unseemly refractoriness. The Orleanists and Legitimists dropped at once the discussion of their rival dynasties, and M. Thiers and Berryer united zealously to bring the President to his senses. They still considered him a mere child in politics, and regarded his late mutiny as a juvenile freak, which a little discipline would cure. The extra allowance which in a confiding moment they had voted him was promptly cut off. The Ministers of the President who, in imitation of English usage, were members of the Assembly and belonged to the Monarchical party, were threatened with proscription. So intemperate in conduct were these enraged leaders of the majority that there was imminent prospect of the Government coming to a stand-still from the want of co-operation between the Executive and the Legislative, and worse still, the country was in danger of being thrown into violent commotion from their open hostility. In truth, a collision was aimed at by the Monarchists with a view to plunge poor France once more into all the horrors of a Socialist revolution, for, said they, "after the deluge we must come."

I heard this odious confession frequently in the mouths of Monarchists, whose hope was not only to get rid of the President, but to make France despair so entirely of political redemption as to cause her to relapse into Monarchy for a century to come. This fact ought to speak trumpet-tongued to all classes and all countries as a proof of the unscrupulousness of politicians when interest or ambition inspire them.

The President was aware of their heinous design, and determined to thwart it. Instead of rushing into violent warfare with the Assembly, he frequently yielded to the tyranny of the majority. Sometimes he changed his Ministers to gratify their caprice; at others, he withdrew propositions for the good of the country which the Monarchists ridiculed or opposed. By this cautious manœuvring the President lulled the anger of the *coryphées* of the Assembly, and confirmed their old delusion that, after all, he was only an unruly *gamin*, who could be managed by their superior adroitness. One result of this state of things was the prolongation of the Republic. The President had no intention to assail it; the Monarchists wished to upset it, but not till all was ready; the Republicans were anxious, of course, to preserve it. Danger environed it, but its existence was more seriously imperilled by its own organic defects than by the animosity of its enemies. There were many sensible people who, caring more for the welfare of the country than the success of parties, thought that as the Republic was existing the best thing was to get it into good working condition, so as to make a permanent thing of it. All that France wanted was stability, and the Republic might, if properly organized, become the best neutral ground for parties of all shades to meet on, and where their contests might be pursued without trampling on the tranquillity of the nation.

Some set to work penetrating the mysteries of the far-famed British Constitution, which either from the perfection of its machinery, or the skill with which it was administered, had for many years secured for England a large share of order, liberty, and material prosperity. Other publicists directed their inquiring glance across the Atlantic, and began to investigate the handiwork of the sages of '87, which had hitherto solved the problem that order and prosperity were compatible with equality of classes and complete liberty of speech and action. The journals and reviews of France teemed with Constitutional discussions; but from want of practical knowledge, the best intentioned writers so obscured and complicated the subject, now treating it too philosophically, and then too elaborately, that the middle and lower classes, who were anxious for their own sakes to know the difference between a good Constitution and a bad one, gave up the hope in despair. To make the confusion worse, the ablest Monarchical writers, who had the most journals at command, misrepresented everything with so much art that if the Abbé Siéyes himself had come back to life he would have been cruelly bothered how to decide.

I remarked that the shrewdest polemists left the British Constitution pretty much to itself, partly because it was not written and depended only on usage, but more, because it was found an ingenious puzzle as it stood, and required no misconstruction to heighten its mystery. Moreover, M. Thiers and the Orleanists desired nothing better than to set up a pattern of the British Constitution in France, that is, a King without power, a House of Peers to play dummy, and a House of Commons to monopolize all the work, with a Prime Minister at its head, absolute master of the Government and country. This was just the thing to suit ambitious statesmen in France and elsewhere, and if all such were as good men and true as Sully and Colbert, the British Constitution might be copied with advantage. The experiment, however, had been tried three times in France, under

Louis XVIII., Charles X., and Louis Philippe, and failed. What the Monarchists most feared was the chance of the Federal Constitution of the United States becoming known at this time in France; for if the ricketty framework of the Republic were readjusted after the American model, the probability was great that neither Monarchy with Parliamentary institutions or without would be seen in France again. Consequently, the pens of the ablest political foes of the Republic were frequently at work disfiguring and belying the undefended charter of '87, consecrated by the names of Washington and Franklin.

I often wondered that no American in Paris took up the cudgels for the sake of truth, if not from patriotic motives—and certainly no one was more competent than Mr. Rives, who had succeeded Mr. Rush as our Minister to France; but his official position probably restrained him.

One day in November, '49, I picked up the *Constitutionnel*, the organ at that time of M. Thiers, and read an essay on our Federal Constitution, which falsified it from beginning to end; and, to my profound surprise, I found it signed with the name of a person professing to be from the State of Ohio. No such individual was known to my countrymen in Paris; and I afterwards discovered that M. Thiers himself was suspected to be the author of the paper in question, but, to add to its weight, had cunningly given it an American origin. My patriotism boiled over at this outrageous *rûse*, and, with the recklessness of a Yankee, who never reflects till he is *in* a "fix," I rushed down into the arena of journalism, resolved to defend the Constitution; but consoled at knowing that neither it nor myself would perish in the attempt. I sat down in my lodgings without a book of any kind, not even a copy of the charter itself before me, and, worse than all, had to write in

French. After pommelling my brains vigorously for a couple of days, I got together a dozen pages or more of manuscript, which expressed all I had to say more or less clearly.

To make the American part of my story more interesting, I drew comparisons with the state of things in England and France. I was rather afraid of being accused of meddling with what did not concern me, and, therefore, handled French affairs with delicacy, whilst I hit right and left at that venerable sham, the British Constitution.

Firing at random sometimes brings a prize; and some time after I discovered that I had winged a splendid one, indeed, as I shall show. I carried off my handiwork to the organ of the Republican party, the *National*, of which M. Caylus was the editor, in place of M. Marrast, and explained the motives that had led to its production. M. Caylus, who had lived a good deal in the United States, thought that a lucid exposition of such a subject would be equally interesting and important, and promised me its early and prominent insertion in his columns.

For several days I enjoyed the tickling consciousness of having "done the State some service;" and as this was the first time, after many vagaries, that I had ever written a political essay, I anticipated, with great relish, the genuine surprise of my friends at seeing me transformed into a ready-made publicist. Alas, for my aspirations! I received at the end of a week my manuscript back again, with a polite note from M. Caylus to the effect that a committee of the editors had perused my lucubrations and decided not to publish them in the *National.* This was mortifying and perplexing. Were my views so commonplace, and the style so bald, as to motive the rejection, which M. Caylus was too civil to say? or had I reflected with too much impartiality on the political bantling brought forth by the Republican party, which the *National* represented? I was not inclined to abandon the job I had begun, and deliberated how to go to work next. I split my essay into three parts—the first on the United States' Constitution, the second on the British, the third on the French—thinking that if I could get the first two doses down the throat of any journalist, I would have less difficulty in making him gulp the last and hardest one.

There was one journal in Paris independent of party, of great circulation, and edited with brilliant ability by the celebrated Emile de Girardin. I knew he dared do all an editor dared, and a good deal more, so I never feared that he would publish my matter if he thought it worth the honor of a place in his columns. I called on him forthwith. He perused my commentaries on the American Constitution with deep attention in my presence, when he said, in his abrupt way,—

"*C'est bien* (This is well); I will publish it."

"I have also attempted an analysis of the British Government," I added.

"If it is equal to this," he continued, "I will insert it."

"These two, however," I remarked, "are only preliminary to a third paper on French affairs."

"Indeed!" he said, with great animation, "I should like to see *that*, and if it does not fall below the rest I will publish it readily."

I was glad to find one journalist in France who preferred the interests of the country to those of party, and was disposed to give all sides a fair hearing in the hope of aiding truth.

The political organisation of France was at this time the vital question, and yet the Republican organ refused the opinions of an American democrat, which the independent journal published.

This fact proves that I have not exaggerated in declaring that in '49 the French politicians, both Republican and Monarchical, were solely bent on their own good, whatever the consequences to their country. On the 21st of November my first sketch was launched on the political world, and the effect was flattering enough to my self love. My countrymen of all grades, after their surprise was over, expressed their satisfaction in round terms. This was highly important, of course, and I was, next, anxious to see what the French thought of the matter. In society I was highly complimented, but the newspapers were silent. This I anticipated, for I thought they would likely be indisposed to contend with me on my own ground.

On the 13th of December I fired my second battery point blank at the penetrable sides of the British Constitution. This did considerable execution. The French of all parties, save the Orleanists, rubbed their hands in private, and exceedingly relished this Yankee bang at the imposing theory of King, Lords, and Commons, so ludicrously evaded in practice. Many of the French said—" This is the first time I ever got a distinct idea of *ce tortillement incroyable, la constitution Anglaise,*" (that incredible *twistification,* the English Constitution,) to which, of course, I bowed low. The English were quite startled at this Transatlantic ebullition. The knowing ones, I mean especially the statesmen in power, resolved at once to *manage* me, if possible, as I will show bye and bye. I must except Lord Brougham, though, whom I met in Paris soon after this, and in thanking me for the allusion I had made to him, said, " he esteemed it both a compliment and an honour." Such language to me from Lord Brougham made me think I had not written atlogether in vain. Still the Paris journals were dumb, though the London *Times* quoted portions of my No. 2.

Last of all came my sugar-coated pill for the French themselves. The Monarchists put on a smiling face, like well-bred people when swallowing anything unpleasant. My Republican friends, on the contrary, indulged in a deal of grimace, and uttered their dissatisfaction in tones not loud, but deep. To my unalloyed astonishment the French press, so celebrated for its intrepid spirit of controversy, refused to enter the lists of discussion, and contented itself with simply quoting a paragraph here and there from my letters to suit some party purpose. I was not forced to conclude that my views were considered too crude for refutation, for in private I received the most flattering compliments from the first men of France and other countries. Several English journals reviewed me at some length, and the *Spectator* more especially did me the honour of a criticism of several columns and of striking power. It was undeniable, therefore, that the journalists of Paris hesitated to pick up the gauntlet, because my facts were indisputable, and my treatment of them entirely candid and impartial. I sought not to favour the projects of party, but to interpret politics in such a fashion as to entice the nation into a clearer inspection of its own interests. To avoid a discussion that might have been detrimental to the designs of party, but in that proportion advantageous to the country, was, doubtless, a judicious step on the part of the political leaders who controlled the press of Paris, but it was proof at the same time that their motives were both selfish and unpatriotic.

I have said enough of these newspaper effusions to excite the curiosity, likely, of some of my readers, whom I refer, therefore, to the appendix, where they will find them at full length. To those who take less interest in such arid but important questions I will venture here on a brief summary.

I undertook to demonstrate in my first essay that in both ancient and modern society there were three elements. A leading man or men; an intelligent class; and the multitude. The well known Greek words show they existed then. *Monos, Aristos, Demus*—one, the best, the many. In England, at the present day, the same elements are expressed by King, Lords, and Commons. From this I inferred that a Government to be durable must represent these elements, and that from the world's record society had suffered, and government had perished, because they were either not represented or badly combined together. I showed that the profoundest thinkers of the world, ancient and modern, had declared that this *mixed* government was the best; but, also, that the greatest legislators of all ages had constantly failed to establish a government of this nature. I indicated the errors of Lycurgus at Sparta, and of Romulus at Rome. The great problem then remained, how to unite in harmonious action the three elements spoken of that were naturally hostile to each other, but with common interests. I declared that the first successful instance in history of a mixed Government was the Federal Constitution of the United States. I explained that herein not only was the supreme power divided into executive and legislative, and the legislative further subdivided so as to represent the intelligent class *(aristos)* and the many *(demus)*, but that the grand merit of the sages of '87 was to have found the way to adjust these elemental forces in a manner that all would work; work *equally*, and therefore, lastingly. If my demonstration is logical, and my deductions true, then, it is clear that the signers of the Constitution of '87 are entitled to the "vast renown" of having invented a model Government, which must be coeval with time if *its system of checks and balances are preserved inviolate.* Here is the great danger.

In my review of the British Constitution I showed that a mixed Government representing the three elements unequally, entitled King, Lords, and Commons, sprung naturally from the situation of the country after the Conquest of 1066. From the imperfect balance of these elements it followed in England as in other countries, and ages, that the Government was overthrown, first, by the democratic element in 1640, and next, by the aristocratic element in 1688. I proved that since then the Monarchical and Democratic elements have had no Constitutional existence, and that the supreme power was no longer divided between a mixed Government, but was monopolized by the aristocratic element or intelligent class, which Government is called an Oligarchy. I explained, further, that at all epochs Government had been more or less influenced by four great classes, representing the four cardinal passions of the heart—the love of religion, the love of war, the love of knowledge, and the love of gain—that is, by the priest, the soldier, the thinker, and the capitalist. In ancient society Government was swayed by the clerical influence when Theocracies prevailed. In the middle ages the military influence was predominant when Feudality existed. In recent times the literary influence and the financial influence are in the ascendant. I asserted that the legitimate object of Government, the good of the greatest number, was frustrated when any one or more of these influences biassed it for the benefit of the class represented. I demonstrated, finally, that in England the Aristocratic element in possession of the supreme power since 1688 had, with a view to maintain its supremacy over its rival elements, the Monarchical and Democratic, conciliated the four influences cited, by bestowing, with a prodigal hand, on the four classes represented, to wit—the clerical, military, literary, and financial—rank, wealth, and power. By this policy the Oligarchy had prolonged their sway, but it was done at the cost of the masses.

The political history of France, from the fall of the Roman Empire, afforded me, in my third letter, an admirable field for testing the theories advanced in the previous ones. It appeared that from the fifth century to the tenth the Monarchical element, supported by the religious influence, had wielded the supreme power. The rise of feudality gave preponderance to the aristocratic element, sustained by the military influence. Again, under Louis XIV., the Monarchical element regained the supremacy, but this time in conjunction with the religious and military influences. Finally, in 1789, the Democratic element got the mastery, with the aid of the literary and financial influences; but no combination with its rival elements being possible at that epoch, it lost, in turn, its control of the sovereign power. In '15, '30, and '48, I showed that attempts were made to organize Government on the solid basis of an union of the three elements; but from design rather than ignorance, they were never brought into harmonious balance, and, consequently, their collisions led to successive revolutions.

In seeking to make my analysis of these letters very brief I may have rendered it somewhat obscure, but a reference to the originals in the appendix will, perhaps, enable the reader to comprehend more fully my meaning. Before quitting this subject I cannot forbear relating a simple incident connected with it. I was at a *fête* at the Elysée one night soon after the appearance of my third letter in the *Presse*, when in one of its crowded saloons I encountered the President, surrounded by his usual *cortége*. He extended his hand towards me with more animation than is his wont, and said in a loud voice, "*Mais, vous avez ecri des choses supérbes*" (you have written some fine things). I was sensibly touched by this marked compliment, and made my acknowledgments in a tone of emotion. I thought the occasion, however, very opportune to try my hand at breaking through that reserve no one yet had been able to penetrate. By the existing Constitution the re-elegibility of the President was forbid, and I had pointed that out as an error. I was very curious to know the President's sentiments on this vital point. In the course of my conversation, therefore, I remarked,

"Your Highness, no doubt, perceived an allusion to yourself in one of my letters."

"To myself!" he echoed in a tone of surprise. "No, I did not. To what do you refer?"

"In commenting on the Constitution of '48 I declared that the non-re-eligibility of the President was a grave defect, and one which had been avoided in our Constitution of the United States." As I spoke I watched the countenance of the President, which changed its expression for a moment, for he was totally unprepared for such a side-thrust as this, and he measured at a glance all the importance of his reply. He put his hands calmly behind him, and was just about to speak when Lord Normanby, the British Ambassador, came up to address him, and I was left to speculate upon what he would, could, or might have said on this pregnant point.

CHAPTER VII.

THE VISCOUNT PALMERSTON.

I left Paris in February of '50, and returned thither in August of the same year. During this short interval, the Legislative Assembly had constantly lost ground in public opinion; for, utterly neglectful of the interests of the country, they were wholly immersed in party intrigues. The Monarchical leaders were, no doubt, deeply annoyed at the inactivity forced upon them by the masterly prudence of the President, whom neither seductions nor provocation could swerve from the independent and national path he had traced out for himself. With a view to coerce him into a more pliant course, the politicians of the Right reduced the annual salary they had at first voted him. This was as ineffectual as the largesses that were occasionally held out for his acceptance. The President seemed fully conscious that the eye of the nation was directed upon him and the Assembly; and when he saw the reluctance of the latter to co-operate with him in any salutary measure of policy, he resolved to keep aloof from all connection with their paltry schemes of party aggrandizement.

The fall of Ledru Rollin and the ultra Republicans in June, '49, left the field open to the Assembly, which might, by a business-like and patriotic course, have acquired a complete ascendancy over France. Instead of this, the Monarchists had frittered away their opportunities and character by paltry manœuvres against the President, and a tyrannical persecution of the Republican Opposition.

In the spring of '50 an event occurred which must have startled the videttes of the Right, for it showed them that opinion was going round again to their opponents. The celebrated writer and ultra Democrat, Eugéne Sue, was elected to the Assembly for Paris by a great majority over his Monarchical antagonist. Instead of profiting by this significant warning, M. Thiers and his cohort laid hold of this result as a pretext for putting down universal suffrage, which was nothing else than an act of *felo de se.*

A new law of franchise was hurried through the Assembly and sent in to the President for his signature. Was this only an ingenious trap to involve the President in difficulty? If he refused to sign this unpopular measure, as it may have been hoped, it would afford the Monarchists the longed-for opportunity of making open war upon him. If, on the contrary, he identified himself with this blow at the sovereignty of the people, a great object was gained by destroying his popularity. It must have been an anxious moment for the President; but he wisely decided to risk temporarily the favor of the people, rather than afford the Monarchists an occasion, by his resistance, to throw the country into violent disorder Besides, the Constitution had given him no *veto,* and he could not legally refuse to sign the law of M. Thiers, emasculating the suffrage. The responsibility was on the Assembly, and the penalty was sure to be paid one day or the other.

The position of the President at home, thwarted by all parties, suspected by the patriotic, and, as yet, unknown to the masses, was full enough of perplexity and peril; but he had quite as difficult a rôle to play with the great Powers of Europe. Russia, Austria, and Prussia sympathized with the exiled Dynasties, whilst they still retained their ancient antipathy to the revolutionary origin of the Bonapartes.

These were reasons enough why the Despotisms of the Continent should shrink from fraternization with the French Republic, whilst there was no inducement whatever to enter into friendly relations with a ruler, were he otherwise unobjectionable, whose tenure of power was limited to four short years.

The President made due allowance for the prejudices and fears of the leading States of Europe, and had the wisdom and independence not to compromise his own position, or lower the dignity of France, by employing any unworthy arts to conciliate them. He must have regarded as a misfortune the league of the Continental Governments against him, whilst the Monarchists of the Assembly rightly considered this as the source of their greatest strength, for they all looked forward to the day as not far distant when a second army of invasion would enter France, to establish once more the Bourbon Dynasty. At this critical moment, the summer of '50, the President cast his eyes upon England, which was really in worse odour at this juncture with the Despotisms of the Continent than the French Republic itself. The British Foreign Office was suspected of a lurking sympathy with the revolutionary party, which had so lately menaced every Throne in Europe, and no expression of abhorrence and disgust was strong enough to convey what was thought and felt by Continental Statesmen of that "firebrand" of Downing Street, the detested Lord Palmerston.

On the fall of the Orleans Dynasty and the appearance of the Republic, in '48, the English Ambassador in Paris, Lord Normanby, had immediate instructions to recognize it; and from that moment the English Government had manifested the rational desire to live on friendly terms with France, whatever might be its form of Government. During the two years that had elapsed the

Prime Minister of England, Lord John Russell, had not manifested in his acts or words any wish to cultivate relations with the Prince Louis Napoleon to the extent of compromising his standing with the Continental Powers; still it was observed that the English Envoy was constantly seen at the elbow of the President. It was only known to the initiated few that this assiduousness was in obedience to the orders of the Secretary of the Foreign Office, Lord Palmerston, and that neither the Prime Minister nor the English Court approved of it.

It was little dreamt of at the time by Lord Palmerston, or the President, or any one else, that Lord Normanby, in compliance with secret instructions from the highest quarters, was only paying outward homage to the President, whilst, unsuspected, he was intriguing for the interests of the Orleans Dynasty. It is hardly fair to blame Lord Normanby for this diplomatic jugglery, until it is quite decided whether he was bound to carry out the policy of the Foreign Secretary, or yield to the wishes of still loftier personages. It is clear from this that a double game was playing, which finally ended in a catastrophe, as all trickery usually does. The President felt quite sure of the apparent sympathy of the English Secretary for Foreign Affairs, yet he must have been puzzled at the well-bred distance so steadily maintained by the British Government towards him. The policy of the English Prime Minister at this epoch may be easily explained. As the head of an Oligarchy, he naturally shrunk from too close a connection with a Republic, and, above all, with a Republic on so unstable a foundation as that of France unquestionably was. Besides, the Dynasty and Government of England were bound by ancient alliance, ties of sympathy, and bonds of political interest, to the Continental Powers, and, furthermore, both must have been naturally averse to form too dangerous an intimacy with the nephew of a Sovereign they had chiefly contributed to overthrow, and whose antecedents inspired both doubt and dislike. If in the face of these considerations the Foreign Minister, Lord Palmerston, endeavoured to cement a close alliance with the President of the French Republic, it must be assigned either to his superior acumen that foresaw all the immense advantages to flow from it, or to a reckless disregard of the consequences that might ensue. This is an important question for the fame of this great Statesman, as well as for the truth of history, and it may be in my power to drop some hints that may help to elucidate both.

In August, 1850, I encountered one day, in the street, a person I had frequently met in the *salons* of Paris, the Hon. R. Edwardes, acting Secretary of the British Embassy at Paris. He expressed his satisfaction at my return from my recent trip to the United States, and pressed me with some earnestness to call at the Embassy to see him. Though much in the habit of meeting him in the best society yet I had never cultivated the acquaintance of Mr. Edwardes, for his manners were not conciliating, nor his conversation very attractive. He had the air of a man deeply buried in rumination, and when he spoke it was with the abruptness of a person suddenly recalled from the dream-land he seemed to inhabit. His eyes, however, were sparkling and restless, which showed that his torpid exterior was only a diplomatic cloak to hide his vigilant observation of men and things. He was a man of some 40 years and upwards, and had passed his life in diplomatic service at the different Courts of Europe. He was at the moment filling the post of Secretary of Embassy, to which he expected to be permanently named.

Receiving a second invitation to call on him, I did so, and

we had a long chat on politics. Mr. E. was by no means disposed to express his own opinions, but rather sought in a subtle manner to extract those of others. I perceived his craft, but gave utterance to my sentiments without reserve, as I had no motive for concealment. I spoke of the uncertainty that overhung the destinies of France, and that I could see no solution but in the prolongation of the power of the President, who alone seemed capable of dealing with the tremendous perils that were imminent. I talked of England and her foreign policy, saying that it seemed to me that her best course was to consolidate as far as she could the position of the President, and to enter into the most cordial union with France, as the interests of both nations demanded it. Referring to the United States, I asserted that I saw nothing to prevent the best understanding between them and England and France, since they were all equally bound to each other by mutual interest. These simple views were listened to with great attention by the hon. Secretary of Embassy, and I inferred he approved of them, as he said nothing to the contrary.

We dined together soon afterwards, when it came out that he had read at the time my essay on the British Constitution, and I deduced from what he let drop that I had hit the nail so exactly on the head that no friend of the Oligarchy, much more an official under it, would like to see the blow repeated. I began to suspect forthwith that the astute Secretary had a motive in his friendly demonstrations, and that he meant in one way or another to allay my Yankee ardour to grapple with the mysteries of the British Constitution. Whether in this he was the agent of superior authority, or only seeking by a display of zeal and activity to make his promotion surer, never occurred to me at the time. One day, at the close of August, I announced to him my intention to run over to London for a few days on private business, when he asked me if I would like to make the acquaintance of the Minister for Foreign Affairs, the Viscount Palmerston, for in that case he would give me letters of introduction. It is needless to say I accepted this flattering offer with extreme readiness, though I marvelled at the time how it came to pass that a simple Secretary of Embassy could venture to present a stranger to so illustrious a personage as the Viscount Palmerston. This mystery, like many others, unravelled itself in process of time, which, however, it may not be necessary to explain. I arrived in London on the first of September, and the day following called in Carlton Gardens and left my introduction and card for the noble Secretary of State. On returning to my hotel some hours later I found the card of Lord Palmerston, with the following note :—

Carlton Gardens, September 2nd, 1850.

Lord Palmerston presents his compliments to Mr. Wikoff, and regrets much that as he is leaving London this afternoon, he cannot receive Mr. Wikoff here, but if Mr. Wikoff will do him the favour to come down to Broadlands to-morrow to dine and sleep, and will excuse the want of any company to meet him, Lord Palmerston will have great pleasure in receiving him.

The one o'clock or five o'clock trains from the Waterloo station would bring Mr. Wikoff in good time to Romsey, which is within a mile from Broadlands.

I was not more surprised than flattered at this prompt acknowledgment of my visit, but it was chiefly owing, no doubt, to the fact of his Lordship's leaving London that day for his country seat after the adjournment of Parliament. I took the five o'clock train next day for Romsey, which the time-tables informed me I would reach soon after 7 o'clock. I had, therefore, abundant time to dwell on the good fortune awaiting me in making the acquaintance of one of the leading Statesmen of Europe, and the most prominent man at the time in England. My mind naturally reverted to his long and singular political career.

Lord Palmerston entered Parliament in 1805 at 21 years of age, and only four years later he obtained the post of Secretary of War in the Ministry of Mr. Perceval. This office, to be sure, had not the importance its name implies, for its duties were purely administrative and secondary, yet it seems strange that so young a man, who had attracted no attention during his brief Parliamentary career, should have been chosen for its occupant. This was owing to the influence of the celebrated Canning, whom the young Viscount had conciliated by his personal qualities and social influence. It may be curious to quote a sketch of Lord Palmerston at the epoch in question, wherein no prophetic eye could easily discern the elements of a future Prime Minister:—"At this time Lord Palmerston was a lion *par excellence*, and was little known save for the cut of his coat, the elegance of his horses, his prowess in gallantry, his successes at Almack's, his skill in the waltz, which, some say, he introduced into England, the *painted* freshness of his complexion, and by that mixture of arrogance and *fadeur*, a demeanour at once stiff and careless, which go to constitute what is generally designated as an *Exclusive*." I will not vouch, of course, for the fidelity of the portrait, but the fact that the *sobriquet* of "Cupid" has up to late years been publicly attached to the name of Lord Palmerston, is proof that his reputation of a *Don Giovanni* is not, at all events, exaggerated. However subordinate the functions of Secretary of War, or however insignificant the means by which he first acquired it, yet it is certain Lord Palmerston could not have retained it for the extraordinary period of 19 years, through five successive Ministeries,* without sterling merits of some kind. During all this tumultuous period he made no figure in Parliament whatever, which would make the retention of his place really mysterious, if it was not known that Lord Palmerston was remarkable always for his intelligence, activity, and strict attention to business. After the fall of Fox, in 1806, the Whigs, or Liberal party, bid a long farewell to power, and up to the hour of his quitting office, in 1828, Lord Palmerston's Toryism was above suspicion. The triumph of the Holy Alliance at Waterloo led to the vigorous suppression of Liberalism all over Europe, and the Tories, under Lord Liverpool, governed the country with extreme rigor. Popular principles began to revive at length, and under Canning, in 1827, Catholic Emancipation and Reform were again discussed. The Duke of Wellington took office a year later, and Toryism was once more in the ascendant. Amid all these fluctuations of opinion, Lord Palmerston remained stationary; and whether Whig or Tory swayed the Government, he was still seen carrying his portfolio of Secretary of War under his arm. One could almost suppose they had grown together. It may justly be inferred from this that Lord Palmerston thought more of office than principle, and that he sacrificed his convictions to his interest. Without meaning to slander his Lordship, it may be said, that Lord Palmerston was never troubled with either convictions or principles in politics. He entered political life too early to form them, and his experience soon taught him the inutility of entertaining them. He discovered, doubtless, that in the country and age he lived, expediency was the true secret of Government,

---

* Mr. Perceval, Lord Liverpool, Mr. Canning, Lord Goderich, Duke of Wellington.

and that as maintaining the *statu quo*, and resisting the spirit of the century, were alike impossible, it was plainly the *rôle* of an English politician to concede what was exacted, and to refuse what might be denied. This is the key-note to Lord Palmerston's whole career. After the French Revolution of '30, he perceived that Toryism in England was tottering to its fall, and to escape being buried in its ruins, he followed Mr. Huskisson in his retreat from the Wellington Ministry. Uncertain of the advent of the Whigs, he did not go over to them at once; but, along with Mr. Huskisson, took up an independent position, which left him the option to join any Government likely to maintain itself. For the first time during this interval, from '28 to '31, he turned his attention to acquiring a Parliamentary reputation, and more particularly directed his attention to foreign questions. He made some speeches on the affairs of Portugal and Greece that attracted attention. Both as to affairs at home and abroad his opinions assumed a more decidedly liberal hue than ever before, though he did not go the length of the leading Whigs in their propositions of Reform. When, in '31, Earl Grey planted the Whig banner in triumph on the heights of the Treasury Bench, followed by all his brilliant cohort, Brougham, Stanley, Russell, Graham, Melbourne, to the astonishment of all, and the dissatisfaction of many, he placed the important charge of the foreign policy of the Government in the hands of Lord Palmerston, whose reputation was far below those I have cited, and that of many others.

For ten years the Whigs retained office, save for a brief interval in '34, and for the entire period Lord Palmerston managed the foreign affairs of England. In this lofty position he displayed abilities quite adequate to all the grave questions he was compelled to handle. He began by cultivating the French Alliance with Louis Philippe. He next settled the famous Belgian difficulty by erecting a throne for Leopold. He formed the Quadruple Alliance, which gave the preponderance to England in Spain and Portugal. He pushed on the conquests of England in India, and forced open the ports of China, to the gain of the commercial world. He finished by getting involved in a quarrel with France in '40, and with the United States in '41, which likely contributed to the fall of the Whig Ministry. He remained in Opposition, attacking the Ministry of Sir Robert Peel at times with great vigour, till '46, when he returned to his former post of Foreign Minister, under Lord John Russell. The Cabinet of Sir Robert Peel left to their successors a misunderstanding with the French Government as to the Spanish marriages, which still existed at the time of the Revolution of '48.

As I have stated before, Lord Palmerston recognised the French Republic at once, and studiously avoided further interference. The revolutionary mania that overspread Europe in '48 and '49 afforded ample scope for the judgment and experience of the Foreign Minister of England, and he had a nice course to steer between the tottering Governments of the Continent and the Revolutionary party, for a time so triumphant. It was expected by the latter that the English Cabinet would aid them to consolidate their power, whilst it was feared by the former that if it refrained from doing so it would only be on the condition of a Constitution being guaranteed to the insurgent States in question. The Constitutional Governments of Belgium, Portugal, and Spain, had been mainly set up by the influence of England in previous years, and certainly the present seemed an auspicious moment to Constitutionalize the whole of Europe. What Lord Palmerston might have thought the interests of his country would suggest as the best policy I do not know, but the Ministry, of which he was only an unit, was not disposed to interfere; consequently his *rôle* was reduced to that of a vigilant and humane surveillance of passing events. He was violently assailed by the reactionary party on the Continent for his supposed sympathy with the progressive cause, whilst he was bitterly railed at by the popular leaders for belying their hopes.

A general outcry was raised against him both at home and abroad, and the storm of discontent went on accumulating, till at last it descended on his head in the shape of a vote of censure in the House of Lords, June, '50. Lord Palmerston was really suspected by the Oligarchy of leaning to the revolutionary party on the Continent, and it was thought necessary to eject him from office. The pretext for this was sought in his energetic conduct against the Greek Government, from whom he demanded redress for injuries against a certain Don Pacifico, a naturalized British subject. The truth simply was, that he was struggling against the Russian influence that controlled the petty kingdom of Greece, and was overspreading the East. For this purpose he seized the occasion of Don Pacifico's claims, and restored British influence by a vigorous demonstration at the Court of Greece. To move against Russia at that moment was considered by the Oligarchy as revolutionary, and hence the vote of censure of June, '50. The matter next came before the House of Commons, and it was universally expected that Lord Palmerston would be compelled by a similar vote of dissatisfaction to tender his resignation. The Press was unanimous in its condemnation. The *Times* fired its broadsides at him daily. Public opinion looked on him with suspicion. His staunchest friends apologised in advance for the votes they intended to cast against him. His fall was imminent, when he rose on the 25th of June, '50, and made his memorable defence. He passed in review his foreign policy from the time he took office to the day he spoke; and his exposition was so clear, his justification so complete, and his innocence of all the charges alleged so palpable, that he overwhelmed his opponents, and he was sustained by a triumphant majority of the House of Commons, which a few hours previously was prepared to ostracize him. This speech is one of Lord Palmerston's grandest efforts, and is eminently characteristic of the man. The matter was important and grave enough, but it was conveyed with so much clearness, and in a style so varied—now dignified and serious, and anon playful and sarcastic—as to enchain the attention of his hearers for a period of five hours, during which he traversed an ocean of detail without referring to a note. For a masterly grasp of his subject, for passages of real eloquence, for point and tact, for humour tinged with irony—above all, for a success that was complete as unexpected—this oration has rarely been surpassed in the Parliamentary debates of England. This triumph silenced his adversaries both within doors and without, and the adjournment of Parliament in August left Lord Palmerston firm in his place of Secretary of Foreign Affairs, and as strong in public esteem as a few weeks before he had been the contrary.

It was no other than this remarkable man and veteran statesman, the victor in so many debates, and the hero of so many diplomatic contests, that I was now flying over the South-Western Railway to meet in compliance with the flattering invitation already given. It was not long after 7 p.m. that I reached the Romsey Station, and as it was a bright and balmy day, I decided to walk over to "Broadlands," only a mile distant. I took my course through the village of Romsey, having nothing to recommend it but its extreme antiquity and only famous, in my recollection, as the birth-place of Master Petty, the ancestor of the Lansdowne family, who began life here as a humble weaver. I soon entered the park gates of Lord Palmerston's noble estate, and followed the carriage drive towards the house, stopping every now and then, involuntarily, to survey that delicious landscape which nowhere exists in such perfection as in England, and carried there to the highest point of pictorial effect. The verdant meadow, trimmed with such neatness as to give it the appearance of a carpet of velvet, unrolled its glittering expanse on every side, with now and then a clump of fine trees, picturesquely grouped, to break its monotony. In the distance I discerned, a rare beauty, the flashing surface of a gentle river, sparkling in the sunshine, which disappearing for a moment behind an envious grove again came smiling into sight, as it pursued its meandering course through the soft vale it seemed to nourish. All my political reminiscences vanished instantaneously at the sight of such transcendent charms as these, and I was fast falling into a reverie and beginning to quote Thomson, when a sudden turn of the road brought me right upon the superb mansion of "Broadlands."

I learnt from the footman who opened the door that Lord Palmerston was out riding, his usual exercise of an afternoon, but that his Lordship expressed the hope I would be able to amuse myself about the grounds till his return. I was escorted to my bedroom, and informed that the dinner hour was half-past eight o'clock. As I had nearly an hour to spare, I descended for a walk on the lawn, which ran sloping from the house to the edge of the pretty stream already alluded to; and anxious to improve my acquaintance with it, I strolled along its winding margin, which at every turn afforded some new and pleasing view.

On my return to the house I found its noble owner waiting for me in the library, and he welcomed me with all the easy familiarity of a finished man of the world. My preconceived notions of his appearance and manners were ludicrously disappointed. Instead of the venerable man of imposing mien and solemn gravity—the conjoint result of high distinction, English formality, and advanced age—I encountered a very pleasant gentleman of some fifty years, apparently, perfectly off-hand and unaffected in his demeanour, and singularly vivacious and playful in his remarks, which were accompanied with a sort of running chuckle. After a few moments' conversation, his Lordship suggesting we had but a few minutes to dress for dinner, rang for a servant to conduct me to my room, whilst he hurried off, saying, he would see me directly in the drawing-room.

On repairing thither, I was presented by his Lordship to the celebrated Lady Palmerston, formerly Countess of Cowper, and once the *belle* of her epoch. She was a tall, finely-formed woman, with a handsome countenance, very elegant manners, and, apparently, still in the prime of life. There was the same polished ease and freedom from restraint of any kind that distinguished her noble husband, and which indicated in both that to high breeding was added the long habit of wide and constant intercourse with society. There was only one other lady present, the Hon. Mrs. W. C——, a member of the family. When dinner was announced Lady P—— rose, and with a charming mixture of affability and *hauteur* offered me her arm, saying, she "would take the stranger into dinner," an honor I certainly would not have ventured to aspire to. The dinner passed off delightfully; my Lord Palmerston talking, joking, and laughing, as though he passed his time doing nothing else. He related several anecdotes, full of point and admirably told. I could not for the life of me imagine I was in the presence of one of the leading men of Europe, who had been a member of the Cabinets that had ended the terrible war against Napoleon I., and began that against the United States, in 1812, and that at this moment had more to do with the destinies of nations than any other man living.

I was not long in detecting, however, that the lively, facetious exterior of Lord Palmerston was but a mask assumed before the world, though always worn with dignity, and that underneath lay concealed that vast intellect, fearless character, and mighty energy, which had raised him, without connection, interest, or wealth, and in the teeth of prejudice, to the position he then held, and which would likely carry him later into the Premiership of England.

On returning to the drawing-room, the Minister left me with the ladies, saying, he would join us at tea; and I learnt afterwards that he was in the habit of retiring to his cabinet for an hour or more after dinner to glance over his despatches, flowing in upon him every day from all quarters of the world. He came in again about eleven o'clock, drank a cup of tea, chatted awhile in his pleasant way, and disappeared once more. He had returned, I found, to his study, where I was surprised to hear he frequently passed part of the night at work. I have since discovered that Lord Palmerston's capacity for labour is prodigious, and his energies, mental and bodily, never flag under any pressure of business. His intelligence, experience, and activity enable him to accomplish everything without appearance of haste or loss of time. Whether it be that his task is congenial, or that his nature demands constant occupation, certain it is that Lord Palmerston labours as incessantly as any operative or farmer's man in England. He requires no recreation, is never seen at places of amusement, and is free from all those fashionable vices so common amongst Statesmen and Diplomatists of all countries. In short, Lord Palmerston is one of those rare men who seem born to carry on the political business of the world; and it is hard to say whether this arises from any special combination of faculties, or from that soaring ambition to govern mankind, that makes labour, trial, and peril easy, nay, attractive, if contributing to that end.

At ten next morning the family were punctually assembled at breakfast, but I found his Lordship more reserved in manner and less inclined for conversation, as though his mind was already intent on the business of the day. After breakfast every one, according to the custom in English country houses, betook themselves to their own mode of amusement, but in bidding me good morning his Lordship asked me to accompany him in his usual ride at four in the afternoon.

I accompanied the ladies in a short ramble over the grounds, 'laid out with exquisite taste, in both the French and English style ; gay parterres of flowers, massed together in the greatest variety and profusion, relieved by sloping lawns and graceful groups of trees. I had fine views of the house from various points, which is an oblong in shape, with wings, and constructed with a nice perception of architectural effect. It is of great dimensions, containing on the lower floor alone three spacious drawing rooms, library, billiard-room, and a dining-room worthy of a palace. On returning from our stroll I was left to dispose of my own time *sêlon mes gouts,* and I passed an hour or so pleasantly in looking over a very choice collection of pictures that adorned the various rooms, amongst which I remarked several rare specimens of Cuyp and Teniers, great favourites of mine. I next wended my way into the library, and what with reading and letter-writing, the hours sped away pleasantly enough.

At four I proceeded to join his Lordship for our ride, and I found him ready at the hour named. As we were about to mount he said—

"I will give you a turn in the New Forest." Having remarked nothing of the kind in the neighbourhood I asked, with some distrust, what the distance might be?

"Only ten miles," returned his Lordship, pulling on his gloves.

Ten miles there, ditto back, thought I, in a sober spirit of computation, besides the turn proposed. I felt I had better come out with a plain statement, whilst there was time.

"If your Lordship is serious," I said, "I shall beg the favour of carrying a pillow along with me, for I am sure to spend the night in the Forest."

"What!" exclaimed the noble Lord, "will a gallop like that fatigue you?"

"I have not strode a horse for these several years past," I expostulated.

"In that case," returned his Lordship, "let us take a walk over the farms," to which I readily assented, and the more so, that the playfulness of the "thorough-bred" intended for me inspired me with secret misgivings that we should soon part company in mutual disgust. To say nothing of fatigue and insecurity I greatly preferred a promenade *à piéd,* since it would afford me a better opportunity for conversation with his Lordship, which I ardently desired. Off we started at a rattling pace, which soon made me suspect I had gained little by the exchange. I was really astonished at the extraordinary bodily vigour of my noble host, which far exceeded mine, though some thirty years his junior, and in sound health.

A group of several fine farms surround the country seat of Lord Palmerston, constituting the estate of Broadlands, and I found them all in high cultivation. The land was too good to require, fortunately, any of those expensive processes of draining, irrigation, and manuring, which has made a science of agriculture in England now-a-days; but his Lordship, confiding in the universality of his genius, thought he could manage his farms as easily as the various States of Europe, and once, in a bucolic mood, undertook it, but he soon found to his cost, as I have learnt, that every business has its mysteries, and that even a great statesman may be taught by country-bumpkins. We stopped a moment to inspect some fine foals, for I discovered that Lord Palmerston shared, in common with his countrymen, that truly national predilection for horse-flesh. At last, emerging into some fine broad meadow-land, the conversation turned to my delight on politics, and his Lordship, without any appearance of reserve, discussed the condition of Europe with his usual clearness and adroitness.

He expressed for France the most friendly sentiments, and deprecated the folly of two nations, with so many mutual interests, ever resorting to unnecessary hostilities; still, I remarked, in passing over late events, he refrained from giving his opinions fully either of men or things. He touched on Italy, and lamented the sad state of things existing there, which he thought it easy enough to improve, if the parties concerned were either willing or knew how to set to work. He said nothing very distinct of Germany, but seemed to think that Austria had made a narrow escape in her late conflict with Hungary, though he refrained from expressing any sympathy with either party. He talked of Russia at more length, and without seeking to underrate the spirit of her people or the vigor of her Sovereign, he showed no apprehension of her vaunted military power and resources. In short, he expressed himself like a man not afraid to cope with her if circumstances made it necessary, and I inferred his opinion was that things were tending in that direction.

He spoke very freely of the United States, and in the kindest spirit. The two nations, his own and mine, he said, were essential to each other, and though occasional jars might arise from diplomatic misunderstandings, still any fatal disagreement he considered out of the question. I made no efforts to ascertain more than his Lordship chose to declare, though I was curious enough to know what were his real notions of policy toward the United States; whether he feared the extension of our territory, and secretly aimed to prevent it. I alluded naturally to Central America, and the squabble then going on between the rival functionaries in that quarter of England and the States, Messrs. Chatfield and Squiers, whose peppery correspondence was creeping into the journals.

"Yes," said his Lordship, "my agent there is displaying too much zeal, and I must recall him."

He refrained from saying what special business he was sent there on, and I thought it would be presumptuous to urge the question further.

By this time we had reached a kind of Observatory on the grounds, which, on ascending, afforded a commanding view of the lovely landscape around. On returning to *terra firma*, we found a large congregation of peasants, of both sexes, just in from the harvest, and who had spied the Lord of the Manor across the field.

"Long live yer Lordship," cried the boldest of the throng, and uproarious cheers followed this mannerly exclamation.

"Well, who's the treasurer amongst you," inquired his Lordship. A hat was instantly held up, when their generous landlord, throwing in a handsome *douceur*, passed rapidly on his way, leaving a roaring sea of enthusiasm behind.

The next morning at breakfast I announced my intention of leaving that afternoon for town, when her Ladyship was kind enough to express regret at my early departure. His Lordship walked with me from the breakfast-room into the library, when he remarked,

"In our conversation yesterday your views seemed to coincide singularly with mine, more especially as regards France and the United States; and if you have nothing better to do, what do you say to aiding me to keep the peace, for I hear that you are a good deal connected with the Press in both countries."

I was as much surprised as flattered at this frank and sudden proposition, which, however, embarrassed me not a little.

"If I thought I could, in my humble way, be of any use to your Lordship," I replied, "and especially to the great cause in question, I certainly should—" I stopped to reflect a moment.

"Well, think it over," said his Lordship, remarking my hesitation, "and let me know. As to compensation, I'll make that easy." With that the noble Secretary of State retired to his cabinet. I was struck with the business-like way he did things, and that he wanted no work he was not willing to pay for.

I had, certes, abundant matter for rumination, but after turning it over in my mind, I was no nearer to a conclusion than before. What puzzled me then and long afterwards was to know what I really could do to make myself at all useful to the Foreign Office of England. To be sure I had relations with the French Press and all the heads of French parties. I was widely connected with the Press and public men of my own country. Yet I was slow to perceive to what account I could turn these advantages, unless I knew exactly what were the wishes and secret purposes of the astute Statesman at the head of the Foreign Office. These I knew nothing about, and, therefore, pondered over the expediency of accepting functions that might be repugnant to my views, or which I might be unable to discharge. My vanity was, certainly, inflated not a trifle at such a personage as Lord Palmerston condescending to enlist my services, but I could not help thinking that he was misled into greatly overrating them. In any case, I decided not to accept his Lordship's offer till I had revolved it further.

Whilst at lunch that day, my gracious hostess proposed a short drive to the old church of Romsey, which was one of the curiosities of the neighbourhood, and that I had ample time, her Ladyship assured me, to see before starting. Nothing could be more interesting than its quaint antiquity, as I found on inspection, and I surveyed it with that peculiar relish which an American only can feel at sight of objects hallowed by the associations of another age, and stamped by the corroding footprints of time. So habituated are we to what is new and fresh in the handiworks of man—so accustomed to associate with what is old ideas of meanness and inferiority, emanating from sight of the rude and clumsy structures of our colonial state some ninety years agone, that when on coming to Europe we contemplate, for the first time, "the solemn temples, the gorgeous palaces, and cloud-capt towers," encrusted with the rust of centuries, and alive with the memories of great men and startling deeds, denoting the wealth, taste, and civilization of times long anterior to the discovery of our Continent, we experience a rush of emotion as novel as overpowering, and which, for a time, breaks up and confounds our settled preconceptions and deep-rooted illusions.

The splendid piles of continental architecture awaken wonder and admiration; but far other chords are touched by the ivy-crowned and unpretending village church of England, such as the one I am speaking of, where the simple slab, inscribed with the familiar Saxon name, brings vividly home to an American the touching fact that the country of his birth is but an off-shoot of the parent-stock around him, and his prejudices melt, and his sensations change as he recognizes that so far from the new and original creation he fancied himself, he is none other than the recent descendant of some English pilgrim. The impressions of an American on visiting Europe vary naturally with the temperament and character of the individual; but the coarsest mind cannot fail to undergo strange modifications, whilst the reflecting and sensitive must vibrate to its innermost depths. It is natural that England should appeal the strongest to American thoughts and feelings; but language, literature, and descent apart, there is a picturesque beauty in its landscape, a neatness and comfort in its homely, but decent villages, a real grandeur in its castles and lordly mansions, with a teeming richness in the broad lands that surround them, that inspire the unimpassioned with earnest admiration, whilst they waft a poetical nature into the regions of enthusiasm.

I remarked, amongst other objects of interest, in the Church of Romsey, a plain marble tablet to the memory of the father of Lord Palmerston, whereon his virtues were feelingly recorded in choice Latin by his dutiful son.

In bidding adieu to my noble host, I informed him that I would do myself the honor of writing in two or three days my reply to his flattering proposition. As I had spoken of visiting Berlin before returning to Paris, Lord Palmerston was so kind as to give me a letter to the British Chargé d'Affaires at that place, which I accepted with a profusion of thanks.

CHAPTER VIII.

A VISIT TO THE FOREIGN OFFICE.

On my return to London I renewed my deliberations on the novel and seducing prospect of entering into connection with the British Foreign Office. I had at the time another scheme in my head, which had temptations of its own, and promised ample remuneration for the time and attention bestowed on it. Still political occupation was more to my taste, and the chance of playing a part, however humble, in the affairs of the three leading nations of the world, England, France, and the United States, was a consideration that appealed not so much to my vanity or ambition, but I hope to less selfish feelings, and which, finally, overcame all doubts and scruples. If I had thought for a single moment that the covert object in view was to entice me into renouncing that allegiance to my native country and her interests, which every right mind and sound heart must cherish as one of the most sacred duties and noblest of sentiments, I should have shrunk from the offer as an insult and a disgrace; or had I supposed that my services would be required for executing the designs and promoting the aggrandisement of England to her exclusive profit, if not to the detriment of her rivals, I would equally have declined the task proposed. Believing, however, that the profound statesman and practical politician at the head of Her Majesty's foreign policy, saw distinctly that the period had arrived not only in the career of England, but the world's history, when the advantage of one nation could not be secured at the sacrifice of the rest, but that nations, like individuals, were mutually dependent, and that Providence had clearly designed the fraternity of mankind by giving to each separate facilities for supplying the wants of all; convinced that Lord Palmerston had the intelligence to perceive this great fundamental truth, the energy to maintain it, and the capacity to apply it; satisfied that his purpose was to foster sentiments of esteem between the three great nations in the van of civilisation—to subdue their enmities—to abate their prejudices—to increase their friendly relations, with a view to enhancing the material prosperity of all, leaving each to decide for itself all domestic questions of politics and morals; forming such conclusions as these, I saw nothing in the offer to become a satellite of the English Foreign Office, that was not honourable and in the highest degree attractive. I abandoned, therefore, all previous projects, gave up my visit to Berlin, wrote to the noble Viscount that I was ready to enter into the arrangement suggested, and went off to Paris to put myself in connection with the Hon. Mr. Edwardes, as indicated by his Lordship in case my decision was in the affirmative.

I was anxious to know what functions would be assigned to me, and I was a good deal more puzzled to divine what I was fit for in the way of diplomatic service. I had no experience of the kind up to this time. My life had been of a desultory and somewhat vagrant description. After scrambling through the University, running through a course of law, I had given the most of my time to travelling, interspersed with episodes rather more eccentric than profitable. To be sure, I had always taken a deep interest in politics in the largest sense. The government of mankind had ever seemed to me the most mysterious and complicated of problems, and in traversing the nations of Europe and Asia, I was not so absorbed by their amusements as to neglect casting a keen and sympathetic glance at the different conditions of men as shaped and modified by the institutions of different ages. The essays I had thrown off so hastily for a French journal conveyed, in part, the results of my observations and reflection. Still, I had never been trained to any administrative work, or employed on any political mission of any kind. The idea, therefore, of putting on diplomatic harness—receiving *secret* instructions—of being employed on *occult* jobs, or engaged in mystifying to unravel mystery, and this, too, for a foreign country, usually regarded as a foe to my own; all this, there was no denying, had the charm of tremendous novelty, but it had a drawback in my utter inexperience to thread these winding labyrinths. I had a shrewd suspicion that either my Lord Palmerston or the Hon. Mr. Edwardes had given me more credit for address, for knowledge of the intricate ways and subterranean avenues of diplomacy, than I possessed, and I anticipated, therefore, not a little amusement at the ludicrous mystification that was sure to ensue. As my diplomacy must be improvised for want of experience, I felt certain that I should, in sea phrase, be cutting across their bows in the most comical fashion just at the moment probably they thought me astern. There is nothing more exciting than a practical joke when the responsibility is not upon yourself, and the oddity of my being called upon to play the *rôle* of Sir Patrick O'Plenipo in real life enlivened my imagination, and sharpened my faculties for all the strange adventures that might befall me. There was only one thing firmly settled in my mind, and that was not to be entrapped into doing anything discreditable to myself or disloyal to the cause I undertook to serve. For all the rest I was indifferent.

My amiable friend and sponsor, the Hon. Mr. Edwardes, at Paris, to whom I reported myself on my arrival, was just one of those diplomatic mysteries that was sure to lead me astray. He had the air of a man with his safety-valves screwed down, so to speak, full of the most important secrets ready to burst out and scatter confusion, if his power of suppression did not keep them under. This was no affectation of manner, but the effect of usage. I expected my cautious Mentor to take off the mask before his Telemachus, and to initiate me into all the *arcana* I had a right to know before I could hope to make myself useful—but not a bit of it. Whether he thought me accomplished in all the *roueries* of his craft, or wanted confidence in me, or that he really had nothing to confide, quite likely, I know not; but instead of information to guide me, all I got were perplexing hints that led me into out-of-the-way conclusions, and which, without a miracle interposed, would some day carry one or both of us down into some bottomless quagmire of discomfiture. This quiet game of bo-peep was one day interrupted by my diplomatic friend asking me "to write something." This was a startling request.

"About what?" I demanded.

"What you please," he replied. "I want to see your style."

This suggestion was not at all to my taste, and somewhat offensive to my pride. It was treating me very like a schoolboy who is requested to do some ciphering to show his proficiency. I interpreted the real purpose of the Hon. Mr. Edwardes as only to get at my opinions, which I should have been too happy to express, *viva voce*, if he had stated the subject. To write something about nothing is not a very inviting task; but it struck me that, perhaps, I might sail round my wily ally by writing some slipshod matter that would force him into criticism. I do not know whether he penetrated my design, but nothing could be more amusing than his surprise, which soon changed into round abuse, of what I had done. He expressed himself with a hearty bluntness that provoked my mirth.

"That's downright trash," he exclaimed, looking over my manuscript.

"You don't mean it?" I said, affecting astonishment.

"What in the world did you write this stuff for?" he continued.

"Only to oblige you."

"That won't do." And he put my MSS. into the fire.

"What's to be done now?" I queried, laughing outright.

"You must write something I can send over to Broadlands," was his rejoinder.

"Indeed!" I said, growing serious; "that's another affair. But what topic this time?"

"You must select your own."

"Suppose I take the present condition of France," I suggested, with a knowing look.

"That will do," he replied, with a smile.

I saw I must make an effort on which my fortunes depended. I didn't like the job at all, but there was no help for it, and so I set to work. I began a pamphlet with a French title, *la France, que veut elle,* (What does France wish), and then proceeded to solve the enigma after my own fashion. In discussing the condition of France, I naturally commented on the state of Europe generally, and added some side-views of Lord Palmerston's policy, which I earnestly applauded. An episode on the growing power of the middle class I took some pains with. After writing a portion of the above, I sent it into my literary taster, and he expressed himself with the same pithiness as before, but in a more complimentary tone.

"Admirable!" he asserted, "nothing could be better."

"Shall I finish it?" I enquired.

"By all means, it's just the thing."

When my task was done, I waited patiently for the next move, for my probation had slackened my ardor somewhat. In a short time after this I received an intimation from the Hon. Mr. Edwardes that I had better make a second visit to Broadlands, and report myself to Lord Palmerston, who would give me the requisite instructions as to my work. He desired me to carry my MSS. along with me to lay before his Lordship, as he had only conveyed to him his opinion of it. Inferring, of course, that he had authority for such advice, I left Paris in a day or two for Southampton, only seven miles from Broadlands, whence I wrote to its noble owner that I had come again to England at the suggestion of Mr. Edwardes, and would be flattered by an interview with his Lordship at such time and place as would suit his convenience. I thought it likely he would name a day to see me in London. I despatched my note by a messenger, and the same afternoon received the following answer:—

Broadlands, 16th October, 1856.

MY DEAR SIR—

I am still here, and shall remain here for ten days longer, therefore, if you wish to see me, you must do me the favour to come here. Can you do so this afternoon? We dine at the same hour as when you were here, and you will find your room ready.

Yours faithfully,

HENRY WIKOFF, Esq. PALMERSTON.

I was not a little gratified at the cordial tone of this invitation, which showed that I had not lost ground in his Lordship's good opinion. I drove over to Broadlands before dinner, and was received with even greater kindness than before. I found several distinguished persons enjoying the hospitality of the Foreign Minister, and amongst them some members of the Diplomatic Corps. The morning after my arrival I handed my *brochure* to his Lordship, who feared he would not have time to peruse it, but desired me to come to his cabinet during the afternoon, and talk over matters. It was clear that Lord Palmerston was entirely satisfied with the information conveyed to him by Mr. Edwardes of the soundness of my views. I waited upon his Lordship before dinner, whom I found hard at work at a high desk, in a spacious room, surrounded by bookcases. He bid me be seated, and, saying that he had not had a moment during the day to glance at my lucubrations, begged me to give him a brief analysis of what I had written. I did so, when he simply remarked that I had gone over a wide ground, and that he was sure I had done justice to it. Though pleasant in his manner, his Lordship seemed indisposed to talk politics. I touched delicately on French affairs, to which he responded briefly. Without premeditation, I asked him what he thought of Louis Napoleon's chances. This was coming too close, I could see, for the noble Secretary turned abruptly round on his chair, got up, put his back to the fire, and then said, with great caution, "Well, he has made no mistake yet." This was explicit enough for a Minister of State. It was apparent that Lord Palmerston thought favourably of the future of the French Prince President from his unqualified encomium of his past. To say the President had made no mistakes amid the trying difficulties he had contended with, was to award high praise to his statesmanship.

I then declared to Lord Palmerston my readiness to enter into the arrangement he had proposed, when, expressing his satisfaction, he desired me, on going up to London, to call on Mr. H. U. Addington, Under Secretary of State, at the Foreign Office, his *alter ego*, as his Lordship styled him, and that he would shape my matters to my liking.

I left Broadlands the following day for London, where, upon my arrival, I called at the Foreign Office, in Downing Street. I was shewn by the messenger on service into an ante-room, a large dingy apartment, where, after giving my card, I was desired to wait till Mr. Addington was disengaged. After a brief detention, I was conducted into the private room of the Under Secretary of State. He was a man of some fifty years and upwards, very erect in stature, with a cold and formal manner, and a severe expression of face. He desired me to be seated, and proceeded at once to business.

"Lord Palmerston informs me," he said, "that you are to be employed in the Foreign Office."

"Yes, Sir," I returned, with an affable smile, which was quite thrown away.

"What do you expect in the way of salary?"

"Why, really," I said, hesitating, "I have not thought of the matter."

"I have instructions to arrange it," continued the Under Secretary; "will you say what sum will do?"

I saw that ceremony was wasted on this model of an administrator, so, after reflecting a moment, I replied, "Four or five hundred will do to begin with."

"Very well. Your salary will be five hundred pounds a-year, paid quarterly, to begin from the first of this month."

As my utility was quite uncertain, I thought this compensation very liberal, and was going to say so, but a glance at the impassive countenance of the Under Secretary checked me. His business was simply to carry out the instructions of the Minister, a mere matter of routine, in which he had neither interest nor responsibility. Finding that Mr. Addington was standing quietly with his back to the fire, wholly absorbed, apparently, with holding up his coat tails, I rose, and inquired if he had any instructions to give me?

"No, I have not."

"Shall I call, then, another day?"

"Where is your address?"

"London Hotel, Albemarle Street."

"I will write to you when I am instructed."

By this time I was congealed down to the frigid level of Mr. Addington's manner, and so bowing with the utmost gravity, I retired without uttering another word. The sunshine out of doors soon restored me, and as I strolled homeward across St. James's Park, I found myself in a rather buoyant state of mind. Five hundred a-year suddenly added to the income of a single man, is not at all calculated to excite disagreeable emotions, and I really wondered how the Under Secretary could display such extraordinary apathy in doing so pleasant a thing by anybody. But that was not all. There was the dignity of my new calling. To find one's self abruptly translated into the upper air of official life, with no more effort than in stepping in and out of the ascending machine at the Colosseum; to feel yourself no longer one of the common herd, who have never had to do with affairs of state; to imagine that in the great diplomatic machine which is at work all the world over, you are henceforth to figure as a screw of more or less importance, with the reserved power always of disturbing its movements if you can't aid them; to know, in short, that you are actually enrolled on the staff of the British Foreign Office, with Lord Palmerston at its head, and £500 a-year to back you, without being able to comprehend by what magic you ever got there; if all this was not enough to make your blood tingle and your head quite giddy on a fine bracing day in October, I would like to know what would. It is easy to imagine that, in this elastic frame of feeling, and with so pleasant a prospective before me, I awaited, in perfect beatitude, the solemn summons of the Under Secretary to return from whence I came, and receive the mission I was destined for. To me, by this time, it was a matter of extreme indifference how I was disposed of, for, as the Roman boasted that "Every road led to Rome," I might with equal confidence feel that every employment led to honor. In the course of a few days I received the following note:—

Mr. Addington presents his compliments to Mr. Wikoff, and, by desire of Lord Palmerston, requests that Mr. Wikoff will call on Mr. Addington at the Foreign Office this day, between 2 and 4 o'clock p.m.

Foreign Office, 22nd October, 1850.

I complied punctually with this invitation, and was received in the same matter-of-fact way as before.

"I sent for you," said Mr. Addington, raising his head from his stand-up desk and dropping his eye-glass, "simply to inform you that it is not quite decided where to employ you; that is now under consideration."

"Very well, Sir," I returned in my blandest tone, and with a smile meant to be irresistible, "I am at your disposition."

"When that point is settled," continued the Under Secretary, just as grim as ever, "I will send for you again."

"Anything further?" I asked, after a brief pause.

"Nothing for the present."

A mutual salutation ended my second visit to the Foreign Office. Without doubting for a moment the Under Secretary's admirable adaptation to his office, I inwardly prayed, whilst there was yet time, that I might not fall under his chilly supervision. I feel an involuntary reverence for one of your phlegmatic men, free from the aberrations of passion, whose judgment must be sounder and their conduct more regular than that of weaker people, but so little is my nature in harmony with these, that I shrink up like a sensitive leaf when I come in contact. To my surprise, only two days later, came a second *appel* from the Foreign Office to this effect—

Mr. Addington requests that Mr. Wikoff will have the goodness to call on him at this office either to-day or to-morrow after 2 o'clock, p.m.

Foreign Office, 24th October, '50.

Brief as it was I recognised something less repelling in this note than in the first, and I began to hope that Mr. Addington would gradually relent when he had once overcome that invincible repugnance to strangers, characteristic of an insular people, but carried to the verge of impoliteness by an English aristocrat. I called promptly at 2 o'clock p.m. of the day I received the above note, and was admitted to Mr. Addington's sanctum a moment after sending in my card. I had augured correctly, for tho' Mr.

Addington's countenance underwent no relaxation, at least nothing approaching to the frivolity of a smile, yet its sternness had subsided. His manner, too, tho' not positively pleasant, had far less of the *odi profanum vulgus* in it. I began to cherish the fancy that I should yet creep through the crevices of his official armor. Putting his back to the fire, his favorite attitude, he said—

"Well, it is decided you are to go to Paris."

"I am very glad of it," escaped me involuntarily.

"It is thought you may be more useful there."

"I hope so," was my answer, tho' secretly considering if such was likely to be the case.

"I think," continued Mr. Addington, "that you will be put in connection with my colleague, Lord Stanley of Alderley, whose functions are more political than mine."*

I was near expressing my satisfaction at this without reflecting, but checking myself I simply said—

"Very well, Sir."

"When are you ready to leave for Paris?"

"To-day, if necessary."

"Suit your convenience," said the Under Secretary rather blandly, "and on your arrival report yourself to the Marquis of Normanby, to whom I will give you a letter."

"As you please, Sir," I replied, "but if it will save you any trouble, Mr. Edwardes can introduce me in my new capacity, for I know his Lordship already."

Little did I dream at the time of all the trouble this unlucky suggestion would cost me. The Under Secretary reflected a moment—

* There are two Under Secretaries of State connected with the British Foreign Office, the one permanent, whose duties are chiefly administrative, and the other appointed by the Foreign Minister of the day, and who retires with him from office.

"Very well," he remarked, "let Mr. Edwardes introduce you. The less written the better." The caution of the experienced official revealed itself in this shrewd phrase.

"Have you any instructions to give me?" I enquired.

"Your instructions as to France," returned the Under Secretary, "you will receive from the Embassy at Paris, but our policy towards the United States will be explained to you shortly, either by Lord Palmerston himself, or through another channel, as he may direct."

I bowed my acquiescence.

"As there is nothing to detain me longer in London, I shall be off at once to Paris," I remarked.

"It would be just as well," replied Mr. Addington, moving towards his desk, "and I wish you a pleasant trip over."

Making my profound acknowledgments for this unexpected act of courtesy, I took my *congé*, and retired.

It may have been only a methodical mode of proceeding, but it struck me there was exceeding caution in the way the Foreign Office was dealing with me. It could not be that any doubts were entertained already as to my fitness for the duties I was to be entrusted with, for the views expressed in the experimental *brochure* I had been called on to write, seemed to give perfect satisfaction; but it might be that the policy of the Government towards France and the United States was of such a delicate and important nature that care was necessary in imparting it to a person that might not appreciate it, or who might possibly be averse to carrying it out. Up to this time all that I had said or written was conscientiously conceived and loyally uttered, but so practised a diplomatist as Lord Palmerston might infer more or less than was meant.

I was, as yet, wholly ignorant of the employment to be assigned to me, or of the tasks to be executed, still my mind was firmly made up to do nothing repugnant to my convictions, or contrary to what I conceived to be the true policy to pursue. How far a Statesman of Lord Palmerston's extraordinary ability would suffer independence in a humble subordinate remained to be seen. I was entirely satisfied from all that had transpired that the policy of the noble Secretary of State towards France was to favour the interests of the Prince Louis Napoleon so far as he could go without positive interference with the domestic affairs of the nation. I apprehended no disagreement with his Lordship on this ground, for all my hopes of France were founded on the extension of the President's tenure of power.

But, as regards the United States, I did fear the possibility of coming into collision with the opinions of Lord Palmerston, though I had seen nothing in what he had said on my first visit to Broadlands to justify such an apprehension. The subject, then, however, was only alluded to, not discussed, and it might turn out that his Lordship entertained conclusions in many points opposite to mine. I felt duly conscious of my littleness alongside of a political Titan of the force of Lord Palmerston; still I was convinced that I knew far more of my own country than did any European Statesman, no matter what his skill or experience. This was an advantage I never meant to yield.

I knew what should be the policy of England towards the United States, but I did not know whether Lord Palmerston would look in the same direction as I did. The traditions of the Foreign Office, and the prejudices of his class, might bias his views; or had he the force and the desire to rise above both, if he saw the interests of his country demanded it. This I believed. Should it turn out otherwise, then, my tenure of attachéship to the Foreign Office would be short-lived, for I never could consent, calmly, to obey instructions that I considered, on superior knowledge, to be disastrous to the cause I had undertaken to serve.

CHAPTER IX.

A DIPLOMATIC TRIUMPH.

I received the hearty congratulations of the Hon. Mr. Edwardes, on my return to Paris, at the final consummation of my connection with the Foreign Office, and in return I made him my warm acknowledgments for the part he had in the matter. We dined together at the *Café Philippe* by way of celebrating the event, and over our *demi-tasse* I made known to him, amongst other details, that Mr. Addington had offered to me a letter for the Marquis of Normanby, but that I had reserved for him the satisfaction of presenting me. My friend's countenance underwent a marvellous change.

"A letter to the Marquis of Normanby, did you say?" and he regarded me with astonishment.

"Yes," I repeated, surprised in my turn, "Mr. Addington proposed my taking a letter to the Ambassador, explaining my position, but I suggested your presenting me to him would do as well."

"Indeed!" he slowly responded, and sunk into a fit of deep reverie.

I was singularly puzzled at the strange mixture of wonder and disappointment manifested by Mr. Edwardes at so simple and natural an incident. After cudgelling my brains for awhile, I broke in upon his meditations by abruptly asking what there was in my bringing over a letter to the Ambassador that struck him as so very odd.

"Why," he said, rousing himself, "I thought the thing was to be on a different footing altogether."

"How so?" I enquired.

"I supposed," he continued, "that the Ambassador was to know nothing at all of your connection with the Foreign Office."

"Indeed!" I said, beginning to get a little perplexed, "with whom, then, was I to consult in Paris?"

"With me, of course," returned Mr. Edwardes, "and I cannot understand the motive of this new arrangement."

Here was a hitch at the very start of my diplomatic career, and it seemed ominous.

"Well, what is best to be done?" I demanded, after a pause in our conversation, "the matter had better be settled in one way or the other."

"You are right," he returned, "it had better be decided, so I will write to-morrow over to Broadlands to know if you are to be presented or not to the Marquis of Normanby."

"It's of no great importance, after all," I declared, "for I shall report from time to time direct to Mr. Addington as to what I am about."

Whether Mr. Edwardes thought it worth his while to write or not, I don't know; but in touching on the same topic a few days later, he seemed anxious to divert me from seeing the Ambassador.

"What's the use of your going to Lord Normanby?" he remarked, "he would only turn you over to his Private Secretary; that would be the end of it. I am far fitter than he is to advise with you. Never mind Lord Normanby—we can get on without him."

This was the tenor of his remarks whenever the subject came up, but it was clearly the first intention of Mr. Addington I should meet the Ambassador. I was in doubt whether it had been differently decided, or whether Mr. Edwardes was anxious to monopolize me for objects of his own. Fearing I might get into some difficulty, I was half disposed to go direct to Lord Normanby, but I was reluctant to risk offending my friend Edwardes, whom I liked in spite of his oddities. Still my position was an embarrassing one.

Before beginning such a job as I had in hand, I ought, as a matter of course, to have consulted at length with some competent party relative to my proceedings at Paris. I knew from my conversations with Lord Palmerston at Broadlands, that his intentions were pacific towards France, and highly friendly to the President of the Republic; but there were a multitude of minor details upon which I might from time to time require information, and which I was not likely to get from Mr. Edwardes, who either played dummy, or, more likely, was quite in the dark himself. I regretted deeply enough I had not brought the letter Mr. Addington had offered me to the Marquis of Normanby; but I was not disposed to be idle, and began to revolve what I should set about, even without instructions.

It was palpable enough that the best interests of England and France, material and moral, required a thorough understanding between them; and there was nothing in the world to prevent this but the violent prejudices which grew out of old feuds and actual ignorance of each other. These prejudices were kept daily alive by the bitter fulminations of the French Press against England; and to soften, if not extinguish these, I thought my attention had better at once be directed. It was certainly a very droll task for me to undertake. An American and a Republican to set about reconciling the fiery journalists of Paris with *perfide Albion*, as England was then styled, and which, whatever their differences amongst themselves, they cordially disliked, was really an enterprise that may have testified to my pluck more than it did to my common sense. Yet I was inspired by so noble a cause, for the smallest success would contribute more or less to the good of these great nations, and to the general interests of humanity.

I saw that in approaching the Editors of the Paris Press, who were wild with party spirit, I should be obliged to appeal to their interests rather than to their patriotism or philanthropy; but though I should use political arguments, I had no political views to propagate, my sole purpose being a closer approximation between the French and English people. I drew comfort from the reflection that whatever might be thought of the eccentricity of my projects, no doubts could be thrown on my disinterestedness, for I meant, of course, to conceal my diplomatic connection with the English Government, that would add to my importance, but diminish likely my chances of success.

In November, '50, the entire Parisian Press were writing with the keenest acrimony against England, and the great guns of journalism were as rapid and fierce in their abusive discharges as those of smaller calibre. The first journal in circulation at that moment was *Le Siécle*, exceeding 40,000 daily. It advocated the moderate Republic, and was conducted with great ability and earnestness of tone. The *Siécle* had taken the popular side from its origin, and its escutcheon was free from stain of inconsistency or corruption. I regretted to see this powerful journal, bitter as it was able in its diatribes against England, doing so much mischief, and I selected it as the first and most important mark for me to circumvallate as best I could.

I procured a letter to its Editor, Louis Perrée, and made his acquaintance. We had several friends in common amongst the politicians of the day, and pleasant cordiality soon sprang up between us. After an interview or so, I took a pliant moment and touched upon the delicate chord of *perfide Albion*, and the remarks of an American on such a subject were listened to with curiosity. He was surprised at the elevation I gave the topic, for instead of discussing Oligarchies and Republics, or questions of territory and power, I spoke only of the interests of civilization involved in a friendly understanding between such nations as France, England, and the United States. These simple views coming from a quarter so unexpected produced a decided impression; but I held stronger batteries in reserve, which were destined, however, for another party; for after a long conversation, the Editor-in-Chief said:

"I would like you to see M. Lamarche; he writes all our foreign articles, and has our entire confidence. Converse with him, and convince him if you can." So saying, he wrote me a few lines of introduction to the Editor specially charged with the foreign department of the *Siécle*, and I took my leave with thanks.

I followed up my advantage by calling immediately upon M. Lamarche. I knew something of his antecedents, and they were all against my hopes. He had seen both military and naval service under the first Napoleon, and had the ill-luck to be taken prisoner by the English, and to be detained till the close of the War in the hulks at Portsmouth. There was reason enough for his prejudice against the English, and I regretted to have so tough a subject to begin with.

Nothing could be less conciliating than the manners of M. Lamarche, I found, on first acquaintance. He had all the *brusquerie* of the French soldier, without being tempered by the usual suavity of French courtesy. His face had a crabbed rather than a stern expression, but his eye redeemed it, for it sparkled with intelligence, not unmixed with goodness. His voice was harsh, but his articulation very distinct. Though rough, he was exceedingly off-hand; and I was quite at home with him in five minutes. He talked with great volubility; his information was vast and various, and his memory of men and events was prodigious. It required no little nerve to make head against such a torrent of ideas and recollections as poured like a Niagara upon the overpowered listener of M. Lamarche.

In my first interview with this very superior man, I was singularly struck with the unalloyed common-sense of all his views and opinions. The French temperament is ardent, and a calm and exact perception of things is rare, especially on political topics, where their feelings mostly run off with their reason. M. Lamarche had seen a great deal of the world; his knowledge was copious, and his mind well balanced. Upon this I built my aspirations. His thirst for information was intense; and he never talked with any one without seeking to learn or teach him something. An American was a curiosity and a study for him, and he drew mercilessly on my experience. At the time I met M. Lamarche he had two favorite antipathies—England and slavery. Nothing could be unluckier for me. I saw him several times before I ventured to touch the first of these tender spots, and when I did he went off in one of his bursts of bilious vociferation that almost dismayed me. I prudently drew him out several times in this way on different occasions, and never once essayed to remonstrate. I knew my boldness would have the better effect when I once began to speak, my mind freely. M. Lamarche only knew me as a patient listener and hardly dreamt I would ever venture to turn upon him with the vigour of an assailant.

The day came, and it was over a pleasant dinner we took together, and which I secretly hoped would render him more pliable to the impression I desired to make. We soon got upon politics, the only subject he relished; and the United States was discussed in every point of view. He fell foul, as I expected, of our peculiar institution of slavery, and, admitting all he said on abstract grounds, I defended it in a practical point of view, and asked him to suggest a remedy for the evil. I kept him chafing violently against this favorite horror of this till his polemical spirit was somewhat subdued, when I whisked him suddenly over to England.

"I see, M. Lamarche," I said, "that you are always battering away at your nearest neighbours, the English."

"*Ah, ces sacres Anglais!*" (those infernal English!) he exclaimed, with ineffable disgust, and emptied his champagne glass at a draught, as though washing down a mass of unpleasant souvenirs.

"Do you know," I replied, in a pleasant tone, "that I am surprised that a man of your extraordinary intelligence should give way to a prejudice that belongs more to the 17th century than to the 19th; a prejudice, too, that your reason must condemn, that your national interests oppose, and, above all, that your aspirations, as a Republican, require you to overcome."

I don't believe M. Lamarche ever had so nauseous a bolus so unexpectedly administered to him, and coming, too, from an American, whom he regarded as a fellow foe to "*ces sacres Anglais.*" He was dumb for a moment, and stared at me with his eye twinkling and flashing like an enraged bull at some daring Picador advancing on it, lance in hand. He went off, as I expected, in a perfect hurricane of words for half-an-hour, which I affected to listen to with the most courteous attention, whilst I was carelessly awaiting to see the real effect of my words after the fumes of his choler had cleared away. I calculated accurately, for, finding I made no reply to his denunciatory phrases, he came round to the point where I knew I had touched him vitally.

"*Mais quel horrible paradoxe vous avez dit là!*" (What a horrible paradox you have uttered), he said, at length, "when you state my hopes as a Republican are damaged by assailing the aristocratic institutions of England. It is just the contrary—" He stopped and looked curiously at me.

"It is no paradox," I replied. "I repeat it is an egregious error, nay, worse, a downright absurdity in the Republican party of France, to assail England in so unmeasured a manner." I went on whiffing my cigar quietly.

"*Une absurdité!*" articulated M. Lamarche with difficulty, and continued gazing at me as though quite staggered.

"Why, what can be clearer!" I returned. "What is a Republic if not a Constitutional Government? and where can you find in Europe any model to justify your theories against the despotic creed but in England? The English Government may be an Oligarchy, yet it is not an Oligarchy of the middle ages, but a Parliamentary Oligarchy, the very thing you Republicans sought to establish in 1848, but are not likely to succeed in. The only chance to save the French Republic, is to copy from the country you are daily disparaging from mere prejudice, now quite out of date. I am far from recommending Parliamentary Government to France, which, before all countries, requires a vigorous Executive, but England is the only nation in Europe, or the world, where representative institutions have existed for centuries, and where they have brought forth the fruits of civil and religious liberty, that have flourished in still greater luxuriance thousands of miles away from the parent soil, in the United States. Now, it is surely not your object, M. Lamarche, nor that of any sane Republican, to write down representative institutions and which the *Siécle* was founded expressly to uphold; then why do you decry England instead of eulogising her? You are not obliged to praise the aristocratic features of her Constitution, which I, as an American, do not like, but remember, that in England only, of ancient or modern times, the principle of representation has flourished and endured."

I knew my time had come, and I went on hammering the nail on the head in this fashion, resolved to pin down for ever, if possible, the anti-English hobgoblin that haunted the fancy of my new friend. M. Lamarche was a soldier before he took up the pen, and true to his craft, he endeavoured to make a bold front of it; but I saw his better part was cowed, that his mind misgave him. His face had a troubled appearance. He kept cracking up the filberts before him with astonishing vigour, exclaiming occasionally, during my tirades, "*ah ca,*" or letting drop a phrase from the camp "*ventre bleu,*" yet he did not seek to interrupt me. There was a tremendous commotion going on inwardly I could see, for logic was wrestling against the prejudice of years.

"What you have said there is striking," he declared, rising to go.

"Yes, strikingly simple," I replied.

"*Il faut y refléchir*" (it is necessary to reflect), he continued, and "I will lay what you have said before the Council of Editors to-morrow."

I was surprised at the progress I had made.

"I beg you to do so," I said, earnestly, "for the Republic is in a critical state, and the policy of its best friends is doing it more harm than its worst enemies."

I felt convinced that I had got a firm grasp on the common sense of M. Lamarche, and I anticipated a favourable result. His intellect and character, both would join to prevent his persisting in a false view, having once perceived it. Only three or four days after this he invited me to dine with the leading Editors of the *Siécle*, M. Bernard and M. Louis Jourdan. I accepted readily, as I desired nothing better than to increase my intimacy with this powerful organ.

I found my new acquaintances, like all Frenchmen, whatever their grade or occupation, perfect men of the world, easy-mannered, free from pretension, fine talkers, and full of spirits. We discussed all manner of things as dinner went on, and when the servants left us, M. Lamarche turned short round in his off-hand way and desired me to explain to his colleagues the views I had expressed the other day to him. I now saw the purport of my introduction to these gentlemen, and I declared my mind as frankly to them as I had done on the first occasion. To my extreme satisfaction, M. Lamarche sustained me, and to cover over his own conversion, he set to work adroitly to convince his *confréres* that the *Siécle* was on the wrong tack in assailing representative institutions, even, though, unfortunately, they existed on the soil of *perfide Albion*.

Two or three more dinners followed this, and I rejoiced at this admirable opportunity of familiarising myself with the Republican mind of France in its moderate phase. The end of all this was, first, that the *Siécle* ceased abusing England; second, that it began to treat her with fairness and favour, and last, though most surprising of all, instead of representing Lord Palmerston daily as the Mephistopheles of the political world, it admitted his ability, and discussed his policy impartially. This was my first success over French prejudice, which, however, is so nearly worn out that it required only a direct appeal to common sense to vanquish it. The plainest proof that the *Siécle* saw that its mission was falsified in attacking England with her parliamentary institutions, is that to this day it has persisted in the tone I ventured to suggest was the proper one.

The astonishment of my *fidus Achates*, Mr. Edwardes, knew no bounds at seeing the most influential journal in France drop its bitter hostility to England, and take up the cudgels in her behalf. He called it a triumph, and thought me adequate to any effort after that. A distinguished friend of Lord Palmerston, when he heard of it, declared, "I had by that single exploit earned my paltry salary ten times over." For my part, I was content that I had a share in rescuing enlightened men and a leading journal from mistaken conceptions of French policy, and so paving the way to a better understanding between France and England.

My easy success against formidable odds encouraged me to persevere in the same line of action, and I next turned my attention to the much read journal of the well known Emile de Girardin, *La Pressè*. It was conducted with great vigour by its owner, Girardin, who employed the best talent he could find in its various departments, besides contributing to it daily the productions of his own unrivalled pen. The tone of *La Presse* was unfriendly to England, but its attacks were chiefly levelled at Lord Palmerston. I thought it might proceed from personal dislike, or, perhaps, from mistaken views of the character and motives of the English Foreign Secretary. I felt no delicacy in approaching E. de Girardin on the subject, for I knew him intimately, and I was quite satisfied if my representations convinced his mind he would abandon at once his spiteful clamour against Lord Palmerston; for Girardin, though "nothing, if not critical," was never unjust from mere love of censure.

It turned out just as I suspected. Though so prominent a man for so many years, Lord Palmerston is the least understood of any Statesman in Europe. He is accused everywhere of being the enemy of everybody, which is so far true that he maintains the interests of England with a hand no less firm than skilful. Foreign Statesmen find it impossible to outwit him, whilst his ceaseless activity gives them no rest. If they take their eye off from him for a moment, they find some advantage lost, and in their rage they pelt him pitilessly in the columns of the official journal from St. Petersburgh to Washington.

The policy of Lord Palmerston is intensely national, and he *will* push English influence, and advance English interests, in every quarter and against everybody. Perhaps his zeal may sometimes be indiscreet, and he risks more than he can gain, but, on perceiving this, he retreats with a dexterity that confounds his opponents. Just at the moment they are prepared to crush him in the corner, where at last they've got him, they discover to their consternation he is not there, but smiling pleasantly at them from another point. There are some who think that Lord Palmerston is so fond of a joke that he cannot restrain his love of fun in the gravest matters, and that he plays with politics as a kitten with a ball, but I am in the habit, on the contrary, of regarding Lord Palmerston as one of those vigilant mariners who knows that the vessel of state, like other craft, sails best and straightest when the helm is kept in constant motion.

When I asked De Girardin flatly why he so often inveighed against one of the cleverest men of the epoch, he exclaimed in his rapid way :—

"*Pour mille et mille raisons*" (for a thousand reasons).

"*D'abord*" (in the first place) I said.

"*D'abord,*" he repeated, hesitating, as though completely posed. It was probably the first time he ever reflected why he attacked him. Recovering himself, he said :—

"*C'est l'ennemi acharne de la France*" (he is the ferocious enemy of France).

"Do you think so?" I replied, doubtingly.

"*Comment*, is there any question of it?" and away he went into an angry description of the outrage committed against France in 1840, when Lord Palmerston gave a lesson to Mehemet Ali in Syria.

"You must admit, Monsieur de Girardin," I said, after he had finished, "that it is an imperious necessity for the English Government to maintain their footing in Egypt, as it is their highway to India?"

"*Soit*" (Be it so), he answered.

"Why, then, you admit that Lord Palmerston only did what he would have been a coward or a traitor not to do in 1840. It is clear that it was not to offend France, or to diminish her influence in Egypt that he attacked the Pasha, but it was to save India from peril, which France had certainly no wish to see endangered. It was a bold act, but a necessary one, and the French are too valiant to condemn courage when occasion calls for it."

"It was pusillanimous in our Government to suffer it," returned M. de Girardin, "but that poor man, Louis Philippe, sacrificed everything for peace."

"It would have been madness in France," I continued, "to make war with England in '40. What interest had France to prevent Lord Palmerston struggling to keep the high-road open to

India? None in the world. A great outcry was raised against M. Thiers and Louis Philippe at the time by the Opposition orators and journals, but the Government knew public opinion forbad a suicidal war on such trifling grounds."

"*Mais ce* Lord Palmerston *travaille toujours et partout contre la France*" (but that Lord Palmerston is always working in every place against France), exclaimed De Girardin.

"What proof have you of that?" I demanded.

Whilst he was trying to rake up the proofs, I went on to say that I had indubitable proofs that Lord Palmerston's sympathies were wholly French; that, besides his admiration for *la grande nation,* he knew that the interests of his own country imperatively demanded a fraternal alliance with France, and therefore it was impossible for him to risk a rupture by working against her secretly, or otherwise."

"It must be strong proof, indeed," declared de Girardin, incredulous, "to make me credit that."

"Lord Palmerston used almost this very language only a few weeks ago."

"To whom?" cried de Girardin, astonished.

"*A votre serviteur,*" I replied.

"To you?"

"To me."

"*Comment donc,*" said de Girardin, his curiosity getting the better of him, "*expliquez moi tout cela*" (explain all that to me).

I then began to speak of my recent visit to Broadlands, and related all the pleasant and sensible things said of France by the noble Secretary of State, and of his desire to cultivate in the interest of both nations the closest ties of amity. I might have added an additional proof of his sincerity by stating the object of his engagement with me, but I forbore doing so.

M. de Girardin was visibly softened by my positive testimony as to the sentiments and character of Lord Palmerston so widely opposite to the opinions he had always entertained. We talked the matter over for some time, when the aggressive journalist seemed inclined to rally again.

"*Mais il se méle de tout*, my Lord Palmerston," (but he interferes in everything, my Lord Palmerston) he exclaimed, as tho' reluctant to give up his prey.

"*Et vous*" (and you), I said, laughing loudly, "what is there your impetuous activity does not interfere with? Woe to all Governments if ever you become Minister for Foreign Affairs." M. de Girardin was obliged to laugh in his turn at this just retort, and he added good naturedly—

"*Eh bien!* I see I must be careful how I handle your noble friend hereafter."

He was as good as his intimation, for I remarked that *la Presse* took from that time a different view of Lord Palmerston's character and acts.

Finding my victories so easily gained, I was not inclined to relax my exertions, but went on from conquest to conquest, even till I succeeded somewhat in subduing the deep-rooted asperity of Amedée Achard, whose Anglophobia was so rabid that he spared not even the cut of Lord Normanby's coat, when no other object to vilify presented itself.

I often met the sparkling *feuilletoniste* of the *Assemblée Nationale* at the pleasant dinner table of M. Vandenbruck, of the American banking house, Green and Co. I used to rally him on his worrying propensities. I threatened him once, if he did not suspend his attacks upon the unoffending Ambassador, that I would some day carry him off to the Embassy *vi et armis* and present him. The chance of such a *contretemps* befalling him had its effect, and by degrees Lord Normanby's name disappeared from the weekly ragout served up so piquantly by Amedée Achard.

In short, I discovered that not only was the character and dispo-sition of the British Foreign Secretary totally misunderstood by the Press of Paris, but that my representations of him were so acceptable as to lead to an entire revolution in their opinions and expressions concerning him. I consider this, certainly, a most desirable result, as the prejudice of long years against Lord Palmerston was likely to militate more than anything else against that harmony and cordiality between the two nations so specially invoked by his Lordship. With a view to disabuse the minds of multitudes, as well as to remove arguments from the hands of those whose interest or passions urged them to seek the estrangement of England and France, the idea occurred to me to draw up a conversation with Lord Palmerston, not an imaginary one, in the style of the celebrated Landor, but an anonymous one, so far as the collocutor of his Lordship was concerned, and I knew that I could procure its insertion in nearly every journal of Paris *et la Banlieu*.

I made a sketch of this sort, putting as exactly as I could re-call them his Lordship's words into his own mouth again, but at the same time giving a precision to his language, that would pre-vent it being "strained to grosser issue" than was desirable. I felt duly sensible that even in making an anonymous report of his Lordship's political views, every care must be taken not to expose him to criticism or unpleasant comment. I thought that I managed the thing with requisite caution, and when I finished the job, I laid it before my diplomatic *surveillant*, Mr. Edwardes, anticipating new congratulations upon the felicity of my conception.

To my astonishment he fell foul of my scheme with a vigor of denunciation that for a moment shook my notion of its propriety to the base.

"What a horrible idea!" he said, holding up his hands as if thunderstruck.

"Indeed," I said, fumbling my MSS., and looking, I dare say, as Desdemona did when she asked "what innocent crime she'd committed?"

"Throw the stuff into the fire," he continued, "and don't think another moment of such an outrage."

By this time I had recovered my composure, and so I asked him to explain himself a little clearer, if he wanted to convince me.

"Explain myself!" he demanded. "Why, do you think, after publishing a gentleman's conversation, you would ever be admitted to his house again?"

"That's a very high-bred notion of yours," I replied, seizing his idea at last. "Nothing could be more proper in the abstract, but nothing more irrelevant on this occasion."

I was half disposed to say absurd, but did not.

"Irrelevant!" he echoed, as much shocked as ever.

"What is more common now-a-days," I persisted, "than to publish conversations with distinguished men living and dead, and what can be more harmless, if every trait of the literary portrait revealed is to the honour and advantage of the party depicted? You know how much I have accomplished in overcoming prejudices by true statements of Lord Palmerston's sentiments, and what possible objection can there be to doing this in a more comprehensive way, since the object to be gained is so important."

I soon discovered that argument was thrown away on my obstinate friend, who was swelling to bursting with an overstrained sense of propriety, which I thought was entirely inapplicable to the case; but I found it impossible to reduce him to my view of the matter by reason or logic, and so I decided at once to bury in the recesses of my portfolio the excommunicated manuscript, which, beyond a doubt, was likely to effect much good, without any great damage to *les bienséances*. I had reason to believe, however, that the warmth of my friend Mr. Edwardes on this occasion had its source in another incident I see no objection to relating.

I happened to encounter Lord Normanby, the Ambassador, at dinner one day, and on reminding him where I had the pleasure of meeting him occasionally in London some years before, he expressed his readiness to renew my acquaintance, and desired me to call on him. I did so a few days later, and naturally enough in the course of conversation, I alluded to my connection with the Foreign Office, which I took it for granted had been mentioned to him by Mr. Edwardes, as he had promised to do. Lord Normanby's surprise was extreme. He knew nothing at all about it, and therefore I was under the necessity of giving him some explanation, referring him to Mr. Edwardes for further details. It turned out, however, that I gave Mr. Edwardes great umbrage by this seemingly harmless act of mine, which I regretted but could not understand. He never vouchsafed me any explanation. I felt sure that Lord Palmerston never intended my appointment to remain unknown to the Ambassador at Paris, as is evident from Mr. Addington's offer of a letter, and how was I to know that Mr. Edwardes had neglected or forgotten to mention it. This incident, trifling as it was, led to consequences more grave that I may possibly mention in their place.

That the Foreign Office might not remain in ignorance of what

I was about, I wrote over to Mr. Addington some brief details of what I have related above, and added such items of political information as I thought would be interesting if not useful. I received soon after the following reply, which I considered satisfactory, as it encouraged me to continue my missives :—

Private. Estcourt, 27th December, '50.

DEAR SIR,

I have received your letter while *en congé* in the country, and have transmitted it to my colleague, Lord Stanley (of Alderley), for Lord Palmerston's information.

It will be better that you should address your letters in future to Lord Palmerston, or to Lord Stanley (marking them "*Private*") through Her Majesty's Embassy at Paris.

I am, Dear Sir,
Yours faithfully,
H. U. ADDINGTON.

It was clear enough to me from this letter that Lord Palmerston desired to be kept informed of my proceedings in Paris, and the direction given me to forward my reports to the Foreign Office convinced me that I was not responsible to Mr. Edwardes, though it was apparent enough that he wished to assume my diplomatic guardianship.

CHAPTER X.

THE GAUNTLET RAISED.

Whilst occupied in the manner above related, my attention was constantly alive to passing events. Every succeeding month brought with it some new phase of the contest daily growing more distinct between the aggressive Assembly and their intended victim, the President. At length, in January, '51, the mask was thrown aside by the Monarchists of the Assembly, and no pains were henceforth taken to conceal their intention to get rid of the Prince Louis Napoleon at the earliest practicable moment. Presuming on his weakness they had, at first, endeavoured to dragoon him into obedience. Finding him less pliant than expected they next essayed the arts of flattery, and the coarser corruption of bribes. Discovering that he was as reluctant to yield to seduction as to dictation, and as blindly convinced as ever of the President's incapacity, the Monarchists lost their temper, and M. Thiers launched the famous phrase which was regarded as a sentence to execution. "*Il faut en finir*" (it is necessary to put an end to this), declared the aspiring arbiter of the destinies of France, and the majority of the Assembly set their wits to work as to the best mode of suppressing the unhappy President, who, by refusing to become the tool of faction, had incurred their puissant displeasure.

The Republican minority vastly enjoyed the fatal struggle now about to begin between the Monarchical majority and the President, whom they alike detested, and both of whom they desired heartily to see overthrown, in the expectation of jumping into their places, and so getting back to power again. Calculating, in the grim spirit of Iago, "now whether he kill Cassio, or Cassio kill him," they felt sure that the result must be to their advantage. It was, indeed, melancholy to a passive spectator, like myself, to see a great and noble nation like France become the mere sport and toy of so many political *gamins*, and all its vast interests jeopardised, and the lives of thousands endangered, merely that the leaders of this party or that might wear the embroidery of Ministers of State, live in sumptuous palaces, and receive the homage of the crowd.

Such has been the pitiful history of the world, but I felt the time had come in France, as elsewhere, when politicians must do something else than merely cabal and intrigue to wield the Sovereign power. In the depth of their selfishness and the ardor of their ambition, I saw that the politicians of the Assembly, both Monarchists and Republicans, had lost sight of this grave truth or more probably were entirely ignorant of it. Such is the vanity of man that your keen politician is too apt to overrate his tricks, his cunning, and devices, whilst he ignores that piercing common sense of the masses which now-a-days is a *fait accompli*. When in the pride of intellect, and with all the pomp of oratory, M. Thiers, from the height of the Tribune, avowed his unfeigned contempt for the "vile multitude," I pitied his infatuation and deplored the fate that awaited him—the infallible punishment of his ignorance or obstinacy. The "vile multitude" has governed France since 1789, and what has been the fate of all who have sought to guide it against its knowledge of its true interests, both Monarchists and Republicans?

I built my faith on the President's future from his accurate knowledge of the past, and his evident comprehension of the present, as revealed in his daily conduct. He seemed to recognise the fact that there was a power in France greater than that of the Assembly or his own, the power of public opinion, and that his chances of duration depended upon his ability to interpret its wishes. With the daring of Œdipus, he undertook to solve the riddles of this terrible sphynx. Order, and liberty, so far as compatible with order, and the material development of France —it was thus he propounded the enigma of the future. As far as it depended on him he struggled to carry out these conclusions of the popular mind, and steadily avoided, his crowning act, to mix himself up with the factious proceedings of the Assembly.

The President felt his strength increasing gradually as his character became better known, not in Paris merely, but in all parts of France which he visited in his summer tours. His speeches, clear and concise as his Uncle's, but appealing to the sense rather than the passions of the people, convinced them the President understood their wants and interests. The acclamations which testified to their satisfaction at such a discovery were translated by the cynics of the Assembly as the homage of the "vile multitude" to a great name.

In the winter of '51, the President began to prepare himself for the conflict he saw approaching—and his acts of daring resolution now and then astounded the leaders of all parties—but they attributed to caprice and temper what was the result of courage, sagacity, and decision.

There was one event worth recalling, as it arrested the attention of all France. I have spoken already of General Changarnier as a guest of the President at the dinner I have recorded. He was, then, high in the esteem of the President and the public both for his military reputation and grave character. The President invested him with the command of the First Division of the Army, as well as of the Garrison of Paris, a total of some 150,000 men. This was a high mark of confidence, but the execution of his duties left nothing to be desired, and the relations of the General with the President were for a long time harmonious and cordial. Holding so important a command, including the military control of the Capital itself, made General Changarnier a very desirable acquisition, and the leaders of the Monarchical party sought to win his ear, and seduce him from his allegiance. The rapid rise of Changarnier, and the popularity he enjoyed, had, no doubt, elicited a soaring ambition, and weakened his judgment. It was hinted to him that he might play the part of General Monk over again, and restore the exiled Dynasty. Deceived, like the rest, by the quiet deportment and silent habits of the President, the General began to think himself the better man of the two, and to wonder, no doubt, why he should not be President as well as General. Certain it is, he lent himself to the seductions practised on him, and joined the camp of the Monarchists.

This was soon known to the public, who thought that he had no business to take any part in politics, but ought to confine himself to his military duties alone. The Monarchists thought, and Changarnier also, that his popularity with the Army was so great, that the President would not dare displace him, lest a military rebellion might ensue. A great many people thought so too.

Things went on in this critical way without offering the President any open cause of rupture.

An incident occurred at last which not only afforded one, but led to another important result. During the course of the autumn, the President ordered the Army of Paris, some 60,000 men, to be manœuvred in portions, at different times, on the plains of Satory, near Paris. The President attended these Reviews, and astonished some of the old Generals, inclined to sneer at him, by taking the command, and displaying his capacity to manage a *corps d'armée* in the field. General Changarnier was also there as General-in-Chief. As the work was hard both on officers and men, consuming the greater part of the day, the President thought it would be no great outrage on military discipline to order refreshments to be served during the hour of repose allowed. Champagne was furnished for the officers, and the men were supplied with a sausage and biscuit. This was known beforehand as the President's intention; and a great outcry was raised in the Assembly for this odious attempt, as it was stigmatized, to corrupt the Army, and convert it into a Prætorian band.

This nonsense levelled against the President had an effect not anticipated. It offended the Army, who thought the Assembly and its leaders must put a low estimate on their honor and intelligence to declare that a sausage or a bottle of wine could degrade them to the level of Commodus' guards. The Assembly thus lost the respect of the Army. General Changarnier, along with his political associates, condemned in harsh terms supplying the Troops with refreshments during the exercises alluded to, and on one occasion marked his displeasure by quitting the field. The schism between the President and his recalcitrant General was now beyond remedy, and the Monarchists and Changarnier himself only yearned for the President to venture to lay his finger upon him. No doubt plans were organized for a military *emeute*.

It may have been a couple of months later, when most people had forgotten the event, and just when the Monarchists were wrapping themselves round with the comfortable conviction that the President held them in too much awe to risk the consequences, that the news spread through Paris that General Changarnier was *destitué*, deprived of all his commands, and consigned to private life, whilst his important functions were bestowed on another.

Great was the rumpus thereat, and ominous were the threatenings that ensued; but whether the Monarchists found the Army not inclined for mutiny, or dreaded to venture upon so formidable an experiment, it is hard to say; yet, it is certain, their indignation evaporated in empty words, whilst it was circulated that Changarnier was loading his brain with a tremendous oratorical charge, which was to be fired off at the President the very first occasion. The day came, and I had no small difficulty to get a place in the diplomatic box at the Assembly. Its vast galleries were overflowing with an excited auditory, and every member of the Legislative body was at his post. Expectation was on tiptoe, for no one knew what the ex-General of the Army of Paris might in his anger say or threaten.

When he ascended the Tribune the silence was profound. His manner, however, was not that of the man I had often seen at the Elysée Palace, calm and haughty. His brow was dark, and his eye revealed the commotion of his mind, but he had the air of an antagonist already vanquished and cowed. His speech was exceeding brief, and only betrayed the bitterness of his heart. He made some vague and spiteful allusions to the President, but ended by saying he sheathed his sword only to draw it again when dangers menaced the country. Whether the General had taken counsel of the men who had provoked his downfall, or obeyed his own discretion, it is certain his speech had more the tone of a whimper than a tirade, which, however, would have damaged him far more than the President.

The effect of this decided act on the Assembly and the public was remarkable. The gauntlet which the leaders of the Assembly had so often contemptuously hurled at the object of their derision was at length calmly picked up, and the first blow in return for many words of insult and acts of defiance was administered with so much skill and daring as to shake the nerves of these bellicose orators. It would have been well for them to have profited by this warning, but as the old line has it, "*Quem Deus vult perdere, prius dementat.*"

The public were not a little surprised at this sudden exhibition of a bold spirit and a strong will, which had lain so long dormant in spite of exceeding provocation. The prudence and sagacity of the President was, as I have said, fast securing their hold on opinion, but little was yet known of his real disposition or character. He lived in a cloud of misrepresentation; he was never seen but through thick fumes of detraction, and this was the first time he had forced his way through into the light of truth, and revealed himself as he was. The apparition was startling, but consoling. From that day the public of France took heart; from that hour dated the future of Louis Napoleon; from that event the leaders of all parties began to see the antagonist they had to cope with was, indeed, a modern Brutus, and that something more than ridicule and abuse was necessary to subdue so clear a head and stout a heart.

It was clear, from the debates of the Assembly, which I frequently attended, that both Monarchists and Republicans were bent on running a muck against the President. No such thing as sober and useful legislation was thought of; no measure of utility was ever brought forward by the leaders of parties, and whenever the President, through his Ministers, took the initiative, the politicians of both sides united to vote it down. Nothing could be more unseemly in the eyes of an Englishman or an American than the behaviour of the Chamber on these occasions, and it required uncommon nerve in the Minister of the day to stand his ground against the volleys of gibes and sarcasms which poured in on him from all quarters.

The Parliamentary practice of England had been for some time the custom of France, and the Ministers of Louis Philippe, as latterly those of the President, were in the habit of retiring when the majority of the Chamber pronounced against them. In this way the President had frequently been compelled to change his Ministers, however well-adapted in all respects to the functions they had to fill, or however assiduous and laborious in their discharge. The object aimed at was to disturb the public mind and compromise the President by these rapid changes of Cabinets. As this seriously interfered with the business of the State, the President decided, for this reason, as well to thwart the machinations of the Legislative conspiracy, to maintain his Ministers in office, whether the majority was for or against them, leaving public opinion to note down the cause of this stoppage in legislation.

The "scenes" that frequently ensued the winter of '51 in the Legislative Assembly were far more piquant than decorous, and must have foreshadowed in the mind of the observant stranger its inevitable fate. An orator no sooner ascended the Tribune than he became a target for the splenetic wit of the party to which he was opposed, and the confusion was only increased by the attempts of the party to which he belonged to support him. This disorderly habit of interrupting a speaker prevailed, though to a lesser extent, in the old Chamber of Deputies, under Louis Philippe, and has always characterized the Parliamentary Assemblies of France. It is not so much to disturb the orator, or impair the effect of his discourse, as an occasion sought for by the leaders of parties to display their wit and attract to themselves the attention of the audience. The presiding officer, instead of repressing these unseemly ebullitions, is more apt to encourage them by his example; and a French Legislature, so far from rivalling in dignity and decorum that of England or the United States, more frequently outvies in noise and irregularity their worse conducted public assemblages.

During the winter of '51 the leading members of the President's Cabinet were M. Baroche, Minister of Foreign Affairs, and M. Leon Faucher, Minister of the Interior. The appearance of either of them at the Tribune was something like a signal for tumult. These gentlemen, in sympathy and principle, adhered rather to the Monarchists than the Republicans, and they used all their influence with the former to obtain their legislative support. Party considerations, however, were stronger than patriotic impulses, and they were as often assailed and annoyed by their friends as by their more direct antagonists. M. Baroche, at the Tribune, invariably maintained his dignity and composure, whatever the provocation. A statesman of superior ability, sound judgment, refined taste, and perfect self-control, he often subdued, by his manner and the adroitness of his discourse, the unruly dispositions of the turbulent politicians around him.

It was just the absence of all these conciliating traits that made Léon Faucher's attempts to address the Assembly a scene of tumult that would have startled a spectator unused to the stormy outbreaks of the legislative body at this epoch. There was something incontestably pugnacious in the disposition of the Minister of the Interior, which revealed itself in the vivid flash of his keen grey eye, and the defiant expression of his upturned nose. Each interruption only seemed to rouse his energy and stimulate his spirit of resistance, and leaving the subject of his discourse, he ran off, as it were, in the pursuit of his assailants, and the sharpness of his retorts, and the bitterness of his repartees, often abashed his adversaries, and silenced the boldest brawlers of the Mountain.*

It would be impossible to give any adequate notion of one of these "scenes" without copying the exact report of them which appeared in the newspapers, and that, to say the least, would consume too much space. Every leader of party managed to have his say, and the character of the individual naturally displayed itself in the tone of his interruption. Many French politicians excel in this species of impromptu, and have acquired a notoriety in this way which would not have attended more elaborate efforts. Let us imagine for a moment M. Leon Faucher at the Tribune. The usual hubbub of conversation would instantly cease, for the scent of the inevitable rumpus would draw off every member's attention from ordinary matters, and the whole House would rouse up and seem to prepare itself with the rollicking spirit of mischievous schoolboys, for a scene of excitement and disorder.

The Minister would begin and speak for some five minutes, perhaps, amid the silence of the Assembly, when, suddenly, M. Jules Favre, of the Republican party, would let drop some piquant remark. The Minister would instantly reply with severity.

M. Victor Hugo would, next, send up one of his sarcastic rockets.

M. Montalembert, of the Monarchical party, would then fire off his bomb full of sardonic contempt.

---

* The ultra Republicans sat on the top benches at the left hand side of the Chamber, which was denominated the *Mountain*, an expression borrowed from the first Revolution and similarly applied.

A pungent flash would escape M. Thiers.

General Cavaignac might, then, be tempted to say something curt and cutting.

M. Dufaure, on the cross-benches, belonging to no side, would venture some grave remark of two interpretations.

All this time the dauntless Faucher would be revolving at the Tribune, as though he stood on a pivot, turning his head in every direction, and keeping up a murderous discharge of oratorical missiles of every size and force, which he sent flying in every direction. Of course, the phrase of every leader would be caught up, and echoed by each member of his party, till, finally, the din became deafening, and nothing could be distinctly heard in the general uproar.

What added to the oddity and absurdity of this singular legislative demonstration was the behaviour of M. Dupin, the President.

"*Silence, Messieurs,*" he would cry, with persevering energy; "*le Ministre a la parole,*" (the Minister is speaking) he would shout, again, with imposing determination, whilst he beat his desk vigorously with his ivory hammer. But no sooner had he partially succeeded in restoring order, than, unable to restrain his caustic wit, or curb his strong Monarchical predilections, he would fling at the heads of the Republican party some stinging reproach, charging them with the whole responsibility of the disorder. This manifest injustice could only renew the tumult, which would go on with occasional lulls till all sides were fairly tired out with their morning's pastime.

Such incidents as these have occurred in the annals of the English House of Commons and the American House of Representatives, but they have sprung from some sudden source of excitement which momentarily overturned the ordinary gravity, the customary propriety, of these business-like bodies, whereas this utter forgetfulness of all dignity and unjustifiable neglect of all duty by the Legislative Assembly during the whole of its spasmodic existence was a matter of constant and familiar occurrence. Wrapped up in a sense of their own importance, and absorbed in the pursuit of party objects, they were wholly unmindful of the ruinous effect of such frivolous and discreditable conduct on the public mind of the country.

In the Constitutional history of France there is no instance of any Legislative body so insensible to the interests of the nation, and so regardless of opinion, as was the Legislative Assembly of '49. I can recall no act of its whole career inspired by a spirit of patriotism, or dictated by a laudable anxiety to elevate the condition of the country or improve the situation of the masses. All that was done that had not a party motive tended only to benefit one class to the detriment of the rest.

A notable proof of this was the vote of the majority to maintain intact the oppressive tariff of the last reign, which enriched the manufacturer to the impoverishment of the labouring class. To the disgrace of the Republic of '48 this odious relic of class legislation was left untouched. The Republic of '89 showed less reverence for the venerable monuments of abuse bequeathed to them by the unjust laws of other times. When the reform of the tariff was mooted in the Assembly in '51, M. Thiers was the zealous champion of the monopolists.

Ascending the Tribune, he delivered one of those brilliant harangues which, though repugnant to the conviction of his hearer, enchain him by the force of its argumentation, its lucid expositions, and elegant diction. No man could seem less calculated to achieve oratorical triumphs than M. Thiers. His short stature, ungraceful person; his shrill, discordant voice; his very eye concealed by glasses; the stranger would regard his appearance at the Tribune with indifference, if not aversion. His masterly intellect and charms of language soon overcome all obstacles, and command admiration alike from friend and adversary. Pity that such gifts should be sacrificed on the shrine of party aggrandisement or of personal ambition.

For hours M. Thiers laboured on the occasion in question to distort the plainest truths, and to disguise sophistry in the specious guise of reason. In the face of common-sense, and despite the recent experience of other countries, M. Thiers endeavoured to show that a scale of imports, in some instances prohibitory, and in others most disproportionate, was to the advantage of the nation and the good of the poorer classes. The shade of Colbert, the patriotic founder of the French Tariff, might well have been invoked to denounce doctrines that so grossly perverted the rational purpose he sought to accomplish by means not more moderate than skilful.

The clear vision of the public, however, was not bewildered by the audacious sophistries of M. Thiers; and though he was applauded and sustained by the unanimous vote of the Monarchical party, it was not the less perceived that both he and they only aimed to enlist on their side the wealth and influence of the manufacturing class. Is it to be wondered at, after all I have related, that the leading Statesmen of France should, one after the other, fall lower and lower in public estimation? Is it at all strange that the Legislative Assembly should, after such displays of party bigotry, neglect of duty, and violent excesses, sink into general contempt? Was it not natural and logical that the nation should begin to doubt the capacity of any Parliamentary body, without check or responsibility, to wield the Government of the country?

The President could not fail to see the bent of the public mind; but he calmly and prudently awaited the signal which the rapid current of events was destined soon to bear him. Amid the violence of party conflicts, M. Thiers must have had some terrible misgivings, as well as a prophetic sense of the retribution that awaited the faithless politicians of the day; else why, in his impatience at some act of party insubordination, did he cry from the height of the Tribune, "*l'Empire est fait*" (the Empire is upon us). Was it the hand-writing on the wall that transfixed his gaze?

CHAPTER XI.

A MISUNDERSTANDING.

What services it may have been supposed by Lord Palmerston it might be in my power to render him in France I know not. From my connection with the Press of Paris, and occasional appearance in its columns, he may have anticipated my possible utility in that influential quarter. His knowledge of my intimacy with the prominent French Statesmen of the day may have led him to expect I should gather from these various points of view some definite indications of forthcoming events. It is certain, however, that he counted for sure upon my seizing every opportunity and using all my experience to support his policy and make known his dispositions towards the United States.

It was no doubt intended that this should be my special field of action; the most important, and most productive scene of my diplomatic exertions. This was my own opinion, and I felt all the responsibility and difficulty of the task. The relations of Great Britain with the United States, though intimate beyond what had ever existed between two nations before, still were ever doubtful and uncertain. That interests so vast and complicated, as depended on the friendship of these two countries, should be exposed to sudden ruin, was, in truth, a gigantic evil, and it well became those whose opportunities or whose position fitted them for the enterprise, to look into the hidden causes of this perilous state of things, in the hope to remove or extinguish them for ever.

It seemed a perfect anomaly that countries like England and the United States, bound together by every reason, moral and material, that could influence humanity, should ever and anon cast looks of distrust and anger at each other, and be hurried, at times, almost to the verge of hostilities.

This was a mystery eminently worth investigating, and I felt a keen relish to set about the matter. Lord Palmerston had not deigned to favor me with his opinions thereupon, but simply, as I have related, expressing his wish that such a condition of things should cease, he confidently left it to me to employ such means as in my judgment appeared the most efficacious to effect his purpose. In looking at the history of the two nations I saw nothing to justify, at the present day, jealousy or dislike. The rebellious colonies of '76 threw off the supremacy of the mother country, and by force of arms achieved their independence. This, once acknowledged, the bitterness of the contest died away, and amicable relations succeeded. The haughty indifference of England to their rights once more compelled the young and spirited States of America to assert their dignity, and the sad spectacle was presented, again, to the world of kinsmen arrayed against each other in deadly conflict. This unnatural war soon ceased, and the amazing results of the peace that has since prevailed have not only softened the memory of past feuds, but served to inculcate the wisdom of eternal friendship and goodwill.

Why is it, then, that clouds should still hover over an alliance so natural and so necessary to the welfare of both? It cannot be doubted that the harsh and acrimonious tone of the English Press for many years past towards the United States has engendered the suspicion amongst them that the sentiments of the community it represents were unfriendly, if not hostile. Is this inference just, or the contrary? It would be most illogical to suppose that the dispositions of the commercial world of England were anything else than favorable to their best customers, for interest coincides with every other consideration to draw into the closest bonds of amity the great trading classes of the two countries. In assailing the institutions, and disparaging the society of the United States, it is, then, evident that the English journals have in past years belied the opinions and compromised the interests of the commercial community of England. It follows, therefore, that the Press have given utterance to the prejudices of the political class which in England represents the aristocratic interest, and which has hitherto not only monopolised the Government, but exercised an undisputed sway over society.

It is in the nature of things that the aristocracy of England should regard with distrust and aversion the democratic institutions of the United States, and that they should deem it their interest to asperse them. It is natural that they should seek by misrepresentation and abuse to preserve the popular mind of England free from the infection of American doctrines, and unbiassed by the influence of American example. It is from their inspiration, therefore, that the English Press has teemed for many years in book-form, pamphlet, and journal, with libellous attacks on the institutions, character, and usages of the United States. This long course of literary aggression awoke a spirit of resentment in the American mind, and has tended more than any other cause to create and foster those feelings of irritation that I have already said expose the friendly relations of the two countries to sudden rupture.

Happily, however, the increasing power of the commercial classes has obliged the aristocracy of England to reconsider their inimical proceedings towards the Union, and these literary attacks have of late diminished in virulence, and at the time I am recording they promise to cease altogether. The sagacity of the aristocratic class displayed itself in this judicious change of conduct; for they could not but see that they endangered their own safety in jeopardizing the vast interests of the nation they aspire to govern. Have they, in truth, yielded so entirely to the suggestions of a calm wisdom, as utterly to abandon their jealous fears of the American democracy, or have they only obeyed the common dictates of prudence in disguising their outward expression? This was an enigma I had not yet been able to solve. Lord Palmerston declared freely the expediency of a pacific policy towards the United States, and there his instructions ceased.

I pondered over this important point most anxiously, as well I might, for a mistake, I felt aware, involved not merely the termination of my connection with the British Government—a secondary consideration—but it would infallibly destroy all my hopes of achieving the great end I had in view. Did the aristocratic Government of England honestly desire to lay the basis of a real and permanent alliance with the United States? This was the weighty problem I had to work at and decide for myself, for it was not a question that I could with diplomatic propriety put to the noble Minister for Foreign Affairs. I felt no disposition to evade the point, or shirk the responsibility attached to it. If I threaded the labyrinth safely success would reward me, but if I were lost in its mazes the cause would console me.

It was certainly a most satisfactory event to the friends of both countries that the English aristocracy had determined, at length, to give up an unprovoked system of detraction. It was a still more conclusive act, that the leading Minister of the English

Government had thought fit to require the aid of an humble American like myself to deepen and strengthen the mutual relations of Great Britain and the United States. But was it the policy merely of the British Minister to preserve the semblance of friendship, and to keep up an intercourse, softened by acts of civility, but limited to considerations of interest? Or, trampling on traditional dislike, narrow prejudice, and groundless apprehensions, was he acting on a deep conviction of the necessity of lasting concord between the nations? There was a way to test this vital question. If the British Government rightly understood their interests, and were inspired by no senseless jealousy of American principles, not merely would they eschew an unwise depreciation of the United States, but, more important still, they would carefully abstain from raising obstacles to her growth, or seek in any way to clog her prosperity. This was the touchstone I meant to apply.

Not only by means of journalism, but by all the devious windings of diplomacy, the successive Ministers of England had for years steadily endeavoured to arrest the natural expansion of the American Union. A policy more unjust or absurd than this it was difficult to conceive. Unjust, because a nation fulfils its necessary mission in spreading the fruits of its superior civilization. Unjust, because Great Britain has exemplified this truth in her long career of conquest, which she has employed every means to maintain and extend. Absurd, because in restricting the extension of the United States they forbid the creation of additional markets to swell their own revenues. Absurd, because in aiming to prevent what they could not defeat they succeeded only in rousing the worst passions, and in braving the risk of eventual hostilities.

Had the English aristocracy lived to see the folly of this delusion, and had they the sagacity to abandon it, like so many others they once cherished; was it reserved for Lord Palmerston the glory and wisdom to stamp with his reprobation a policy so barren and so pregnant with danger? Could I doubt it; for my employment else would have been a mockery? If, perchance, I had any misgivings of this, yet, as a conscientious man, there was but one course open to me. Loyalty to the cause I had espoused was not circumscribed in my view to passively enforcing the policy of any particular Minister. Such a position I never would have assumed; and I thought Lord Palmerston was displaying, not diplomatic caution, but the large purposes he entertained in leaving me sole arbiter of the best means to adopt. Regarding the reputation of the Foreign Secretary as identified with the interests of his country, and relying on his patriotism, I believed he would readily endorse my views and plans when he saw them broadly tending to the advantage of all.

It might happen, peradventure, that disinterested and comprehensive as the plans of a great Statesman should ever be, and above considerations of self or class, still, that Lord Palmerston, bent on the welfare of the nation, might, even then, radically differ with me on the conclusions I acted on. I feared rather than anticipated this. Profound as was my respect for the experience and ability of his Lordship, I felt confident of my superior knowledge of my own country. No foreign Statesman has or ever will comprehend it, so unlike its origin and influences to the standard they alone are familiar with. Knowing from observation and study the character and interests of the United States, I considered myself a better judge, not only of the manner a pacific policy could be carried out, but likewise of the way that the advantage of Great Britain might be equally promoted and secured. Happily, I saw from the first that the good of both were not merely compatible, but, to a great degree, largely identified. I trusted to the sagacity of Lord Palmerston to perceive this, whilst I earnestly hoped that neither prejudice of class or clique, or morbid jealousy of a growing Power, would induce him to condemn the convictions I had arrived at.

Finally, I admit that I hesitated for a moment on the risk I was needlessly running. A temperate support of the English Government in the American Press, a cautious opposition to American ideas, so far as they conflicted with the favourite dogmas of the English world, would not have exposed me to any attack on my patriotism, whilst they would have tended towards the "pacific policy" Lord Palmerston had in view. Such easy labour as this would have ensured all requirements, and sheltered my office and salary from all the rude contingencies that might otherwise assail them. I declare that it was not thoughtless temerity, nor undisciplined ambition, that carried me beyond this line, but simply the honest hope, the anxious aspiration, to remove shallow causes of difference, or substantial grounds of complaint, and to lay down in their place, between Great Britain and the United States, the foundations of a solid friendship and a durable alliance, not more necessary to their mutual interests than conducive to the welfare of mankind.

In November, '50, I began writing to the Press of the United States, both north and south. In my correspondence I took some pains to give impartial and careful expositions of English politics, which in the United States are variously understood, from the conflicting representations of party organs and biassed critics. Further than this, I began to assert that both England and her Government were fast outliving the bigotted views of their own interest, and the selfish apprehensions of American progress that had ever characterized them. Aware of Lord Palmerston's unpopularity in the United States, I endeavoured to impart more correct notions of his character and dispositions. Honestly lauding his abilities, and praising his zeal and activity in promoting the welfare of his country, I sought to palliate his imperious tenacity, and somewhat pragmatical habits. However devoted to national interests, I endeavoured to show he was not perversely hostile to those of other countries, and, least of all, to those of the United States. I enlarged on this point with some warmth, and maintained it against no small opposition.

Advancing beyond this, I made no scruple of saying that neither Lord Palmerston nor the English Government felt either alarm or annoyance at the growth of the Union, or the extension of her territory—that they felt no disposition to check the one or retard the other—that leaving it to the United States to consider what was due to the rights of others, and to the preservation of its own character, they were more disposed to encourage than deprecate legitimate aggrandisement. I maintained that the favourite proclamation of the "manifest destiny" of the Union by enthusiastic editors; or the vague yearnings of energetic orators for the widening of the "area of freedom," so far from inspiring dismay in England, only enlivened the joyful anticipations of her manufacturers for new markets and increased consumption, whilst her Government, sensible of the importance of this calculation, and mindful of its own foreign policy, saw nothing to apprehend, and had no disposition to interfere.

I avoided saying aught that could minister to a lust of conquest, which, in fact, I knew did not exist in the United States, for what with the moral scruples of some, and the political doubts of others, any territorial additions to the Union by violent means were likely to meet with more serious opposition at home than abroad. This was novel information, indeed, to send to the American Press, and was so utterly at variance with the known policy of the British Government, and the settled convictions of the American people, that it was received with surprise and incredulity. These assurances, whether founded or not, were soon known, on reflection, to be so consonant to reason and so clearly in keeping with the interests of both countries, that they began to work their way and find believers. I might cite as proofs of this the efforts of two influential journals, one at the North, and the other at the South, to know who was their anonymous correspondent, and if this was objectionable, to enter into negociations for the permanent continuance of the correspondence.

No journal I addressed refused to insert these conciliating sentiments, and I was even surprised to see the organs of the ultra Democracy give them a prominent place in their columns. One result, alike important and satisfactory, was achieved by this experiment, and that was to discover that no jealousy or dislike of England has any deep root in the minds or hearts of their descendants beyond the Atlantic, and that it only requires the mother country to adopt such a policy, political and commercial, as manifestly harmonises with the sense and welfare of both countries, and is congenial to the spirit of the age, for an alliance to spring up between Great Britain and the United States that would redound not only to their material prosperity, but offer a spectacle of moral grandeur that would inspire the philanthropist, and bring forth such a harvest of untold blessings as to cause the "morning stars to gather together and sing for joy."

I refrained from troubling the Foreign Office with specimens of my American correspondence, as it was a subject that neither Lord Palmerston nor Mr. Addington would give a written opinion on, so

I laid it before my diplomatic counsellor, Mr. Edwardes, with whom I always remained in connection. The tone and matter were both no doubt very foreign to all his preconceived notions, and I hardly expected a very cordial approval from him of ideas that to a man of routine, and bred up in the old school of tradition, must have seemed something like flat treason to British interests and British supremacy. I was not disappointed in my anticipations, but I had already given to my worthy coadjutor, with all his foregone conclusions, such a series of violent shocks by my eccentric views and unforeseen flights, that he submitted to this new infliction, if not with resignation, at least with the grimness of utter despair. I requested him to forward his opinions of the correspondence to Lord Palmerston, and let me know the result.

It so happened that Mr. Crampton, British Minister at Washington, was in Paris, *en congé* for a few days, whilst my letters to the American Press were under the consideration of Mr. Edwardes, who thought fit very sensibly to submit them to his inspection, as I discovered one day on going into the Embassy, where I found Mr. Crampton quietly perusing my new treatment of an old subject. No man was better adapted, from his long residence in the United States, as well as from his moderate character, to pronounce upon my speculations, though it might well happen that from one cause or the other his conclusions were the reverse of mine. At all events I was glad enough that my recent diplomatic feat was not entirely at the mercy of Mr. Edwardes, who might too precipitately censure it from unacquaintance with the subject. A joint report would now be made to Lord Palmerston, and unless both were mortal to me one might serve to neutralise the other. I felt some concern for the upshot, as may be gathered from the reflections already uttered, but it was not so much for the glory of being instrumental, however humbly, in getting the British Foreign Office at last on the right track in its American policy, as, really, for the desire to see England and the Union no longer drifting about on seas of prejudice, the sport of political jealousies and official caprice. Mr. Crampton, whom I met, as just stated, forebore any comment on what he had read, which I considered suspicious, but it may only have been prudent. Mr. Edwardes, for a week or so ensuing, wore a manner that daily grew, as I thought, in importance and reserve. He looked somewhat as I suppose a Leyden jar must feel when suddenly charged with its electrical contents, quite ready and willing to go off in an explosion at the first touch. All this was ominous, and I began to think it high time to "set my house in order," lest I might be taken unawares.

Towards the close of February, '51, I received one morning a note from my friend, Mr. Edwardes, who, though wrapped in a thunder-cloud, still let a smile of sunshine fall on me at intervals. He wrote, as always, in a friendly strain:—

MY DEAR WIKOFF—

If it is convenient to you, I should be very glad to see you here (at the Embassy) this evening, as an idea has struck me.

Yours very truly,

Monday. R. EDWARDES.

P.S.—Should you come, pray let it be early.

There was nothing positively alarming in this. An idea may strike one man without its knocking another down. I could very well comprehend the possibility of my friend being suddenly seized with a violent fit of conception, and his requiring the presence of some familiar hand to relieve his mind, and get him over his trouble. That he dreaded the inconvenience of being left too long in solitary possession of "his idea" is evident from his soliciting me to come "early." Was it, perhaps, something delightful he had to impart, and yearned to make me happy? Or could it be that, with the horrible eagerness of an executioner in a hurry, he was anxious to despatch his victim without allowing him the luxury of a last kick?

I was ruminating lazily over this suggestive note, in all the comfort of my morning gown after breakfast, and exhaling the while the fragrant essence of a choice *regalia*, when, an hour having scarcely elapsed, a second missive in the same distinct hand was brought in by my valet. It read thus:—

MY DEAR WIKOFF—

If you will have the goodness to look in upon me *to-morrow* instead of this evening, I should be very much obliged to you. I beg your pardon, but I have a person with me who is about to start for England, and I have to speak with him on business.

Yours sincerely,

Monday. R. EDWARDES.

Wherefore this sudden postponement? What had become of the "idea?" Had it evaporated, or submitted to bottling under wire pressure? But why were both it and me shuffled off so strangely till to-morrow? Ominous word! I recited forthwith Macbeth's touching soliloquy on "To-morrow," and found consolation therein. Yet, disturbing thought, who could be the "person," whose business was so pressing? Was it only some diplomatic Hamlet, who cried "Ho! for England?" or perchance an amiable "Queen's Messenger," who was to be the bearer of some confidential communication on the score of knick-knacks to be brought over on his return?

I lost myself again in a wholly new labyrinth of surmise, which had finally to give way to more active occupation. Be the import of the coming interview what it might, I felt myself quite adequate to the event, and with the dauntless front of Byron when he exclaimed, "here's a heart for any fate!" I felt myself fully prepared either to rise to higher functions, the possible reward of loyal efforts, or to fall back again into the unofficial throng, where the Foreign Office found me, unconscious of its mysteries, and undazzled by its illusions and emoluments.

At the pleasant hour of twelve the following day, and enlivened by a glorious sunshine, I took up my well-known line of march for the British Embassy, where, gaily mounting the staircase that led to the apartments of the Acting Secretary, I made my *entrée*, all radiant with smiles, and buoyant with expectation. That estimable functionary, arrayed in all the splendour of a showy *robe de chambre*, received me with an affability that left me the freest option to infer anything most congenial to my excited fancy. Lighting his cigarette with singular imperturbability, and then politely pushing the box towards me, he sank gently back into his capacious arm-chair, as though gathering himself up for the effort he was about to make. He reminded me—I say it not unkindly—of some diplomatic Dandini who was on the verge of imparting "a secret most important" to a luckless Pompolino, who had fallen unwarily into the toils of a practical joke. After giving me time to enjoy the aroma of the scented weed he whiffed, Mr. Edwardes began:—

"I have a bit of advice to give you, my dear fellow."

"Need I say how happy I shall be to receive it," was my reply, in the blandest tone.

"Well, then, I think you had better resign."

Recovering my breath as well as I could after this murderous blow, so gently administered, I exclaimed:—

"Wherefore?"

"Why, the Ministry at home, you see, is very ricketty."

"Well, what then?" I enquired.

"Should Lord Palmerston go out of office, of course your appointment ends."

"So be it," I continued, "but why resign before then?"

A short pause ensued, which I employed in rapid cogitation.

"Depend on it," Mr. Edwardes resumed, "you had better resign at once, and take a sum down than"—

"Than what?" I said, as he hesitated.

"Than risk getting nothing beyond what you have received."

My adviser then crossed his legs, and set about smoking in earnest, as though relieved of the business he was charged withal, and was deeply conscious he had nothing more to say. The "idea" had exploded; the secret was out, and it came with a plumptitude that well nigh staggered me. Instead of being "Lord Chancellor, already," I found myself worse off than the aspiring Pompolino just quoted. There was no mistaking the motive of this friendly advice. "Resign" meant, in plain English, "you've gone and done for yourself, so take a gratuity and get about your business." I recollected, however, that my connection with the Foreign Office was none of my seeking. At Broadlands, as related, Lord Palmerston proposed what only after some hesitation I had accepted. If his bargain turned out a bad one it was no fault of mine. Dismissing me in this summary way was hardly diplomatic or polite. I resolved, therefore, on the instant, to put the Foreign Office to its trumps, and to compel all parties, before I had done with it, from its illustrious head down to its passive subordinate at Paris, to try their skill with me in a regular diplomatic " set to," all Yankee as I was, untutored and unannealed. Throwing the remnant of my cigarette in the fire, and rousing myself from the short fit of reflection I had indulged in, I renewed the conversation:—

"Your suggestion, my dear Edwardes, is certainly well-timed, but I don't see the least necessity for my acting on it."

"No!" he drawled out, rather puzzled.

"I should regret to see Lord Palmerston leave office," I continued, "for the sake of the country; but it is not right for any one to abandon him at such a moment. No; I prefer to risk my salary a thousand times first, and will console myself with the souvenir of the small services you have been good enough at times to praise so highly." This was a thumper totally unlooked-for by the Acting Secretary, who, no doubt, had the check in his pocket which he thought would completely smooth over my prompt exodus from the Foreign Office.

"Eh, what's that?" he said, burning his fingers with his cigarette, and sliding in and out of his chair, looking unutterably nonplussed.

"What, you won't resign?"

"Could you really expect me to be guilty of such a rat-like proceeding?"

"But think, my dear fellow," said Mr. Edwardes, getting keenly anxious about my future welfare, "if the Ministry goes out, which, *du reste*, is certain, it is all over with you."

"Alas, and alack-a-day!" I sighed as I smiled.

"It's all nonsense," urged the excited Secretary, "to throw away a sum in hand. Remember, if the Cabinet retires, Lord Palmerston has no further control over the funds of the Foreign Office."

"But his successor has," I remarked carelessly, looking up at the ceiling.

"His successor!" exclaimed Mr. Edwardes, getting rather perplexed. "What in the world have you to do with his successor?"

"Do you forget," I asked, "that my engagement was made by the year?—and I suppose it was done in good faith."

"But who could have anticipated this fall of the Ministry?"

"Why, I admit that such a contingency occurred to me, but as neither Lord Palmerston nor Mr. Addington spoke of it, I concluded my engagement would survive it." From the rapid changes in the Secretary's countenance I perceived that he was conscious of drifting, like Wolsey, "far beyond his depth," and that he had better hasten back to his starting point if he wished to escape the dangers of the unknown sea that laid before him.

"Then you won't resign?" he demanded again.

"It would be a pusillanimous act," I replied disdainfully.

"And you refuse a sum down?"

"Do you really think me so sordid?" I said reproachfully.

"Will you take another cigarette?" inquired poor Edwardes in utter desperation.

"Anything to oblige you," and I helped myself. Seeing him *aux abois*, as the French say (lost in the woods), I got up, and saying I would drop in again in a day or two, I bid him good morning.

There is no disguising that I felt both surprised and annoyed at this abrupt and equivocal mode of putting an end to my connection with the Foreign Office. It has been seen that I never had contemplated, much less sought a position not more novel than embarrassing. I knew myself unprepared by experience, and was doubtful of my capacity to fulfil the duties that might devolve upon me; and my difficulties were tenfold increased by the strange manner I was dealt with from the beginning.

The frank expression of my opinions on my first visit to Broadlands evidently met the approval of Lord Palmerston; else why did he propose my joining the Foreign Office? I was then put to the test of a written expression of them in fuller detail, which so entirely concurred with his views that he transferred me to Mr. Addington's hands to settle the minor point of salary. I expected on this occasion some precise instructions from his Lordship or his adjunct as to the specific functions I was to perform, but was simply informed that I was to be employed in Paris; and a letter to the Marquis of Normanby, the British Ambassador there, was offered to me. It was intended, perhaps, I should receive my instructions from him; but Mr. Edwardes, who had hitherto acted on behalf of Lord Palmerston, declined to introduce me to him.

I was left, consequently, to the sole guidance of Mr. Edwardes, from whom—and I say it without any ill-will to him—I failed to receive either advice or assistance that could serve me in the least. I saw him constantly, and had much conversation with him; but I found either that he was wholly ignorant of the duties I was expected to perform, or that he was enjoined to leave me to my own inspirations. I went to work, then, as related, on my own account; and I leave my readers to judge whether my successful attempt to pacify the hostility of the French Press against England, or my equally innocuous effort to sow the seeds of a fraternal alliance between the two branches of one family, England and the United States, were not likely to do rather good than harm; and that, independent of my salary, whether I did not deserve something better than the severe censure conveyed to me so unexpectedly in the request of Mr. Edwardes for my resignation.

The pretext alleged of Lord Palmerston probably going out with the Ministry was, I considered, a mere subterfuge, for I knew it was not the habit of the Foreign Office to turn all its *employés* adrift with the accession of every new Cabinet. It may have been that Lord Palmerston felt some delicacy at transferring to his successor, amongst his diplomatic effects, such an unprecedented novelty as a Yankee "chiel," that might be "takin' notes." Perhaps he may have become sensible of having done a rash thing in letting into the Foreign Office, as stuffed full of mysteries as the British Museum of curiosities, an American with his national habit of "guessing," unnaturally stimulated by so piquant an atmosphere. And, peradventure, I did not wholly waste my time; and were it consistent with my self-respect, I might, justified by the provocation received, in lieu of the present volume, possibly give to the lovers of the marvellous whole chapters of "guesses," that would prove I was no bad hand in solving diplomatic riddles.

It may not have been the case; but if the noble Foreign Secretary was alarmed at his own indiscretion, a rare fault in him, there was only one course to be taken, due alike to the fact of the connection having been thrust on me, as to its having been made by the year, and perhaps not less due to the services which had been acknowledged, and that course was to summon me to London, where Lord Palmerston or Mr. Addington might have deigned to give me some sufficient reason for closing my engagement, with such offer of compensation as the circumstances seemed to warrant.

I say compensation, not for the services spoken of, for they had another motive than a mere pecuniary one, but for the sacrifice made of other engagements when I agreed to accept that of the Foreign Office.

In every case I felt that some consideration was due to me, and the more so that I was painfully conscious that my secret connection with the English Foreign Office might expose me to the stigma of being regarded by my countrymen as a " British spy," should it ever become public, and I not have the means, perhaps, consistent with my obligations, to make its true nature known.

Right or wrong, these were my reflections in dwelling upon the incident that transpired in the apartment of Mr. Edwardes, and which, though treated rather jocularly at the time, I was decided to bring to a somewhat more serious *dénouement*.

CHAPTER XII.

A TRIP TO LILLE.

As I have already described, the Monarchical parties of France were heart and soul engaged in wrestling with the President for the future possession of France. M. Thiers was bent on setting up the Orleans dynasty again, with the Duchess of Orleans for Regent, and himself, disinterested man, for Prime Minister and King *de facto*. M. Berryer was quite as anxious, from more chivalric motives, to restore the old Bourbon sceptre to the nerveless grasp of its last inheritor. These two factions were working in perfect unison tò undermine the President, hoping at an early day either to consign him to the dungeons of Vincennes, or to send him off with a *carte blanche* for foreign travel, according to circumstances. As for the President, though sorely pressed by secret intrigues and open resistance, distrustful of friends and beset by foes, he bore himself calmly, though warily, confident in his resources, and buoyed up by his resolution to protect the nation, as far as it was in his power, against the league of reckless, desperate politicians who were again ready, with parricidal hands, to rend her to pieces in the eager thirst for the *spolia optima*, for power and its emoluments.

The admirable address of the President had succeeded thus far in keeping the conspiring factions at bay; but as the manœuvrings of Fontenoy were followed by the conflict, so it was equally sure that interests so antagonistic as those represented by the Assembly and the President must one day not far off measure their deadly pretensions against each other. Meanwhile, the Republican party, seeing their Monarchical rivals wholly absorbed in a struggle with the President, thought the time a favourable one for making a little political capital, by getting up a demonstration in behalf of the destitute lower classes, whose manifold woes were an admirable theme for eloquent tongues.

A debate on this really important topic broke out in the Assembly the winter of '51, that I am speaking of; and after a deal of asseveration and denial on both sides, several prominent members of the Republican party, honestly solicitous to know the truth, determined to make a pilgrimage to one of the largest manufacturing towns of France, and investigate for themselves the exact state of the case.

They did me the honour to invite me to join them, which I most readily accepted, not only for the gratification of mingling in their attractive society, but also to enjoy so excellent an opportunity of getting a close inspection of the actual condition of the operative poor of France. I knew all these gentlemen well; and I dare say some outline of the simple incidents of our trip, as far as I can recall them in the lapse of five years, as well as a careless sketch of this remarkable group, who wore no disguise before me, may be of interest to my readers.

The party consisted of the Prince Napoleon Bonaparte, cousin of the President; M. Emile de Girardin; M. Blanqui, of the Institute; M. Victor Hugo, and Charles Hugo, his son; all of them members of the Assembly, save the latter, who presided over one of the Republican organs of the day. They had selected the town of *Lille*, some ninety miles north of Paris, for their investigations, the exciting accounts that prevailed of the sufferings of the poor at that place, who were represented as living like rats in cellars underground.

The day of our departure was fixed, and it was settled that we should rendezvous at the Railway Depôt, to take the evening train at eight o'clock. I reached it only a minute before starting, and should never have discovered my party but for the excessive good-nature of the Prince Napoléon, who was standing outside, at the door of the carriage retained for us, on the look-out for me. We had only four hours to reach our destination, and part of the time was spent in sprightly conversation. Though intimate with each one of our party, save M. Blanqui, and accustomed to their society, still I was surprised and amazed at the change that came over them all the moment we had got some few miles out of Paris. It seemed as though they had left all the cares and responsibilities of their several positions behind them, and in presence only of familiar friends they threw aside as an encumbrance their conventional demeanour, abandoning themselves to the unrestrained inspirations of their natural dispositions.

I soon perceived that M. de Girardin was the *gamin*, the mischievous urchin, of the party, and he soon impregnated the rest with his overflowing gaiety. The natural dignity of the Prince melted away into joviality; the thoughtful reserve of Victor Hugo was lit up with smiles; whilst M. Blanqui, dismissing all the gravity of the Institute, struggled in joke and repartee with the arch-instigator of all the fun. I had seen a great deal of M. de Girardin before this, and had grown equally accustomed to his severe and abrupt manner when in editorial harness, with his mind in full action, as well as to the easy and *degagé* humour habitual to him in society. This new phase, however, was totally unexpected, and reminded me of Emelia's line in the play. "It is not in a year and a day that we know a man!"

It was deeply interesting to me, an amateur psychologist of the first water, to watch the sportive gyrations of the master-intellects about me. It was not so much a spectacle of intellectual athletæ pitting their wit against each other as of so many playful elephants indulging in gambols out of pure wantonness. There is to me something exceedingly refreshing in the sight of distinguished men unbuttoning the jerkin of their dignity, so to speak, and bending down to the level of ordinary humanity.

In the United States or England you can never see this thoroughly done. A renowned Yankee, or an illustrious John Bull, never descends from his stilts, but under protest, as it were. All their struggles after the playful and facetious smack of awkwardness and affectation, ludicrously reminding one of a giraffe's attempts at grace. Your Frenchman, now, of whatever grade, slides as easily and naturally from the grave to the gay as an expert vocalist from the upper to the lower register of his voice, and seems quite at home in both moods, for he never seeks, like the afóresaid, to mix up dignity with frivolity; and for this reason a Frenchman never appears absurd when, in common parlance, he is playing the fool. However, all this comes of different customs, climates, and what not, and there is no use, therefore, railing at the one whilst enjoying the other.

The exuberance of our party at last gave way to fatigue, and by the time we reached Lille each one of us seemed trying hard to rub a hole through the cushion his head reposed on, under the oscillating effect of the railway. In plain English, we were all buried in sleep.

It was between midnight and one o'clock in the morning that we found ourselves wandering about the streets of Lille in search of the leading hotel of the town, for we could discover no guide at the station to assist us. There was something impressive in the stillness that overspread this busy hive of industry. The hum of labor was hushed. Neither creak of machinery, nor the clatter of looms, broke upon the silence of night. The operative, whether in cellar or garret, rested from toil, and his deep repose might have been envied by many a Sybarite who tossed sleepless to and fro on his luxurious couch. Our search was successful, and after rousing the drowsy porter we made good our *entrée* into the *Grand Hotel de Lille.*

The fresh air of the night had stimulated appetite, and there was a general cry for *poulét froid* and whatever accompaniment that was handy. To our chagrin we had to content ourselves with two or three bottles of Bordeaux *ordinaire*, and some bread and cheese, for the Cerberus of the larder had long since vanished into some remote garret, where discovery was hopeless. I had little doubt that if some of the names of our party had been sounded the alarum would soon have spread, and Boniface would have turned out in all haste at the head of his white-aproned battalion. But to the sulky porter, aroused from his first sleep, was reserved the exclusive honour of supplying, with very small portions of bread and cheese, the cousin of the President, the first *litterateur*, and the first publicist of France, to say nothing of the distinguished representative of the Institute. Our hunger made our modest fare very acceptable, and M. de Girardin presided, with his usual impartiality, over the exact distribution of our limited supply.

Bedrooms were the next object of our solicitude, but an active search by our awakened janitor only brought four to light, of which one was assigned to the *Institute*, the other to *La Presse*, the third to the French Academy and son, whilst the Prince was good enough to share the fourth, a commodious double-bedded room, with me. In the thirst for adventure that carried Cook around the world, I made the tour of my quarters of the night, and after navigating my way through various closets and *garde-robes*, I lit upon a door in the wall, which, opening cautiously, I found led to an elegant salon, unoccupied, a grate all arranged for lighting, and candelabras stocked with *bougies*. I announced my prize with all the pride of an explorer, and proposed ordering up what was left of our Bordeaux, and carrying on our chat. But the "Academicians," as the Prince styled the elders of our party, decided to go to bed, whilst the Prince, young Hugo, and myself, sat down by the comfortable fire, and discussed for an hour or so the future destinies of mankind.

The next morning, at eight, M. de Girardin came dancing into the Prince's room as chirping and merry as the night before, and reminded him that he had a hard day's work to do, for it was settled that we should return to Paris late that night, as the daily debates in the Assembly were important.

"*Ma foi*," I said, startled from a sound sleep, "I thought the *coup d'etat* had broken out at Lille by mistake." I alluded to the accusation made every day against the President in the Assembly, and journals of Paris.

"I hope," said M. de Girardin, rubbing his hands at the prospect, "such an event as that will not catch the Prince in bed."

"Don't you think," I asked, "that would be the best place for him. You wouldn't have him oppose his cousin making him heir to the throne, whilst as a *republicain honnête* he could not assist at such a transformation."

"Bravo," cried the Prince, springing lightly from his bed, "*voila*, a dilemma for you to extricate me from, *mon cher* de Girardin, whilst I am making my toilette."

Before nine o'clock we were all assembled at breakfast. By

this time the landlord had discovered his illustrious guests, and his attentions were unbounded. By ten we all sallied out, furnished with the names of the streets and lanes chiefly occupied by the pauper population, for to avoid being known the Prince and his distinguished friends desired not to take a guide who might let their names transpire. We were all provided with memorandum books and pencils, to note down the worst cases of destitution we should encounter; and without knowing what might have been the feelings of the Prince and M. Victor Hugo, I felt sure that the best polemist of the day, M. de Girardin, was quietly anticipating some splendid cases of misery that he might bring to bear with all the power of his pen against the Monarchical party he was then furiously belaying.

M. Blanqui was a stout Conservative, and voted with the Majority, and he jocosely told M. de Girardin that he would watch him close. A half-hour's walk brought us to the part of the town we were in quest of, and our party lost no time in diving curiously into the numberless recesses where poverty had fled for shelter. Apologizing, with that easy politeness so entirely French, for the friendly intrusion into their humble homes, the Prince and his friends began enquiring of these hapless creatures the details of their condition. We mounted from room to room to the garrets, and thence descended into those cellars which had been the theme of mysterious allusions in the Assembly and the Press, where it was intimated that misery in its most hideous aspect reared its ghastly eyeballs in silent rebuke of the Government and society that tolerated it. We had been an hour hard at it without coming across such a case of appalling destitution as to set the recording pencils a-going.

We found lots of old men and old women, and young women with children huddled together in pretty close quarters, but the rooms were not dirty, and were well enough lighted and ventilated. The occupants were decently clothed, and clean often to neatness. They looked healthy, and with the buoyancy of the French in every condition, were lively and chatty. The cellars under ground were comfortable enough, generally floored over, and accessible to light and air, quite as much so as the area-rooms of London houses. They were warmed by stoves, and supplied with sufficient furniture—a good bed always holding a prominent place.

"But where do the poorest amongst you live?" was more than once demanded; and some tattered ciceroni, expecting a franc for his trouble, would lead us into more houses and cellars, fac similes of those we had left. Occasionally we met touching cases of hardship, where sickness or death had lent its terrible aggravation; but nowhere did we find those spectacles of revolting wretchedness that made the heart sick with horror.

All had food, however scanty; but the culinary skill of the French never deserts them, and more than once I tasted the *bouillon* on the fire, and found it highly palatable. After visiting many of the famous *caves sous terre* (cellars underground), I remember exclaiming that I would prefer a residence in any one of them, a hundred times over, to the apartment of Prince Louis, in the dreary citadel of Ham, and I little dreamt at the time that I was destined ere the year was out to occupy something far less inhabitable.

"*Eh bien*," said the Prince to me frequently, as well as his brother members, "what do *you* think of this?" for coming as I did from a new country, said to be without poor, they were naturally curious to know how I was impressed with what I had seen.

"Frankly, gentlemen," I replied, "my mind is greatly relieved;

for instead of the rosy-cheeked and merry-hearted paupers, for the most part, that I have been passing with you in review this morning, I expected something far different and worse. If this is an average sample of your poor population, I thank Heaven that France is so well off; and, believe me, if you were to inspect the manufacturing towns of England, or to enter the abodes of the emigrant class at New York, you would find a strata of humanity in every point of view lower and more pitiable."

I should not forget to mention other peculiarities that, in fact, belong rather to the national character. These poor people were not merely lively in temper, but naturally intelligent, and their deameanour was easy without vulgarity, and polite without servility. Even before '89, the French lower classes were never so coarse and brutal as in other countries, which in some degree arose from the pleasant terms of familiarity on which the upper classes always mixed with them. As no provision is made by law for the poor in France, they are compelled to support themselves by labour, but where age or sickness incapacitate them, as was the case with some that we visited during our rounds, charity steps forth to their relief, which is usually administered with discrimination by the parish priest. Our visit was a God-send to some afflicted souls, for in every instance of this sort, the commiseration of the Prince and his friends was exhibited in positive proofs; and, doubtless, if it had been known from what illustrious hands the gift had descended, it would have been still more highly appreciated.

In the history of Lille this was probably the first time that such unwelcome haunts as these had ever been explored by a Prince of the blood and some of the leading men of France; and the motives that inspired them, though not free from political alloy, yet did honour to humanity. The results of our investigation were all in favour of M. Blanqui, who made merry at the misconceptions of his Republican *confréres*, who had honestly believed the case much worse. The memorandum books had been but little in request, and neither the Tribune nor *La Presse* were likely to electrify the community with startling details of destitution, that would have lost none of their repulsive interest in the tones of thunder that would have made them known.

As far as political objects went, the trip to Lille was a failure, and the Majority and the Government had a happy escape of it; but it pleased me to discern in the physiognomies of the Prince and his friends, not the blank disappointment of politicians who had missed an "effect," but such symptoms of honest satisfaction as patriots and good men would naturally feel to find any class of their fellow-men less unfortunate than expected. Before we had completed our tour the rumour that our party contained some *haut personnages* began to spread, and a crowd commenced, in consequence, to accumulate. The marvellous likeness of the Prince to his uncle, the Emperor, attracted every eye, and the possibility of a Bonaparte being amongst them was getting up a commotion from cellar to garret that threatened an enthusiastic explosion, but which the Prince and his party thought it best to retreat from, and so all haste was made back to our hotel.

The news of such remarkable men being, even, in *incognito* at Lille was not likely to remain long a secret, and it had already reached the ears of the celebrated manufacturers, Messrs. S——, who were waiting at our hotel to invite the Prince and party to visit their extensive premises, the resort of all strangers passing through. The invitation was readily accepted, and a couple of hours were soon spent in the inspection of the varied details of this mammoth establishment.

It would require too much space to dwell on this point, but what struck me more than the machinery, which was equal in all respects to anything I had seen in England or the United States, was the healthy and decent appearance of the operatives. Messrs. S—— have earned a just distinction by the care they have given to the moral, as well as the bodily, health of their workmen, numbering some hundreds; and amongst the not least interesting features of their vast *fabrique* are school-rooms, where the instruction is gratuitous, and well-constructed bath-houses. These humane attentions to the comfort and improvement of their men are abundantly rewarded by the perfect order and regularity that distinguish this model enterprise.

Before leaving, the Prince and party inscribed their names on the book of visitors, at the request of Messrs. S——, who, turning over a few pages, pointed out the names of Louis Philippe and all his family, who, only four years preceding, had done this noble establishment the honour of a royal visit. What a commentary was conveyed in this close conjunction of such names as Bourbon and Bonaparte! The Messrs. S—— were invited by the Prince to join us at dinner, which turned out a downright feast of Sardanapalus. Our landlord, out of respect to his guests, as well as to make amends for his shortcomings of the previous night, set his *batterie de cuisine* in full motion, and certainly acquitted himself *à ravir*.

But I shall remember this sumptuous repast for other reasons. The Messrs. S—— were highly-intelligent men, and Conservative in their politics, as capitalists with such vast responsibilities would naturally be in times of disorder such as then prevailed. They found an adherent in M. Blanqui. M. de Girardin and the Viscount Victor Hugo were known as ardent Republicans and something more.

The Prince Napoleon leant decidedly to popular doctrines, but was not an ultra. Such materials as these, brought into close contact under the influence of a good dinner, were not likely to remain long dormant. The conversation at first turned upon industrial topics, which the Messrs. S—— treated with great ability, but by degrees it veered towards the delicate ground of politics.

M. de Girardin, in the same spirit of mirthful provocation as the night before, indulged in a series of playful sallies at the expense of the "Majority," but M. Blanqui showed no alacrity in taking up the cudgels for his side of the Assembly. At last, the Prince, by way of seconding his aggressive friend, opened a direct attack on the cautious member of the *Institute*.

"*Mais quavéz vous à dire?*" (but what have you to say for yourself?) demanded the Prince, and he followed up his question by a spirited but pleasant sally of several minutes.

This forced M. Blanqui into the field, whose information was immense, and facility of elocution remarkable. He made a vigorous but amusing onslaught on the Republican party, taking care to point his heaviest guns at those zealots, *ces rouges*, of the Press and the Assembly, "whose fiery apostrophes," he remarked, "only meant for political effect, might light up a conflagration that would not only consume them, *pas un grand mal* (no great harm), but burn out everybody else." This applied specially to M. de Girardin, who laughed as heartily as the rest of us, and to M. Victor Hugo.

I kept my eye on the latter, who smiled occasionally, but it was like the gleam from the thunder-cloud. M. Hugo, unlike most Frenchmen, seems to have no *penchant* for talking. His mind is of the meditative cast, and he ordinarily expresses himself in short, quiet phrases, replete with force and point. His nature is inclined to slumber, but it is the repose of the lion, and when aroused to aggression his strength is something fearful. The admirable hits of M. Blanqui served to stimulate him, and that *vis inertiæ,* which is a trait of powerful minds, that seem to shrink from their own action, gradually gave way.

Stretching himself up to his full height, he began in his slow, measured way to reply to M. Blanqui, till by degrees the flood-gates of his eloquence burst open, and he dazzled us all by a pyrotechnic display of those brilliant declamatory periods—now flashing with satire, then almost hissing with bitterness, which give a *cachét* to his oratory, and deeply impresses his hearers. Intensity is the feature of M. Hugo's character; it is the poetical element. *Poeta nascitur non fit.* Whatever his opinions he believes in them ardently, and they come from his lips almost sparkling with the heat of the furnace they have passed through. Though he converted none of us to his views, we believed him sincere in his faith.

This unexpected rehearsal of a "scene" at the Assembly, minus its disorder, must have been a treat for the Messrs. S——, who rarely got to Paris, and they seemed to enjoy it vastly. Our dinner broke up rather late, and our party returned to Paris the same night in as high spirits as they left.

It is needless to say that no mention was ever made in the Assembly or out of it of this Republican foray into the quiet lanes and alleys of unsuspecting Lille, or of the "plentiful lack" of political ammunition found there. This pleasant excursion for all the parties concerned has hitherto gone without a chronicler, but its simple incidents may be read with interest by some, identified as they are with such remarkable persons, and illustrating as they do the state of things in '51.

It is singular, indeed, to contemplate the strange fate that in so short an interval overtook every one of the small group I have just cited. The Prince Napoleon, then cousin of the President, and one of the leaders of the "Left," is long since cousin of the Emperor, and in close proximity to the throne.

Emile de Girardin, then a fierce polemist, dashing and foaming through the columns of the *Presse* like a mountain torrent, has laid down his jaded pen, and turned his mind to more practical purposes. He may have lost something in personal importance, but his country will gain by the energy, then running waste, being turned into a more profitable channel.

Victor Hugo, then, one of the Chiefs of the Republican party, before the year was out had abandoned France. He has persisted since in his voluntary exile, giving ever and anon a bitter utterance to his stricken hopes in a fierce tirade against a Prince who not only protected France from anarchy, but who as surely saved his head from the guillotine. For I remember well the remark of M. Hugo to myself and others one evening at his house the winter of '51. "People often come to me," he said, "in alarm at the chance of disorder breaking out, and they implore me to protect their lives and property if anarchy should get the upper hand. But I tell these good people to despair of aid from me, for in the whirlwind I am as likely to perish as the rest." His tone was solemn like that of a man who foresaw his doom. It was inevitable, for had civil war broken out in France in '52, which the *coup d'état* alone prevented, not a single party leader, Republican or Monarchical, would have escaped the fury of the people.

Girardin saw this as well as Hugo, for he remarked to me one day, that "before the year is out I don't know where the waves of revolution may carry me. Perhaps I may leap on a plank of safety, and go over to your country."

"Take care," I replied with a shake of the head, "that you do not come first in contact with the plank of the guillotine."

"*Ma foi,*" he said, smiling, "*c'est bien possible.*"

What can better demonstrate than this the vertigo that had seized the French politicians in '51? for here they were not only exposing their country to ruin, but risking their heads to gratify their lust for power and their hatred for rivals.

How strange that in the silence of exile the reason of Victor Hugo has not risen above the virulence of party, and that with the vindictiveness of the Parthian, he should still launch his envenomed arrows against the invulnerable front of the Prince, in whose skilful hands eight millions of his countrymen have deposited the sovereign power. How nobler far, how more worthy his character, his fame, his memory, that shaking off henceforth the vulgar associations of party, and soaring again into those lofty regions of literature, where he has left such memorable trophies of his power, he should, to the glory of France and his own honor, dedicate his genius to the creation of some other imperishable monument, that would add a new laurel to the graceful chaplet that decks his brow, more lasting than the gaudy halo that crowns political triumphs. If insensible to the magnanimity of Napoleon III., if deaf to the entreaties of family and the appeal of friends, will he, dares he to resist the mute expectation of France that would listen again to the melodious accents of his neglected lyre, and would respond once more with delight to the new and thrilling manifestations of an intellect, as versatile as it is grand.

Of the rest of our little party, Charles Hugo, with the pertinacity of his father, clings to exile. M. Blanqui, alas, is since dead. As for my humble self, I, like the rest, have had my share of vicissitude, and, *nolens volens*, was made to suffer the rigors of fifteen months imprisonment at Genoa, through the active instrumentality of two officials of Her Britanic Majesty's Government, Messrs. James Hudson and Timothy Brown, of unpleasant memory.

CHAPTER XIII.

A REPRIEVE.

The English Cabinet, of which Lord Palmerston was the Minister of Foreign Affairs, did not resign after all, as Mr. Edwardes had predicted. There were, certainly, rumours to that effect, and such an intention may have been entertained, but Cabinet Ministers in England, as elsewhere, have a relish for place and emolument, which they are in no hurry to sacrifice if it can be avoided. I kept up my visits as usual to the British Embassy, and asked Mr. Edwardes one day if he did not approve of my sensible conduct in declining to act on his suggestion of resigning on the ground he had alleged, and which had turned out utterly fallacious.

"Well, I was quite sure," he replied, "that the Cabinet would go out."

"But if I had resigned for no other reason, as you proposed, would not Lord Palmerston have blamed me for a precipitate step?"

"Really I cannot say," he returned, and he showed symptoms of wishing to change the conversation.

"But do you still advise my resignation, on any other grounds?" I continued.

"No, no, I have nothing further to say about it," he answered in an embarrassed manner. "When you go over to London you will see Mr. Addington and discuss that point with him."

"You are right, there," I said, "he is the proper person to consult on that matter." The subject then dropped, and Mr. Edwardes never alluded to it in any way afterwards.

I was sometimes at a loss how to view this singular incident. Could it be possible that the acting Secretary, from some motive of pique or other, had ventured on a stroke of diplomatic *finesse* to get me out of his way? If I had indiscreetly acted on his advice, and sent in through him my resignation for the reason he had advanced, no explanation might ever have followed, and Lord Palmerston would only have inferred that I was tired of my situation. On mature reflection, however, I dismissed this supposition, for it is hardly likely that Mr. Edwardes would have risked all the consequences of such a gratuitous and daring act. For him to suppose that at a word, or a hint, I would, without provocation or cause of dissatisfaction, throw up my situation, was absurd. Besides, he had spoken of a "sum of money down," which he could not have presumed to offer if he had not had authority to do so. It was plain, therefore, as deduction could make it, that it was an ill-considered attempt of the Foreign Office to get rid of me by a side-wind.

If this should turn out to be the case, I was obliged to conclude that my mode of seeking to establish a permanent alliance between England and the United States had not been approved of by Lord Palmerston, for I remembered that my efforts towards disarming the hostility of the French Press against England, her government, and institutions, were at the time highly praised, and marvelled at. Neither the British Embassy at Paris, nor any of those pensioned Diplomatists that make this gay capital their frequent place of abode, had ever essayed, much less accomplished, so desirable an end for the interests of both countries. If it was proposed to terminate my connection with the Foreign Office on this ground, I should rejoice at my downfall with all the fervour of a martyr, for my faith was profound that it was only in the mode I had initiated—viz., an abstinence from all intrigues against the United States, that perfect concord could be inaugurated between the two nations who stood in such earnest need of each other.

I felt as sure as that the sun would continue to shine that the day would come, and that before long, when aristocratic prejudice or mistaken views of British interests would give way to more correct and enlightened convictions, and that the policy of England, instead of thwarting the developement of the United States by occult intrigues, or open combinations with other Powers, would more wisely seek to profit by the immense advantages that must result from their inevitable growth and extension.

It was as plain as an axiom that the interest of England, political and commercial, was to conciliate and strengthen the United States; and it was certain that if her Oligarchy did not discover this in time, the clear sense of the middle classes would require them to give up the helm of State to wiser hands. I was deeply convinced, therefore, that I had acted a loyal part towards England and her Foreign Minister, when in my correspondence, and by other means, not less effective, I had urged this new plan of conduct towards the United States.

I never doubted at the time that Lord Palmerston's anxious object was to approach closer than ever before to the United States, for England was in danger of a league of Despots, who considered her free Press a standing cause of disorder in Europe. Lord Palmerston himself was denounced as a "firebrand" in every Court of the Continent; and, uncertain as was the direction France would take, it was, I conceived, a judicious policy in his Lordship to tighten the bonds of amity with the Union, which would not have hesitated, by a spontaneous burst of feeling, to lend her co-operation to rescuing the liberties of the world, had the armies of Europe sailed towards England. I was really surprised, therefore, under all the circumstances, that I had given offence to the noble Foreign Secretary by advocating a policy so many motives combined to recommend.

It may be supposed, after the event I have related, that my position was anything but pleasant. Led to suspect that I had forfeited the confidence of Lord Palmerston, and that my services, however zealous, were no longer acceptable, I felt anxious either to lay down the trust I had conscientiously performed, or to receive such explanations as would enable me honourably to retain it. In compliance with Mr. Edwardes' intimation, I decided to let the matter lie over till I went to London in April to draw my quarter's salary, when I doubted not that Mr. Addington would be ready with adequate reasons to justify the abrupt close of my engagement.

Meanwhile I went on with my functions as usual, keeping my gaze, however, earnestly bent on every-day's indications of a portentous crisis in the affairs of France. Any chance of conciliation between the Monarchical or Republican parties and the President was out of the question. *Their* aim was the sovereign power which he wielded, but what *his* purpose was, whether he meant to retain it by force, or to leave them to seize it at their pleasure, was the absorbing enigma of the epoch. Suspicion and apprehension took every shape of accusation, and both the Press and the Assembly echoed to loud assertions that the President was organizing a *coup d'état*, a violent usurpation of absolute power. Every species of intrigue, every form of provocation, was employed to extract his secret, to get even a clue to his unfathomable designs.

It was all in vain. In public and private he wore the same imperturbable front, he preserved the same moderation of language, and continued to turn the same serene smile of indifference alike on seductions or covert treachery. In spite of the meagre allowance accorded by the Assembly, he managed to keep up his receptions at the *Elysée*, and the gay world flocked in crowds to share his hospitalty. I remarked that officers of all grades of the Army thronged to the Palace on these occasions, and I thought there was a lurking something in the expression they wore that indicated not only devotion to the President, but a fixed purpose to sustain him against any foul play or insidious machinations that might be attempted. The Assembly had fallen in the estimation of all classes in France, but their inconsiderate comments on the reviews of Satory gave, as I mentioned, serious offence to the whole Army.

At all these *fêtes* the President mingled freely with his guests, and partook gaily in the diversions of the hour. To the surprise of many he did not scruple even to dance when the whim took him, and this was railed at by the grey-beards of the Assembly as a frivolity inconsistent with his high position.

Ce n'est pas un homme sérieux (he is not a man of sense) they never ceased to declare and to believe, but whether the President really sought to mislead them and to disguise his profound intentions under a mask of assumed gaiety, or whether he merely indulged a passing and not undignified caprice, it were difficult to pronounce.

One of the singular and original features of this extraordinary man's character is a species of moral hardihood, which has always made him dare to do what his judgment or taste considered unobjectionable. No exaggerated notions of his rank prevented him ever from taking part in ordinary recreations, or seeking such amusements as other men find palatable. For this reason he excels in all light and graceful accomplishments, and in riding, or driving, fencing, or waltzing, or even skating, he has few competitors. It is not unusual, certainly, that a Prince should so employ his leisure, but that a man of such superior intellect, and of so grave and thoughtful a character, should find enjoyment in pastimes generally considered the prerogative of common men, seems, apparently, strange and inconsistent.

In reality it is not so, for the severest personages that history records have in secret disported themselves in a manner they would have openly shrunk to avow. The grim Richelieu had his hours of *abandon;* whilst the stern Cromwell's favorite relaxation was, on finishing his dinner, to roll up his napkin and throw it at the head of one of his familiars, which was the signal for a general volley all round. As earnest as Richelieu, and as unimpassioned as Cromwell, the Prince Louis could never have descended to vice or buffoonery, which his taste and dignity both forbade. His peculiarity has been in resisting that conventional affectation that is thought necessary to high rank, and in calmly daring to follow the bent of his disposition, regardless of the comments of the world of gossip.

I remember an instance of this in London, '47. I heard it remarked on more than one occasion, at that time, by certain titled friends of the Prince Louis, that he was much in the habit of frequenting the country house of a very estimable gentleman, but not much known in the fashionable world. It was thought by his haughty friends somewhat derogatory to a Prince of his high pretensions, that he should bestow his society familiarly on individuals, however respectable, yet too far below him in the social hierarchy. Presuming on his good nature, and my long acquaintance, I ventured one day to repeat the observations I had heard.

"*Vraiment*," said the Prince, with a pleasant smile of incredulity. "They say nothing against the respectability of Sir —— ?"

"Oh, not a word," I returned. "Simply that it is not just the sort of place your Highness should habitually visit."

"I should be sorry to shock the parties you allude to," observed the Prince, "but, really, I see no alternative. Sir —— and family are very amiable, and nothing can exceed their civility to me. I cannot see any good reason why I should deprive myself of the pleasure of going to their house."

This was the honest expression of his mind, which ignored with suppressed disdain such trivial guides to conduct as were only to be found in the prejudices of rank.

What he was in exile he remained in the splendour of his new position, and as President of the Republic he passed along through the brilliant saloons of the *Elysée*, easy, unaffected, composed, kindly addressing old friends, and smiling affably on new.

There was one attraction the less at the receptions of the President in the Spring of '51, and that was the "graced persons" of the leaders of the Monarchical parties, Thiers, Môlé, Berryer, Montalembert, *et id omne genus*, who fondly fancied some two years before that they were the real masters of the Palace, where their puppet played the empty *rôle* of presiding over its festivities. The Republican Chiefs had never from the outset frequented the *Elysée* in any number, and it arose, doubtless, from the active part taken against the President's election, which had ended in so disastrous a defeat for themselves.

At the period in question, March, '51, all parties and all men were plunged in a Serbonian bog of doubt and perplexity. Beyond the close of the Presidential term, May, '52, nothing could be discerned. The future spread out like a vast and blank expanse, darkened by thick and threatening shadows, but without one distinct or fixed object to arrest the mind or console the gaze. I turned my eyes wistfully in every direction. I sounded every oracle and drew forth the reflections of every observant and dispassionate mind. Still it was ever *vox et preterea nihil.* All was surmise, fear, or hope. The optimist and the pessimist had an unlimited range to indulge their respective fancies, and the vast body of hearers who were swayed by them, drifted helplessly onwards to the solution which for better or worse awaited them.

In all France there was one man only at this time, and he, seemingly, the most unconcerned, who had clear and definite ideas as to the future, which lay plain and sure before him. Whilst others speculated, he planned; whilst others hoped, he resolved; and when others shrunk from the inevitable abyss France must cross, he boldly, confidently, approached it. Over it the President meant to leap. Would France follow at his bidding? Her salvation and his were wrapped up in that portentous doubt.

As birds are known to fly hurriedly to and fro before the coming storm, so parties and men, at last, began to change positions anxiously and to provide for their safety in schemes and counsel. I discovered that the moderate Republican party, having changed their tactics and abandoned rusty prejudices against England, was quite disposed to make advances towards her Government, and would have been exceedingly content to come to some tacit understanding under certain contingencies. Lord Palmerston, however, was too experienced a statesman and too crafty a diplomatist to compromise himself by an indiscreet word when such information reached him. It was well, and no doubt satisfactory for him, to know that if France should fall once more into the uneasy lap of party politicians, that the only really practical and progressive amongst them all considered their interests as identified with the English alliance.

What were the secret conclusions of his Lordship as to the future of France, or what his unavowed bias, it is useless to speculate upon; but I see no harm in venturing the belief that he put no small confidence in the *avenir* of the Prince Louis. His practised eye must have measured with singular accuracy the caution and skill of the President's consummate manœuvres, amid amazing difficulties. He must, also, as carefully have estimated the damnatory effects of the factious and disorderly career of the Legislative Assembly. He rightly judged, no doubt, the power of the President's name, the popularity of his conduct, his decision of character, and his dauntless will.

In the confusion and terror of a crisis, Lord Palmerston must have foreseen all the benefit to be derived from such advantages as these.

"He has made no mistake yet," was the significant phrase of his Lordship, at Broadlands, October, '50, and the President had been not less felicitous in the interval that had elapsed. The sympathies of Lord Palmerston, if such a word is applicable to a Statesman of his *calibre*, must, therefore, have leant towards the Prince Louis, and he must have contemplated his retention of power against the most adverse chances as highly probable, if not desirable.

Whether as an Englishman of the old school, and one of the Oligarchy, he retained any prejudice against the name of Bonaparte, it is utterly idle to consider; for a purely political machine like the noble Foreign Secretary, if I may use the simile, works solely with calculations, not sentiments. It was enough for him to see the President's final success probable, to desire it, and to adapt himself, with all the readiness of a pliant politician, to the results that would grow out of it, seeking to extract from them all the profit his policy demanded.

I deem this to be an impartial, however imperfect, sketch of the situation at the beginning of April, when I went over to London in quest of Mr. Addington's quarterly check, as well as of some definite information respecting my longer connection with the Foreign Office. I called promptly, and was received by the Under Secretary with his usual formal civility. In reply to his ordinary question of "what was going on in France," I conveyed just such an exposition as I have detailed at greater length above.

He listened with his accustomed gravity, and in his favorite attitude before the fire, nodding his head or uttering an idle exclamation in the approved official fashion. Having quietly digested all I had to say, the Under Secretary turned to business, and moving towards his desk filled up a check on Drummond's Bank with that easy unconcern people usually feel when they dispose of other people's cash. I signed, as usual, a receipt for the amount, and Mr. Addington was on the point of making his parting salutation when, to his surprise, I sat down again.

I believed him fully aware of all that had occurred; still, for form's sake, I considered it best to make known to him, as though he did not, all that had transpired between Mr. Edwardes and myself, recapitulating every detail, and winding up with my reflections thereon. The Under Secretary had passed years enough in the Foreign Office to know how to accommodate himself in manner and language to all possible emergencies; and though he may not have anticipated a proceeding so direct, and, perhaps, a little presumptuous on my part, still he met it with a composure, if not utterly stoical, at least in harmony with his mystic functions.

Mr. Addington may have expected that as he showed no desire or intention to refer to the diplomatic passage of arms which had occurred between Mr. Edwardes and myself, that I would in all likelihood be content to "let well alone." This is ancient usage both within and without the walls of the Foreign Office, and before violating it I had given it a passing thought. It was not so much from rampant curiosity to pierce through mysteries, as with a view to pacify my offended dignity, that I determined now that the time had come to receive such explanation as the occasion, I considered, called for.

Having finished my recital, carefully studded with every effect that could possibly add to its weight, I paused, like Brutus, for a reply, mutely wondering what it would be. The Under Secretary had stood the while with his gaze intently fixed on the Turkey carpet, meditating, as I thought, on my words. The sound of my voice ceasing seemed to wake him up, and finding my tale fully told, he raised his head and said—

"Well, I know nothing at all about the matter, and, therefore, have nothing to say."

I fell headlong from the boiling point of expectation to the zero of disappointment.

"Know nothing about it?" I exclaimed.

"Nothing."

"Never heard of it?"

"Never."

There was a chilly dryness in Mr. Addington's looks and words that almost benumbed me. I never had the ambition of Hercules for desperate jobs, and I saw how far beyond my strength would be any effort to force out of Mr. Addington a word it was not his cue to speak. I tried him again, however, on another tack.

"What would you advise me to do?" I asked.

I had never suspected the impassable Under Secretary capable of a shrug, but he gave way to one, as a response, that a Frenchman might have envied. Still absorbed in contemplation of the aforesaid carpet, the Under Secretary stood at bay.

Under any other circumstances I might have admired it, but paralyzed by my rebound from the stone wall (begging Mr. Addington's pardon) I had unconsciously run against, I felt only anxious to pick myself up and be off.

"Good morning," I said pleasantly, as I retired to the door.

"Good morning," repeated the Under Secretary in a tone that to my disordered fancy had all the effect of "don't you wish you may get it?" that is, in reference to what I wanted to know.

From what I have related it has been seen that Mr. Addington, by direction, of course, of Lord Palmerston, had thought proper to ignore the proceedings of his subordinate, Mr. Edwardes, at Paris. Now, what did this mean? Mystery was piled on mystery. It was impossible to doubt that Mr. Edwardes had simply obeyed instructions in his *brusque* effort to oust me, but why should the Under Secretary hesitate to follow up the initiative that had been taken. Was it possible that Lord Palmerston had, meanwhile, been seized with a fit of repentance, and had concluded not to break with me, either from a hope of future usefulness or the conviction that I deserved a better fate?

At all events, it was plain enough that the Foreign Office had beat a retreat and left me still in possession of the field. This might have sufficed any easy gentleman chiefly concerned in pocketing regularly his quarter's salary, but I was not at all inclined to sit quietly down under the Damocles sword suspended over my head. Had I lost the confidence of Lord Palmerston? If so, why retain me a day longer in the Foreign Office? Why not put a prompt, a civil, and satisfactory termination to it? This was what I wanted to know, and was quite decided to ascertain.

On the other hand, if it were decided to go on with me, why not vouchsafe me such indications as would enable me to comply with the views of my chief? Should these turn out different from what I supposed they were, as conveyed in the remarks of Lord Palmerston at Broadlands, September, '50, or were such as I could not conscientiously support, then nothing was left me but to tender my resignation. This was, certainly, the common-sense view of the subject, but it may not have conformed to the diplomatic mode of proceeding in vogue at the Foreign Office. There was this advantage, however, in adopting the former, that it would have left me without cause of dissatisfaction or grounds of complaint.

My interview with Mr. Addington only cleared up one point, viz., that a change of tactics had been decided upon. I was determined *coûte qui coûte* to press forward and know more. I was fully sensible of my presumption in contending single-handed against such formidable odds as the legion yclept the Foreign Office, with such a Colossus as Lord Palmerston at its head. I had little doubt of my ultimate defeat, but my mind, as related, was firmly made up to try my hand at a set-to with the very masters of the art of craft, and failure would, therefore, bring no humiliation. Nay, an advantage would still remain with me in the new experience gained.

True, if I could have possibly foreseen by mesmeric or other means, all the frightful consequences of my great temerity—if I could have dreamt of such an inconceivable concatenation of events, as ultimately put me in the hard gripe of the Foreign Office, *certes*, I should have recoiled in terror from what I looked on at the time as a harmless and justifiable course of action. If the Foreign Office, on the other hand, had been imbued with any prophetic lore, and could, by astrological or other divination, have anticipated the failure of their worst designs, and the final publication of this book, it is quite probable they would have dropped all sleights of hand, however dexterous, and dealt with me in a more rational way.

Having recovered, in a day or two, from my flat repulse at Mr. Addington's hands, I turned my battery, albeit in a curious, not a hostile sense, against my commander-in-chief, Lord Palmerston. I meant to seek an interview with him, and I could imagine no adequate reason why he should refuse it. When I left him last at Broadlands, but six short months ago, I was high in favor, and nothing could I detect, in reviewing my acts or intentions, that of right should lower me. As my employment sprang entirely from his own suggestion, I had positive claims on his attention, and he was, further, bound by his breeding, *noblesse oblige*, to treat me with civility.

I called at the Foreign Office, therefore, one afternoon, and sent up my card to the noble Viscount. The answer returned was—"Lord Palmerston's engaged, but will you wait?" Nothing was more likely than his Lordship should be engaged, and so resigning myself to my thoughts, I set patiently to work at what the French call *faire l'antichambre*. Half an hour elapsed, and I considered this justified me in walking about the dingy, dark room, which at the Foreign Office answers for the purgatory that all expectants, sinners or not, are required to pass more or less time in.

An hour elapsed, but no summons thence. I heard bells ring and messengers moving about the corridors, but the door of my solitary den gave no signs of vitality. Having finished my promenade, I began, by way of distraction, to read over the nearly illegible titles of sundry musty volumes that reposed in undisturbed decay in a respectable old bookcase, that had been kept locked up from time immemorial.

It was a pretty hard job for a man who never got a medal for patience, but I worked through two hours on the slender materials enumerated. Lord Palmerston was still engaged, for I had heard nothing to the contrary. Lord Palmerston's reputation for wit all the world knows, but it was only on this occasion I slowly perceived that he was just as fond of a practical joke. He had requested me "to wait," and he left it entirely to my option to keep waiting or to go.

I decided, after the dose already digested, on the latter, and ringing for a messenger I bid him say, should Lord Palmerston send down, that I would call again. I could scan in the physigonomy of the veteran I addressed an expression not to be mistaken. It said as plainly as words, "if you have not got enough of it, call again." I might be mistaken, but my case began to look worse than I thought it.

The unpleasant probation the noble Secretary had put me through left me to infer that he sought to shirk me, and this symptom in a Minister of State is fatal. But reverting to my common-sense notions, and forgetting that diplomacy loses all its charms if it does not employ circuitous methods, I sat down to write a polite note to Lord Palmerston, regretting that other engagements prevented me from waiting longer at the Foreign Office on Wednesday, and begging the honor of an interview at his leisure. He must answer that, was my reflection as I dispatched my note, and what can he say but that he will see me, or make an excuse for not doing so? One or the other will suffice.

The same day I received the following:—

Carlton Gardens, 15th April, 1851.

DEAR SIR—

You will find me at the Foreign Office to-morrow at five o'clock.

Yours faithfully,

HY. WIKOFF, Esq. PALMERSTON.

All my doubts and suspicions vanished on the instant. This prompt and business-like reply, granting me the desired interview, and naming even the precise hour my visit was expected, scattered to the wind all my brooding fancies, and I saw how much mental wrong I had done the innocent Under Secretary of State, whilst my remorse was keen, indeed, at all my silly imaginings concerning the illustrious head and front of the Foreign Office. The noble Viscount never could have granted, it struck me immediately, this interview, without prevarication or delay, if he were not prepared to come to a definite understanding, and to go on smoothly with my engagement hereafter.

If all I had suspected had been well founded, why the Minister would have availed himself of any pretext, pressure of business or what not, to avoid meeting me, and this might have been expressed in the civilest manner possible. No man ever had a more complete mastery over language than Lord Palmerston, which he employs with such singular skill as to be able to convey the faintest shade of thought.

As I wended my way to the Foreign Office on the day in question, I turned over in my mind the best mode of treating the subject I was desirous to touch upon. I felt the indiscretion of seeking to ascertain what might exactly be the opinions of the Foreign Minister respecting the United States, or whether he thought that I had shewn more zeal than tact in the course I had taken. I felt easy, however, at knowing, even if I had any such intentions, that Lord Palmerston was too old a diplomatist to let me ransack his mind at my leisure. I was quite certain that I would obtain no more than he was disposed to impart to me, and I resigned myself, therefore, the more readily to the modicum of information, more or less, that he would condescend to accord me.

I was at the place of rendezvous punctually at five o'clock, and sent up my card as usual. I waited half-an-hour, but without the least impatience this time, for as my mind was in no suspense about the result, the moments flew by unobserved. A messenger, finally, came in to say that one of the Diplomatic Corps had just called upon Lord Palmerston, and that I would be obliged to wait his departure.

"Oh, very well," I replied, "I shall abide his Lordship's pleasure."

Time rolled on, and by degrees I exhausted all the topics of my gentle meditations. Bless my soul! it occurred to me, at last, could I have mistaken the date of the note and have come the wrong day? I had it in my pocket and examined it. No; there it was, the 15th of April, and I had made no error.

Nearly two hours had elapsed since my arrival, and I thought I might venture to summon one of the officials of the place, and so rang the bell. The intensely respectable individual who had bowed me out the day before presented himself.

"Has the Foreign Ambassador gone?" I inquired.

"I believe he has," was the cautious reply.

"Is anybody with his Lordship?"

"I really cannot say, Sir," was the prudent answer; for the underlings of the Foreign Office are all obliged to respect the observances of a certain diplomatic training. Any bungling of theirs might involve the Minister or Under Secretaries in various unpleasant predicaments, and their dismissal would follow without mercy. They speak, therefore, by the card; and when my interlocutor went so far as to admit, with a qualification, that the Ambassador was gone, whilst I was not immediately sent for, I was seized with a new qualm of suspicion.

I hesitated a moment, and then thought another question might tend to elucidate matters.

"Perhaps his Lordship has forgotten me," I suggested.

"Oh no, Sir," exclaimed the messenger, "his Lordship always places on his desk the cards of those he intends to see, and only removes them after he has seen them."

Cerberus had his cue, for all this meant that as the noble Lord had not sent for me yet, there was the likely inference that he would not send for me at all.

"I will wait a little longer," I observed to the messenger, who retired with a bow of acquiescence.

Now what in the world am I to understand by all this, was my inward and searching reflection as I sat down again to ruminate. A humiliating sense of my inability to cope with manœuvres like these came over me, and as I looked round the dull apartment almost obscured in the shades of evening, I began to wish myself fairly out of this fox's den.

What *did* the illustrious Viscount mean, I kept on repeating as each effort at a solution failed, in asking me to come and see him at the Foreign Office on such a day and at such an hour? There it is in black and white, and I read his note again.

Carlton Gardens, 15th April, 1851.

DEAR SIR—

You will find me at the Foreign Office to-morrow at five o'clock.

Yours faithfully,

HY. WIKOFF, Esq. PALMERSTON.

I perused it mechanically over and over, when, at last, a new light began to pierce my dull brains. Was it possible? Another practical joke of the noble humourist ten times richer than that of the previous day. How could I be so stupid as not to see it before! The same self-contempt at his blindness which overtook Macbeth when "Birnam wood came to Dunsinane," overcame me for a moment.

Lord Palmerston told me in his note that I would find him at the Foreign Office at five o'clock. Well, it was true. I had found him there at that hour punctually. He had never said anything about *seeing* me, though. That was simply an inference of my own, and I had paid for it by kicking my heels there in idle expectation for more than two mortal hours. It must be so. I see the joke now, and a better never victimised me.

I rang the bell once more, when the same deferential man in black appeared.

"Has his Lordship enquired for me?" I asked pleasantly.

"I believe his Lordship has gone," and my respondent unconsciously, perhaps, rubbed his nose with his finger, an indication, as I took it, most significant, and worth a whole volume of dull comment. The truth stared me in the face. I had been the dupe of an admirable *ruse*, and his Lordship must have enjoyed its complete success not a little. Happily, I was not obliged to conceal my vexation from the attentive janitor who stood by to bow me out, for I felt none; but picking up my hat, I took my departure without loss of dignity.

Some may doubt my composure under such a deliberate slight, and think it mere parade. It is astonishing, though, with what equanimity ordinary people bear the brunt of a great man's joke, and as the bully in the play asserted that he always liked any one the better for having fought with him, so I thought, perhaps, Lord Palmerston would relish me the more for having achieved such a jocular triumph over me. What tended chiefly, there is little doubt, to allay any little irritation that I might otherwise have experienced, was my unfeigned surprise to find that such "artful dodges" were to be found amongst the diplomatic apparatus of the Foreign Office, and that they were so highly esteemed as to be employed, when occasion warranted it, by such an adept of the art as Lord Palmerston, the distinguished head of the department.

Up to this time I had considered that jests like these constituted the stock-in-trade of facetious school-boys, but this new experience of mine not only revealed the unlimited resources of diplomacy, but taught me that the simplest means are frequently the cleverest and the best. In my ignorance I had entertained the most profound reverence, almost dread, for the *arcana* of the Downing-street temple, and when first I entered its solemn portals, I ventured forward with cautious step and 'bated breath, lest it might be thought that "fools rush in where angels fear to tread." But as my apprenticeship waxed on, and I became better acquainted with its *modus operandi* and more familiar with the materials used, I discovered, like the novice who gets at last "behind the scenes," that I had been all my life admiring very grand effects produced by very trashy means.

In the present case, see what had been accomplished by a

common-place trick enough, which had served to give a tumble to my conceit, and to protect Lord Palmerston's secrets from my aggressive curiosity. I found myself so effectually tamed down by this unexpected bye-play of the adroit Minister, that I decided forthwith to give up my experiments on the Foreign Office, and to abide the manifestation of its final pleasure with what grace I could.

I abandoned London soon after, and making a short *detour* to revive my drooping spirits, got back to Paris on the 27th of April, a wiser man somewhat than I left it. On calling next day at the British Embassy I found a letter there in the well-known hand of the noble Secretary of State. It ran thus—

Carlton Gardens, April 18th, 1851.

MY DEAR SIR—

I was very sorry to be prevented from seeing you on Wednesday, but if you should be in town on Saturday, the 26th, you would find me at the Foreign Office at five o'clock, or half-past five, on that day.

Yours faithfully,

HY. WIKOFF, Esq. PALMERSTON.

The immediate effect of this flattering missive was to make me quite oblivious of my late bruises, and I was near as possible running over to London to explain why it happened that I was not there on the 26th, the day suggested. But my first emotions soon subsided, and I began to recall the illusions that had led me astray before. In spite of all my deference, the suspicion was getting strong hold of me that if my Lord Palmerston was not a gay, he was, perchance, an arch deceiver.

I looked closer into his note. Was it, in fact, a *bonâ fide* apology for the fun he had played off on me, or was it only one of those formal acts of civility of the hardened boxer, who, after a "smasher," seeks to encourage his antagonist to try it again, by hoping "he has not hurt him." The apparent regret of the illustrious Viscount was highly soothing, but why did he put off the proposed interview to the 26th—a whole week? Was that only to give me breathing time and courage to venture again?

The really suspicious point of his renewed invitation was, that the same language exactly was employed as before, viz., "You will find me at the Foreign Office." No; a joke's a joke, I observed to myself, but it loses all its piquancy from repetition, and before I consign myself again to solitary confinement in that fusty old cell at the Foreign Office for several hours, I will give his Lordship a sly hint that I half divine his intention. If I am mistaken I shall have a more explicit letter, but in the other case I shall hear no more of him. This was my sage decision, and I wrote to him accordingly.

The result showed I had acted sensibly, for in a few days afterwards Mr. Edwardes told me that Lord Palmerston had written to bid him say that "he did not wish to see me for anything particular, but he thought I wished to see him."

"Go to, go to, for an arrant madcap," I was inclined to say with the grave-digger in Hamlet, when I heard this message. It was actually laughing in my face without the smallest consideration for my wounded pretensions. It was just as much as to say, "Well, my Yankee friend and *employé*, if your vaulting ambition to penetrate into the unfathomable recesses of my ambiguous policy is not yet appeased, come on once more—'you will find me at the Foreign Office at five o'clock.'"

In the state of mystification to which I had fallen, it was some comfort to find a companion no better off. For not long after I returned, Mr. Edwardes said to me one day, rubbing his hands in a pleasant sort of a way:—

"Well, what did Mr. Addington say to you?"

"He said," I replied, not affecting to understand him, "here's a check for £125, and will you sign the receipt?"

He looked at me askance, to make sure I was not diplomatising; and reassured by my innocent look, he went on:—

"Yes, but what did he say, I mean, about your resigning?"

"Not a single word," I answered.

"What, not a word!" he exclaimed, energetically, somewhat in the tone that Othello exclaimed, "What, not Cassio killed!" though I don't intend to compare the cases.

"No," I repeated, "not a word, though I did my best to draw him out."

Mr. Edwardes fell back as thoroughly thunderstruck as ever I saw any one. He remained for a time motionless, like Don Bartolo in the opera, and when, at length, he came to, it seemed as though he would never entirely get over his astonishment. I don't think he was ever the same man again.

It was clearer to me than ever before, however, that the first intention was to cut my head off summarily, as attempted through the intervention of Mr. Edwardes, but for some incomprehensible reason, known only to the Foreign Office, a *reprieve* was decided on, and my official life was prolonged. Be it for better or for worse, I was still determined to go on as I had begun, and to continue, be the consequences what they might, to do all that in me lay to cement the happy concord between England and France, and above all, to bury deep the immovable foundations of a lasting alliance between sire and son, England and her once rebellious colonies, now one of the great Powers of the world.

CHAPTER XIV.

THE DIE CAST.

That the leading statesmen of France should have known nothing of the character or intellect of the Prince Louis Napoleon prior to his advent in France, August, 1848, is natural enough; for, an exile all his life, they had no chance of personal observation, and what else they knew of him was greatly to his disadvantage. His attempts against the dynasty of Louis Philippe in '36 and '40 were regarded as nothing short of the acts of a madman, for neither his means nor motives were understood. Besides, it was the interest of the statesmen of the day to heap opprobrium upon him, whatever their secret opinions, for his success might lead to the creation of new men, and their own retirement from the stage of politics.

As far as my own experience went, and I may venture to say there was scarcely a prominent man of France whose opinion I had not sounded in one way or another of the Prince Louis, I do not hesitate to assert that not one of them had the least notion of his true disposition, character, or mind when he was elected President of the Republic, December, '48. It was a settled conviction amongst them all that he was a weak and frivolous person, and composed of just such pliant materials as adapted him exactly for the political tool they ardently desired to get hold of. Louis Philippe had too much cleverness and duplicity to be handled always as suited the views of his aspiring counsellors.

I have in the course of my narrative given passing glimpses of the ominous difficulties that grew up gradually between the President and the influential politicians of the day. To any one who understood the President's real character, and the mistaken opinions formed of him by these party leaders, it was curious, not to say amusing, to watch the development of events, and to note the various phases of feeling the latter successively underwent. When the results of their *management* of the President turned out the very opposite to that intended, whilst his conduct was so different to that expected, they were, at first, astonished, then perplexed, next distrustful, and, at last, furiously hostile.

At the beginning you heard them exclaiming, "*mais c'est étonnant*" (it is astonishing).

Later it was, "*ma foi, je n'y comprends rien* (by my faith, I don't understand it).

Afterwards they began whispering, "*prenez y garde ; méfiez vous*" (take care ; be on your guard).

Finally, they broke out with, "*il faut en finir, c'est à rendre fou*" (it is time to finish—it is enough to drive one mad).

It is natural, I repeat, that French politicians should have misconceived the Prince Louis at the beginning; and I admit that it was no easy matter to read him quickly and correctly afterwards, for his natural reserve was deepened tenfold by the extreme caution his difficult position exacted; but what I do consider very strange is, that, up to the last moment, the keenest-sighted men of the political world should still be wandering about as completely in the dark as to the man they really had to do with, as though they were obstinately playing with him a game of "blind man's buff."

Whether it was that the Prince Louis was a combination such as they had never met before—and there is something in this, for the Prince is neither wholly French, German, Italian, English, or American, but, having lived in all these countries, he has contracted, likely, a little identity with each—or whether, having yielded prematurely to a rooted conviction, they were too proud to confess it even to themselves, I know not; but the fact is positive, that even so late as May, 1851, the idea was still as prevalent as ever amongst them, that the Prince Louis Napoleon was a very ordinary person, without force or capacity for the *rôle* he was enacting.

That it may not be supposed I am indulging in idle speculation, I will mention an expression of M. Dupin's, President of the Assembly, which struck me so forcibly that I have never forgotten it. But first a word or two of this distinguished person.

M. Dupin was a lawyer by profession, and rose steadily to its highest functions. Embarking in political life, he obtained similar elevation there. Eschewing the extreme opinions of all parties, he attached himself to that body of respectable men, who, under Louis Philippe, were designated the *juste milieu* party, which appellation explained their moderate views, and consequent influence in the State. M. Dupin for many years presided over the Chamber of Deputies, and became, at last, in May, '49, President of the Legislative Assembly. It is needless almost to say, that to occupy such positions as M. Dupin retained for years, and to reach to that elevation in the State which was universally conceded to him, he must possess abilities of the very first order.

It is not for this only I select him for a passing remark, but rather that with the intellect he possesses in common with so many of his gifted countrymen, he joins a description of character that is, certainly, rare in France. M. Dupin, in law, politics, and daily life, is one of those serious, practical, and business-like men, that are common enough in England and the United States, but in the land, even, of Henri IV. are *rari nantes in gurgite vasto.* He is almost entirely free of that frivolity, that gaiety of disposition, that for centuries has been a large ingredient in French character, and which, though modified with change of times, is still a prominent trait, even amongst the highest class of men, where it displays itself, if not in manner and speech, at least in levity of conduct or laxity of opinion.

M. Dupin may, in short, be regarded as one of that new school of statesmen that are the especial product of our times, and whose genius is kept in curb by public opinion and popular responsibility. He is one of the discerning few in France who see that the people are too intelligent, and too resolute, to be governed for the mere profit of party, and according to the whims of politicians. For this reason he is admirably adapted, better than any other man I know of, to sustain and administer in France that Parliamentary Government which is the English panacea for the diseased body-politic of every nation.

If such a man as M. Dupin, by the single force of his talents, character, and career, cannot secure the longevity of Parliamentary institutions, it may be logically inferred that the soil of France is not yet adapted to this exotic *d'outre mer.* M. Dupin was President of the Chamber of Deputies, as I have said, under Louis Philippe, and was, besides, an intimate friend and counsellor of the King; yet he failed signally in making the Parliament understand either the exigencies of the epoch or the spirit of the nation. Again, when President of the Legislative Assembly, where it was of vital consequence he should reconcile the Parliamentary party to the jarring and hostile elements around, he forgot his *rôle* so far as to become a partisan, and sacrificed his important functions for the sake of a *bon mốt*.

If M. Dupin could have restrained his sarcastic wit, better order would have prevailed in the Assembly; and if such a man was carried away at such a crisis, it proves that party spirit is yet too strong in France, perhaps, for a balanced Constitution to flourish; and how much more, then, for the plaything called Parliamentary Government?

I have known M. Dupin for several years, so far as a humble individual like myself can know so lofty a person, and have occasionally sought an interview. I was curious, indeed, to ascertain what might be the real opinion of such a man concerning the immediate future of his country, as well as of those who might control her destinies.

I called on him one morning in May, '51, at the splendid residence assigned to their President by the Assembly, and was favoured with a short conversation, though quite a crowd of expectants were waiting in his ante-chamber to see him.

With all his prudence it was impossible for him to disguise the utter vacancy of his mind as to the momentous contingencies of the future; but one important fact leaked out, which did honor to his patriotism, and harmonised with the elevation of his character. Though identified in some measure with the Monarchical party, more from love of order than sympathy with their projects, he displayed entire readiness to lend himself to any political arrangement that offered the best chance of stability.

As the Assembly had declared itself against the re-election of the Prince Louis Napoleon to the Presidency, he considered it useless to take that into consideration; but it was evident that he was quite ready to enter into a compromise with the moderate Republican party, as constituting the best basis for a permanent organisation. General Cavaignac was the admitted head of this party, and I asked him, rather abruptly, what he thought of him.

"*Le General Cavaignac est un homme très digne sous tous les rapports*" (General Cavaignac is a very worthy man in all respects), was his reply, uttered with strong emphasis.

Yet, M. Dupin remembered his failure in '48, when competing with the Prince Louis for the popular favor, and he was fully aware that neither the General nor his party had gained anything since.

The conversation then turned upon the Prince President, of whom M. Dupin spoke in measured terms of respect. He avowed his conduct had been judicious, though I am sure he thought this had proceeded more from irresolution than judgment. He believed the Prince still retained his hold upon the masses, and that this made all the difficulty of the situation.

"Do you think he will retire," I ventured to ask, "at the end of his term?"

M. Dupin hesitated a moment. "*Il aspire au pourpre*" (He aspires to the purple), he said slowly and with much gravity.

"His chances are not bad, I think," was my prompt remark.

"*Non, mais*—" returned the President of the Assembly, and he stopped short.

"*Mais*—" I repeated in a tone of undisguised interest—

"*Mais il n'est pas assez fort pour ce rôle la* (but he is not strong enough to play that part).

M. Dupin certainly spoke from no prejudice against the Prince, or as though averse to his making the effort if he thought fit, but simply from his profound conviction that the Prince had not the requisite force of character or mental capacity to govern France.

It is worth while to give this anecdote, which I trust will not be offensive to the ex-President Dupin, as illustrating the opinion entertained of the Prince Louis by the leading men of France, even so late as the spring of '51.

A grand event had already occurred, which I must notice with some particularity, for it was, in fact, the cast of the die which shaped anew the history of France. By the Republican Constitution of '48, it was settled that the President of the Republic was not re-eligible. This may have been partly meant to gratify, in turn, the ambition of public men, but still more to prevent any popular chief from consolidating his power. It displayed, however, a doubt of the popular intelligence, which came with a bad grace from the Republican party. It proved they had no faith in their own doctrines. Still worse, it was an unjustifiable invasion of the popular will, for had not the nation, invested with unlimited suffrage, the right to choose their own Government?

This was an egregious mistake, which, added to its other defects, rendered the permanence of the Constitution more than doubtful. The popularity of the Prince Louis was so universal that his re-election might be regarded as the national sentiment; and under these circumstances, it was clearly the duty of the Assembly to modify the Constitution and strike out the prohibiting clause in question. As faithful representatives, they were required to respect the popular wish, which manifested itself in every form of enthusiastic demonstration; and as patriots, they were bound to remove with cheerful alacrity so threatening a cause of disorder as grew out of the retention of this presumptuous interference with the will of the nation.

It was remembered that the Constitution had never been submitted to popular approval, and this made the maintenance of any of its provisions, that came into direct collision with the popular desire, doubly unwise, as it was clearly dangerous. This was, indeed, a momentous question. Upon its decision depended boundless contingencies, inconceivable results. If the Assembly were solely anxious for the welfare of France, their course was manifest. They should unanimously withdraw every obstacle to the free expression of the national impulse. Whatever their doubts or dislike of the President of the Republic might be, they had no right to dictate to the nation, or to thwart its purpose.

How blind must they be not to see that any such attempt must recoil upon their own heads, and make the President only the legitimate agent of the national will in putting a violent end to their abused mandate. As patriots, as men of sense, and as sagacious politicians, they had only one alternative, viz., to repeal the Constitutional clause against re-eligibility.

What was their conduct at this grave crisis, involving their own destiny and the national weal?

What was the conduct of the Convention which in '87 framed the present Constitution of the United States? Every clause, every line of it was shaped in accordance with the popular mind, and it was, afterwards, duly submitted to the popular vote for approval or rejection. Just imagine the fate of the signers of this instrument if they had inserted a prohibition against the re-eligibility of the President, lest Washington or Jefferson might be the country's choice. It is easy to conceive the fate of this noble charter, if it had been disfigured by such a clause, from such a motive—it would have been indignantly trampled under foot.

Again, imagine what would have been the conduct of the English Oligarchy any time within these 25 years past upon any question which vitally touched the feelings or interests of the nation. Did they resist the Reform Bill in '32, or maintain the Corn Laws in '45? No, they were too wise to peril their own existence, or to throw the country into violent disorder.

Let us see, now, what was the behaviour of the French Legislative Assembly in 1851. Every man of them knew that the country was in a most critical condition—that the wildest doctrines pervaded portions of the lower classes—that the worst passions of the worst men were aroused—that secret societies stood ready at every dark corner, waiting the signal of anarchy to spring forward and apply the torch and use the poignard, till France became a spectacle of horror to Europe. They also knew that if the Prince Louis Napoleon was prevented becoming a candidate for re-election, no other one remained upon whom the national choice was likely to rally. Did they, with the knowledge of this notorious fact, and in the presence of these dangers, forget party differences, close their ranks, and, deliberating together as patriotic Frenchmen, decide to expunge the prohibitory clause, and thus extinguish all cause for alarm, and all pretext for usurpation?

Behold. The proposition came before the Assembly. The Republicans opposed the amendment in a body. They braved all consequences, as they thought their party must gain by confusion. It rested with the Monarchists to decide the question, as they had the majority. *They deliberately voted to maintain the clause against re-eligibility*, and thus arrogantly set at defiance the known wishes and the dearest interests of the nation.

It was perfectly known to all those who mixed in political circles at the time, that their object was to get rid of the Prince Louis Napoleon; and to gratify their personal hostility, they went to the length of risking some terrible catastrophe. They had another object, besides, which was to do away with the Republic, and they felt quite confident that their vote against amending the Constitution, which would only ensure its longer duration, must precipitate some revolutionary demonstration, which they meant to seize upon for restoring the Monarchy.

Whatever may be thought of the want of nationality, or the utter deficiency of correct feeling of the Monarchists of '51, still something might be conceded to their desperate courage if they had based their calculations upon anything like a reasonable basis. But in doing away with the Prince Louis, and in overthrowing the Republic, what chance, the most remote, existed for setting up the Monarchy in their place? The feeling of the country ran strong against both branches of the Bourbon family, and any attempt to restore a Legitimist or Orleanist Prince would be met by the most implacable resistance.

If the nation, however, had entertained no objection to the restoration of the Bourbon Monarchy, was there any possibility of the adherents of the opposing branches ever agreeing which of the two should reign? Would M. Thiers and Count Môlé, on behalf of the Orleans Dynasty, have yielded to M. Berryer and Count Montalembert, representing the claims of Henri V? Unless they were prepared to revive the Spartan Constitution of Lycurgus, which divided the Executive Power between two kings—an absurdity—it was certain that the Monarchists would get to loggerheads amongst themselves, which would, infallibly, throw France into the hands of the Socialists and Communists, who were so utterly incapable of organising a Government of any kind, that ruin and massacre would overspread the land.

Every thinking man, nay, every dispassionate person in France, expressed these opinions daily in the summer of '51. The Monarchists could not, and did not, gainsay them. *Alea jacta est* was their only response; and they began their preparations for carrying out the first part of their programme, the expulsion of Prince Louis from power. Beyond that they neither saw nor calculated. Insurrection was probable, Socialism was imminent, and Anarchy might hold the country in her frightful embrace for years to come, "*Mais, enfin, le jeu est à nous*" (but, finally, the game is ours), was their declared belief; for France, exhausted and bleeding at every pore, must cry out for the Monarchy, which will, then, take new and permanent root.

This was the reasoning of these infatuated, infuriated men in '51. Are such men, so deficient in judgment and common humanity, to say nothing of patriotism, fit to be entrusted with the well-being of Hottentots? Are men, who would sacrifice to private pique or party passions their own safety and a nation's welfare, likely to inaugurate with success the Parliamentary Government of England, or the Constitutional balance of the United States? Such were, doubtless, the reflections of the nation, astounded at so bold and flagitious an act as the refusal to revise the Constitution. Was it likely that a people so sagacious, experienced, and high-spirited as the French would tamely suffer their lives and property; their national character and dignity, thus to be thrown into the boiling cauldron of Revolution, whenever it might suit the whims, or gratify the *mauvaise humeur* of certain politicians?

For my part, I made up my mind at the time that these gentlemen, however brilliant their literary or declamatory powers, totally underrated the intelligence of the great nation they aspired to control, and lamentably misconceived the age they were living in. It is true, they dug the pit which swallowed up Charles the Tenth and his Government of Priests. Not less true, thev prepared the downfall of Louis Philippe and his cohort of Placemen and Jobbers. In this, however, they were simply the instruments of the popular will, whilst they believed that they were only carrying out their personal projects.

It is high time for the politicians of France to learn what the politicians of England and the United States already know: that France, no more than England or the United States, can be governed against its will or interests by any man, or set of men, whatever their skill at intrigue, their moral hardihood, or their arrogant conceit.

As far, then, as it depended on the politicians of the Assembly, Republican and Monarchical, unhappy France was launched once more upon a shoreless sea. The vessel of State, betrayed by her own Officers, was drifting helplessly towards perdition. If her crew did not bestir themselves in time, their fate was sealed.

What thought or said the President of the Republic at this last desperate move of the coalition of parties against him? He was narrowly watched by his antagonists, who eagerly longed for a word, and inwardly prayed for some act of his, that might give them some advantage over him.

The nation, too, turned its earnest gaze upon him as though seeking to investigate if he had the requisite skill and resolution to undertake its defence against the perils which environed it. But he spoke not, nor yet gave sign. His mien was calm, his pursuits uninterrupted, and his resignation to the schemes of his enemies apparently supreme. His purpose, if he had any, remained inscrutable.

The Assembly, perplexed, seemed to repent its temerity. The nation, alarmed, regarded in silent horror the vortex it was approaching. The President, whatever his outward composure, must have pondered anxiously over the part he had to play. Should he abandon the helm, and leave the bark, freighted with such precious interests, to be dashed to pieces, or, Curtius like, should he leap into the gulf, and seek to save the nation if he lost himself? He must have paused in the presence of such vast considerations. Selfish ambition could not alone have nerved him against such tremendous risks as beset his path. It was one of those solemn moments when nothing less than a sense of duty and a conviction of right will inspire a man or a nation to brave all odds, and struggle for the triumph of a righteous cause.

It would have been an act of sheer insanity for him to think of entering the lists against the politicians of France, arrayed in solid phalanx, if he had not known the country was ready to sustain him in its own behalf. Could he doubt it? Had not petitions from every quarter and from all classes poured for months into the Assembly, demanding his eligibility? Had not the sympathies of the nation displayed themselves in enthusiastic shouts in whatever section of France he appeared? What did this mean other than that public opinion approved of his course, and thereby condemned that of the Assembly? It is impossible to misrepresent the situation, for these facts are notorious.

I challenge contradiction when I assert that, in 1851, the Prince Louis Napoleon was endorsed by the opinion of the country; and to the same extent, therefore, were his opponents in the Assembly branded with national reprobation. If, then, he believed himself called upon to champion the cause of France, and felt his courage equal to the grandeur of the emergency, what forbad the act? His oath to the Constitution! What a mockery! The Constitution no longer existed. It had been insulted, violated, and defied in the street and the Assembly by its own authors, till it had become a by-word of scorn. It had been broken through and ridden down by the Monarchical majority, in utter contempt, whenever it suited their purpose or relieved their spleen.

What was the Constitution of '48 other than the ill-contrived pact of the pseudo-Republican party, by which they hoped to secure power in their own hands, and which, fearful of its rejection, they had never ventured to submit to the vote of the country. It wanted the national stamp, and was therefore illegal, according to every Republican theory. Some of its more prominent authors, Louis Blanc and Ledru Rollin, had, by an appeal to arms, endeavoured in '48 and '49 to destroy it, but it was sustained by the necessities of the country till some better adjusted organization should supersede it. Indeed, it mattered little to the country what form of government existed, whether Republican or Monarchical, so long as legislation was in harmony with their interests, and the laws were faithfully administered.

But things had come to such a pass that the Legislature, who alone had the power, treasonably refused to amend the organic law when it was proved that it stood directly in the path of the wishes and interests of the nation. To talk at such a crisis of the oath of the President to a party compact, violated, first, by its own sponsors, and next, abused by those who temporarily sustained it from selfish motives, and which was always wanting in legality, is simply to set logic and reason at defiance.

These were the views entertained at the time by all impartial and dispassionate people, who had no other interest than to see the country saved from the horrors of anarchy which so plainly awaited it. As time wore on, the politicians of all parties began to make preparations for the stormy future now approaching. The Republicans were sore perplexed to find a candidate to represent them at the next Presidential election. So little confidence had they that any one of their known leaders was likely to attract the popular suffrage, that they made up their minds to adopt *un homme du peuple,* some common labourer or workman. They were busy the autumn of '51, seeking to find such an one as would suit their purpose. Could any fact more clearly denote to what a point the Republican party in France had fallen, when they were compelled to resort to such a shift in the hope to save themselves from utter extinction?

As for the Monarchists, they found themselves in quite as serious a dilemma. If they brought forward a candidate for the next Presidency, it would be a formal recognition on their part of the Republican Constitution, a thing detested, and yet it would hardly do to let the period of the election come without making an effort to secure it. They, too, were equally puzzled for a candidate the nation would be disposed to accept.

The third son of Louis Philippe, the Prince de Joinville, was talked of, but his only claim to popularity was founded on the fact of his having brought home from St. Helena the ashes of Napoleon. Could anything prove, stronger than this, the magical power of the name of Bonaparte? and what chance did the proposed candidate of the Monarchical party stand in opposition to the incontestable hold on popular affection of the nephew and heir of the idolized Emperor? But he needed not the mighty spell of his name, for the President had only to come forward for re-election as the rejected candidate of the Assembly, and this alone, if he had no other title, would have given him a majority of millions.

Meanwhile, the party of disorder, with secret societies scattered all over the country, was lying in ambush, joyously panting for the moment of confusion to rise and pillage the land. Let any disinterested mind, therefore, contemplate the situation of France in November, '51, and say what was the duty of any patriot, or friend of humanity, who had adequate means to accomplish his object. The Monarchical and Republican parties had fallen so low in national esteem that any candidate who came forward in their behalf was sure of a condign defeat, and yet, from motives equally disgraceful to them as politicians and as men, they dared to oppose the choice of the nation by refusing to amend an objectionable law.

I appeal to the patriots and philanthropists of every nation. I invoke the memories of Washington, Jefferson, and Adams, and reverentially demand whether the delegates of a people who, false to duty and deaf to conscience, are ready to sacrifice the order and well-being of a whole community, and, perhaps, the peace of the world, to the sordid interests of party and the aggrandisement of individuals, have not abjured their allegiance and forfeited their mandate? In such a case do not all representative rights revert to the power from whence they came, and is the nation not justified when, in its omnipotence, it pronounces sentence upon such guilty dereliction, "Depart, thou unfaithful servants?"

How often in the history of the world have nations perished, and tyranny been perpetuated, by the same criminal indifference to the public good, and the same reckless devotion to personal interests as was displayed by the leaders of the French Legislative Assembly of 1851? Happily, the intelligence of such communities as those of the United States and England have arrived at that point that no body of men, however high in station, or gifted in intellect, would presume to set the national will at defiance, or to make a holocaust of the national welfare only to carry out their party objects.

And it is consoling to know that such iniquities are coming to an end in France; for the significant lessons of 1789, 1830, and 1848, should teach French politicians that the acute and resolute nation they so insolently seek to mislead will not suffer its dignity, its interests, or its destinies, longer to be tampered with, or betrayed.

The future of France, and the safety of the community, were in the hands of the Prince Louis Napoleon in November, '51, and everything depended on the decision he came to. If he thought it best to abide the close of his Presidential term, May, '52, he was certain to be re-elected by an overwhelming vote against all competitors.

It was already settled, in that case, amongst the party leaders of the Assembly, to ignore his election, and to set up some man of their own. That resource was hopeless, for there was no chance of their agreeing together. This was plainly proved, for, in November, they voted to protect themselves against the President, by organizing an army of defence, but they fell out as to the General who should command it. The Monarchists insisted on General Changarnier, but the Republicans called for General Cavaignac. The same thing would have ensued if the Assembly had attempted to choose a President of the Republic. Each party would have adhered to its own candidate, and the country meanwhile would have fallen into anarchy. If anything was to be done to prevent this frightful result, it must have been done at once.

The nation, standing quite aloof from the handful of politicians whom it had repudiated, called on the Prince Louis Napoleon to anticipate the dread signal of civil war, and to take the Government, momentarily, into his hands. The Army, whose patriotism made them nothing more than the exponents of the popular sentiment, and the instruments of the popular voice—this same Army, which in 1830 refused to fight for Charles X. against the nation, and which, also, in 1848, marched out of Paris at the popular demand—now manifested its sympathies for the man to whom the finger of the nation emphatically pointed. And Louis Napoleon, if he was not appalled at the magnitude of the crisis, if his reason was not confounded, nor his heart smitten with doubt, had no alternative. If his courage was firm, and his patriotism equal to risk of life and loss of name, there was nothing left but to march boldly into the Temple, and dismiss the unworthy band who had defiled it.

CHAPTER XV.

THE DENOUEMENT.

My quarter's salary came round again on the first of July, and I set off once more for London, as anxious as ever to know what were the mystical intentions of the Foreign Office concerning me; but, sobered by my past experience, I found myself less inclined to employ any rash expedient to force a solution which I might, peradventure, obtain by more indirect means. It stood to reason that persons of such vast diplomatic experience as those at the head of the Foreign Office, and in the daily habit of threading their entangled way through all sorts of mazy complications, where all the resources of artifice and duplicity were skilfully put into requisition, were not to be driven into a corner and made to avow their hidden purpose by the onslaught, however unexpected, of a subaltern like myself, albeit energetic and determined on effecting his object. I had discovered that much already, and saw the necessity of altering my tactics.

It would require no little ingenuity, combined with a copious mixture of perseverance and sagacity, I felt aware, to escape from my present position in a manner satisfactory to myself. I preferred quitting it, ten times over, to retaining it under the suspicions attached to me, but deeply conscious that I had exerted myself to the utmost to serve all parties, and equally convinced that my efforts had not been thrown away, I felt it my due to know why and how I had given dissatisfaction. An explanation I considered necessary to prevent my falling a victim to some artful intrigue, or some plausible calumny. I had received the most unequivocal approbation for my successful endeavours to soften the asperities of the French press towards England, and there was nothing left, therefore, to find fault with but the view I had taken of the true policy of the Foreign Office towards the United States. If this were so, and to tell the truth I had got information to justify my thinking so, whose fault was it that any misconception had arisen?

I explained my mind on this point most distinctly to Lord Palmerston at Broadlands, when he seemed entirely to agree with me. Had he thought fit to disguise at that time his real opinions, or had he since then come to new and opposite conclusions? In every case I felt my right was unquestionable to press for some sufficient explanation to account for the strange conduct pursued. Besides, I had abandoned other engagements of great value, which I was ready to prove, to accept the functions that Lord Palmerston had thrust on me, and it was unreasonable to expect that I would be bowed abruptly out of the Foreign Office without inquiry or complaint. I considered myself ill-treated, and I leave my readers to judge if I had not some adequate grounds; but I admit frankly that my temper was not in the least soured.

Having recovered from my first emotions of surprise, perhaps a little mixed with chagrin to see my zeal all wasted, I had gradually worked myself into rather a merry mood at the circuitous method and needless strategems employed to effect an object so easily despatched by simpler means. It was not to be expected, however, that the Foreign Office, the very fountain head of diplomacy, would do things in a straightforward way whilst a possibility existed for a display of its peculiar craft; so that I was not only resigned to all forms of procrastination, but constantly on the *qui vive* for new and instructive exhibitions of diplomatic "magic and mystery."

During the three months elapsed, I had thrown away no occasion where I could render service, but I certainly worked with far less zest under the discouragement I had received. I kept up occasional calls at the Embassy in Paris, and was always cordially received by Mr. Edwardes, though I found him a good deal less confiding in his tone and remarks than of yore. Whether this arose from any hint he may have received from head-quarters, or grew out of the perplexed state of his mind as to my ultimate fate, and the mystery that hung over it, I cannot tell, but he no longer indulged in those confidential moods that used to seize him of old, when, with great frankness and no small discernment, he commented somewhat sarcastically on men and things. Far be it from me to abuse these friendly communings.

I called on Mr. Addington the day after my arrival in London, and was received by that very estimable, but exceedingly formal gentleman, with such unusual demonstrations of courtesy, that I felt satisfied at once that the shaft so long held in poise was now to be launched against my official existence. And sure enough, no sooner were the customary preliminaries of check-giving and receipt-signing over, than Mr. Addington asked me with a pleasant tone to be seated.

"I am instructed," he began, without preface, but with much gravity, "on the part of Lord Palmerston, to say, that your engagement with the Foreign Office will close at the end of the year from the time it began—that is, on the first of October next."

I waited a moment, almost expecting him to add the usual complement to a judicial sentence, "And may the Lord have mercy on you."

Finding that he had done, I inclined my head in acquiescence, and said:—

"If such be his Lordship's pleasure, I must submit to it with all grace; but, inasmuch as I have occasionally received praise for my services, and have never yet had any fault found, would it be considered too bold to ask in what manner I have given dissatisfaction?"

"Indeed, I cannot answer you," returned Mr. Addington, with an air of candour, "for his Lordship has given me no information on the subject. I was merely requested to convey to you notice of the cessation of the engagement."

"Well, I must say, if I can do so without offence," I persisted, "that it is rather a singular proceeding. His Lordship offers me the engagement without solicitation; I accepted it at a sacrifice, which I stated at the time, and now, without any reason alleged, I am summarily dismissed. If his Lordship was at all given to caprice, I should be at no loss to account for it, but I am satisfied there must be some urgent motive for the act."

"Why, the fact is," replied Mr. Addington, who seemed anxious to relieve my perplexity, "Mr. Hume and his allies in Parliament make such determined attacks every year on our Government expenditure, that I should not be surprised if Lord Palmerston thought a little retrenchment was necessary."

The pretext was futile enough, for the Foreign Office thinks little of lavishing a few thousands when it has a purpose in view; and my salary of a few hundreds would never have aroused its susceptibilities, if no other motive than economy was at the bottom.

"If his Lordship really thought," I said to Mr. Addington, with an incredulous smile, "that my salary was beyond my deserts, why rather than part on so frivolous a ground, I would request him to guage it according to his fancy."

"Well, really," returned Mr. Addington, getting uneasy at having been betrayed into a surmise, "I don't know anything about the matter. I was simply instructed to notify you in the manner I have done, and no reason for so doing was added."

"Under these circumstances," I concluded, rising, "it would be inconsiderate to encroach longer on your time, or to put you to the trouble of speculating further as to Lord Palmerston's motives. Perhaps, I may yet be favoured with some statement of them from himself." Mr. Addington seemed inclined to say, "Perhaps you won't," to judge from his countenance, but he refrained from so incautious a phrase, and bowed me out with the same marked civility with which he had received me.

I began to feel not a little piqued at making so many efforts, supported by the stoutest resolution, and yet without the least perceptible progress towards the grand solution I had set my heart upon. Here was I, finally, cut loose from my moorings, and drifting down the tide towards the vortex of nothingness that must swallow me, without so much as being able to clutch hold of a straw to afford me the fleeting satisfaction of knowing which way the wind really blew. By degrees I fell to thinking I had underrated my calling all this time, and that there was, really, something in Diplomacy after all. It remained to be seen, though, if it were of such inflexible material as to resist the battering ram of my legitimate curiosity, and I set to work meditating what step I had better take next.

Fortunately I was on intimate terms with a friend of Lord Palmerston, a very amiable and most sagacious gentleman, the late Mr. Peter Borthwick, M.P. I resolved instanter to lay my case before him, and solicit his intervention. I did so. He listened with his usual urbanity, and remarked at the close that he was quite sure that Lord Palmerston, as a matter of comity, would not hesitate to give me some explanation of his desire to put an end to my engagement, and the more so as I had no wish to prolong it. He was kind enough to say he would see Lord Palmerston on the subject, and let me know the result.

Mr. Borthwick was as good as his word, as all remember who knew him that he invariably was, and two or three days after he did me the favor of a visit. Mr. Borthwick stated that Lord Palmerston greatly regretted he had not had the pleasure of seeing me on my previous visit (whereat I winced a little), but that he could see no objection in the world to conversing with me on the notice he had given me, and that if I would oblige him so much as to call at his house in Carlton Gardens, on Wednesday next, at 12 o'clock punctually, he would have great satisfaction at receiving me. I thanked Mr. Borthwick cordially for his kind offices, and secretly applauded myself for calling his influential aid into requisition. Mr. Borthwick added, that Lord Palmerston was too busy when he met him to talk about the matter in hand; but that he accorded the interview asked in the readiest manner, and he had no doubt that I would be entirely satisfied with my reception.

I congratulated myself on my perseverance, which had, at last, brought its due reward; but at the same time I was so much flattered at the noble Secretary of State's yielding to my wish, that I decided on accepting deferentially whatever *éclaircissement* he should deem fit to make, and so let the matter drop. After all, I cared far less to worry his Lordship into assigning a cause for my exit from the Foreign Office, that, really, had no charms for me, than to receive from him at parting that courtesy which he had extended to me at meeting, and which, certainly, I had in no wise forfeited. My pride rebelled at being sent off like an ill-behaved servant without a character, as it were, when I had made such strenuous and loyal efforts to promote the good of all.

I did not fail, of course, to present myself at his Lordship's house, in Carlton Gardens, at noon on the Wednesday designated by Mr. Borthwick; when, on sending in my name, the servant returned with the concise message that "His Lordship was not at home."

"There must be some mistake," I said to the footman, "for his Lordship was to give me an interview to-day at this hour."

"His Lordship is not at home," was politely repeated by the powdered lackey; whereupon I withdrew, consigned once more to a limbo of endless speculation.

Convinced there must be some *mal entendu* I wrote immediately to his Lordship to say that Mr. Borthwick had informed me that his Lordship had named Wednesday at noon for an interview; but that as business might have interfered, would his Lordship be pleased to let me know when it would suit his convenience to receive me. Lord Palmerston did not condescend to reply to me, so I was left to infer that the extraordinary rebuff I had suffered, the first of the kind it had ever been my fate to encounter, was nothing more or less than another ingenious diplomatic device to clap an extinguisher on my presumptuous expectations. Wonderful and inscrutable are thy ways, O Diplomacy, was my awe-stricken reflection, as, shaking the dust of London from my feet, I dashed off to Switzerland to try the effect of its bracing air on my jaded spirits and shattered nerves, for this last and most unexpected "flooring" had for the nonce quite unmanned me.

The experiments I had previously undergone at the Foreign Office in April, were a species of slow, protracted torment, that after a time became bearable; but a sudden prostration from such a height as his Lordship had so cleverly led me up to, was a blow so stunning as to paralyse me for a time, and my recovery was lingering and precarious. There was no boy's play about Lord Palmerston's diplomatic mode of administering "a punisher," I began to perceive, as I slowly regained my senses; and this is one of the prominent characteristics of this remarkable man. But, *en revanche*, he is sportive, even in his grimmest moments, and nothing is more common for him than to utter a pungent witticism over the fallen body of the victim he has just fearlessly demolished.

I did not throw away my time in Switzerland, as I have elsewhere recorded, but in the course of several interviews at Geneva with Mr. James Fazy, the leading radical of the Cantons, a politician of great influence and superior capacity, I took occasion to enforce those doctrines of pacific progress which I believed to be the true policy of Western Europe.

Mr. Fazy manifested the heartiest disposition to draw closer the alliance of the Cantons with England and France, but naturally displayed great repugnance to the repressive policy of Austria, which only kept the spirit of insurrection alive, wherever its Government extended. I entered into some details respecting the character and policy of Lord Palmerston, whom Mr. Fazy greatly admired, but the devious windings of whose diplomacy the Genevese Radical did not, like many others, always understand.

I explained the position of England as one of great difficulty, requiring a masterly hand to conduct it safely along its course, both at home and abroad. The foreign policy of the noble Lord at a period so critical as the present was, seemingly, inconsistent according to the changing position of things. He was anxious to promote the political transformation of Europe nearer to an identity with English institutions, for this must necessarily develope commercial progress, to the certain advantage of English products; but he was equally obliged, for cogent reasons, to avoid tampering indiscreetly with the domestic affairs of other nations. It was necessary to steer with great skill and delicacy between considerations like these; but I remarked that, in my humble opinion, no English statesman ever lived so admirably qualified as the noble Minister for Foreign Affairs for such a task. Mr. Fazy concurred in my point of view, and I left him with his favourable impression of Lord Palmerston none the weaker for what I had said.

On my return to Paris I went on with my usual avocations, and kept up my rounds in journalistic and other circles; for I considered it only proper, as long as I was in the pay of the Foreign Office, that I should give some *quid pro quo*.

In the beginning of October I paid my last visit, as I thought, to Mr. Addington in Downing-street, and received my last quarter's salary, as I supposed. My visit was short, though pleasant enough. I thought it quite useless to try my hand again on Mr. Addington, for there was hardly a weapon in the whole armoury of wheedling he was not familiar with. I was loth, indeed, to give him up in so unsatisfactory a way; but as my eye made its circuit round him, there was something, it struck me, so impenetrable and granite-like in his manner and remarks that I was fain to fall back on an American simile by comparing myself to a "juvenile musquito pecking at the rock of Gibraltar."

I ventured to say, "I have not been lucky enough to see Lord Palmerston yet."

"I am not surprised," replied Mr. Addington, "he is always so busy."

"And yet," I continued, "he always finds time for everything."

"He is wonderfully active," rejoined Mr. Addington evasively.

Before quitting him I dropped a remark or so upon Kossuth, who had just then arrived in England from his Eastern bondage, whence Lord Palmerston had the credit of delivering him. For the first time Mr. Addington exhibited some warmth of manner, and I was relieved to see he had a sentient spot about him, however invisible to mortal eyes. He talked for a moment with something like vehemence, but it would be in bad taste, of course, to repeat what he said.

It is certain that Kossuth turned out a different kind of importation from what the Foreign Office had expected; and I think people, generally, were surprised at his beginning so hastily his bellicose propaganda. The publication he made at Marseilles of his sympathy with the Revolutionary party, and his antipathy to Louis Napoleon, President of the Republic, was considered, I remember, by his friends, as indiscreet, to say the least.

After Mr. Addington, for once, had spoken his mind, he wound up by saying,

"Well, I am glad he is going to your country."

Not knowing whether he meant this in kindness or the contrary, I hesitated whether to thank him or not.

"Is that because you wish to get rid of him?" I asked.

"No, but I think it will be all the better for himself to get there as soon as he can."

"How so?"

"Why, I don't know if it is an effect of your atmosphere or not, but people seem to come faster to their level there, up or down, as the case may be, than in other places. Most of our European celebrities, I observe, soon evaporate there, and trouble the world no more with their greatness."

I was struck with Mr. Addington's just appreciation, which I have conveyed in meaning, if not exactly in his own words; and I was really glad to see that an Under Secretary of State of the Foreign Office had begun, at last, to turn a little of his attention towards the United States, by no means a common thing of yore. I expressed myself in complimentary language to this effect, and added,

"It is just as you say, Mr. Addington. In the United States we have nothing for great men to do or talk about, and they no sooner get there than they find their occupation gone. We give them a *Charivari* on arriving, declare unlimited sympathy for the lofty intentions we give them credit for, and then turn round to our business, and expect them to attend to theirs."

Mr. Addington smiled knowingly at this confirmation of his views, which led him, perhaps, to think, that in spite of former doubts, the United States were not, peradventure, created utterly in vain; and that Providence, in its bounty, might even have meant to benefit the Monarchies of the Old World by making America answer the purpose of a sort of quarantine, where a lot of pestilential demagogues were rapidly restored by democratic treatment to their long-lost common sense. Mr. Addington said nothing of the kind, and may never have thought it; but I inferred that some such reflections may have wandered through his mind, to judge from the serene expression of his countenance whilst I was speaking.

I bid adieu to this amiable and accomplished functionary with sincere respect, and I should be truly sorry if my unceremonious use of his name gave him the least annoyance; but he must see how impossible it was to omit him in any faithful narration of my temporary connection with the Foreign Office.

In compliance with the intimation I had received in July, and with the payment of my last quarter's salary, my eventful relations with H. B. M. Government ceased; still, I was not at all reconciled to the *modus operandi* employed. I felt myself perfectly justified, under all the circumstances of the case—having been invited by Lord Palmerston to join the Foreign Office—having sacrificed other engagements to do so, and having acquitted myself to the best of my poor abilities, whether usefully or not, whilst there—I say I felt myself fully justified in remonstrating against the *sans façon* manner I had been treated. I was, therefore, emboldened to make another, if not a final effort, to induce Lord Palmerston to throw me, at least, a crumb of civility before entirely losing sight of him.

Besides, I was aware that his Lordship, with all his fondness for a practical joke, was, as far as a great statesman can ever be, a just-minded and good-hearted man enough; and that having had his share of fun out of me, he might be induced to treat me with a little ordinary courtesy, if I could only manage to touch his sense of propriety. I was sensible it was no easy job to arrive at that, for how can a politician, much more a Minister of State, ever suffer himself to be guided by those nice and delicate perceptions that influenee well-bred people, without running the risk of compromising that official exclusiveness, that proud isolation, in which it is convenient, if not agreeable, for them to live.

A great man in office must keep himself at a proper altitude above the common herd, else he would lose his necessary *prestige*, besides undergoing endless invasions from "outside barbarians;" and there is no way for him to accomplish all this so effectually as blunting his mind, and extinguishing his sensibilities to the usual standards of social commerce. He is obliged to protect himself by a *chevaux de frieze* of diplomacy, and to resort to every artifice of defence, if he be not driven, at last, to the dire extremity of prostrating his pursuer by officially banging the door in his face. I had regularly gone through all these stages of diplomatic repulsion, as I have honestly related, and it is a miracle that I did not sink under it; but the justice of my cause inspired me, and I still clung to the hope that if ever I could contrive to get behind the official ramparts which concealed the diplomatist, I should have little or no difficulty in convincing the gentleman that I had a case to be heard, if not a demand to be accorded.

I passed nearly the whole month of October in London, meditating and devising some plan to effect a breach in the walls of Downing Street, and having weighed and examined every possible mode of attack, I sat down, at last, with my ideas fully matured, and indited another urgent appeal to the illustrious Viscount. I took care not to throw away a single chance of success, and though I was less solicitous about pecuniary reparation than for the explanation I had most at heart, still, I did not omit to remind his Lordship, that, in my first letter after leaving Broadlands, accepting his offer, I spoke distinctly of other advantages I should renounce, and which I held myself ready to prove.

Sometimes, considerations that partake of a legal claim are successful with practical men, when mere moral or sentimental views are regarded as abstract and of no weight. So I thought, at least, when with the utmost delicacy I recalled this fact to his Lordship's recollection, trusting that such a proof of my alacrity to espouse his views, entitled me, if not to substantial remuneration, at all events, to some *amende honorable*.

I forwarded my statement to the noble Lord, confiding less in the force of my reasoning than in the moderation of my tone, which he could hardly think other than creditable to me, after the eccentric courses that had been adopted towards me. Nearly a month elapsed, and I began to believe my case utterly desperate, when a reply, in the familiar hand of Mr. Addington, was transmitted to me. There was no mistaking, for a moment, the authorship of this document. There was an ingenuity and adroitness in its statements and style, so characteristic of the noble Minister for Foreign Affairs, that I perceived, at once, Mr. Addington had done nothing more than copy out the original sketch.

His Lordship, first, took care to state, in perspicuous language, the motive of my engagement; then, pleasantly sought to diminish its importance, if any, by hinting that my communications were but few with "this office," leaving out, as superfluous, any mention of my daily visits to the Embassy at Paris for months. The gentle intimation conveyed in the simple words, that "no further benefit was likely to result from my services," contain a whole volume of meaning. I saw it clearly enough, that the "pacific policy" I had sought to enforce, in my American correspondence, was not, as I had other reasons for knowing, the "pacific policy" his Lordship at all meant. His peace policy towards the United States, I discovered, was of that rather doubtful description, as never to preclude a chance of war, if it did not really seek to provoke it.

My humble notions of a "pacific policy" between England and the United States went much further. Seeing every reason, under heaven, for these two countries to remain united, I endeavoured to inaugurate a policy that would make war well nigh an impossibility. I was aware, to be sure, that this would not be acceptable to politicians or diplomatists, who thrive, chiefly, on the discord of nations; but I thought that Lord Palmerston measured the wisdom of not compromising such vast interests for the sake of thee excitement afforded, or for displaying his skill in keeping alive old points of dispute, whilst playfully seeking to create new ones.

It was plain enough, my ideas of founding a "pacific policy" were not congenial to his Lordship, and, consequently, he reminds me that engagements like mine, "are, in their very nature, temporary and dependent on circumstances."

I found no fault with the doctrine, and it was quite enough for his Lordship to break off with me, when he once began to doubt the utility of my services. *Quandiu bene se gesserint* was, I admit, the real tenure of such an engagement as mine.

I never dreamt of fastening myself upon his Lordship at th Foreign Office, else I would have taken the usual mode of seeking to ascertain the notions entertained at head quarters and of carrying them out, *fas aut nefas*. It would have been presumption, indeed, in a subordinate to do otherwise; but on the subject of a "pacific policy" with the United States, Lord Palmerston left me the widest margin, confiding, as I thought, in my superior knowledge of my own country.

His Lordship's radical error was in not defining, distinctly, in his first conversation with me at Broadlands, what were his views of a "liberal and pacific policy" with the United States. His diplomatic habit of caution on that occasion involved him in a somewhat serious entanglement; for I would have declined the honor extended to me, if I had not thought his Lordship meant, even at the expense of losing his best *cheval de bataille*, to give up the old system of bickering with the United States, and establish a cordial and permanent alliance. This is the way I understood him as regarded France, and was praised for my discernment. The rule, evidently, did not work both ways.

His Lordship, however, closed his letter by a very handsome act, which was quite as characteristic as the rest. The noble Viscount, in his moments of levity, may be jocose; or in the hurry of business, or in the ardor of debate, may be a little imperious, or a deal too pungent, but never, under any circumstances, is he wanting in generosity or capable of petty calculations. He thought fit, as a matter of tact, not to recollect the advantages I had spoken of having renounced at the beginning, and it was with his usual love of a jest that he expressed his confidence that he had not "bound himself to make good such renunciation." Of course not. Whoever heard of Lord Palmerston binding himself in advance to do anything he might not like to do when the time came?

I must have commented enough on the letter in question to have piqued my reader's curiosity; and shall, therefore, give it without further preface.

Foreign Office, November 24, 1851

SIR—

In reply to the letter which you addressed to Viscount Palmerston on the 31st of October, I am directed to observe to you that the sole object of the arrangement which his Lordship made with you, in the autumn of last year, was to make known clearly, through the medium of the French and the United States press, the liberal, and especially the pacific character, of the policy of Her Majesty's Government.

How far that object has been attained Lord Palmerston is unable to judge, as your communications with this office, since the commencement of your engagement, have been but few. His Lordship is willing, however, to believe that your services may have contributed to forward the desired end.

But you must be well aware that engagements of this kind are, in their very nature, temporary and dependent on circumstances, and Lord Palmerston having seen reason to be satisfied that no further benefit was likely to result from your exertions, and perceiving, also, that economy required that services of doubtful utility should no longer be continued at a considerable charge, caused an announcement to be made to you, at least as long ago as the month of July last, that the arrangement made with you would terminate with the termination of this year.

Lord Palmerston has no recollection whatever of your having declared to him, at any time, that, in order to devote your attention to the object he had in view, you would be obliged to renounce other advantages present or prospective; but he is confident that he in no way bound himself to make good such renunciation.

I am, therefore, directed to state to you that Lord Palmerston considers that the engagement taken with you would properly cease, as already announced to you, with the close of this year; but in order that you may have a full twelve months notice of its cessation, he will continue until the end of June next the rate of payment which you have already received, and on the 30th of June that allowance will accordingly cease altogether.

I am, Sir, your obedient
and humble servant,
H. U. ADDINGTON.

HENRY WIKOFF, Esq.

The only thing that perplexed me in this letter was the evident intention of its noble author to prolong my connection with the Foreign Office, by continuing my quarterly payments of salary instead of giving, as originally proposed through Mr. Edwardes, "a sum of money down." What could be the motive of this new whim? Did Lord Palmerston begin in his heart to regret stripping me of my functions from a premature apprehension of my inutility, or was it an ingenious method to ensure my good behaviour *ad interim?*

The latter was not unlikely, for I had reason to know that the noble Secretary of State entertained some fear that I might allow my recent relations with the Foreign Office to transpire, which would be an annoyance to him, if nothing more. This was an idle dread, however; for though I had no reason to conceal my connection with the Foreign Office, I was by no means so proud of it as to desire to make it public—so, if the continuance of my salary for nine months longer was, in fact, "hush money," it was entirely thrown away. If I had been ambitious of notoriety, or even of a vindictive temper, certes, I had grounds enough for public complaint in the "deep damnation" of my "taking off," and his Lordship is not aware to this hour how far it might be in my power to gratify the morbid appetite of gossip-mongers; for, I repeat, that my connection with the Foreign Office and its hangers-on was long enough to initiate me into many of its mysteries, carefully concealed from the *oi polloi.*

Such unscrupulousness as this, however, would be justified by no extent of provocation, and I give the proof in the harmless recital I have made of my late relations with the Foreign Office, after the singular persecution I have since undergone at the hands of its accredited agents, and which I am about to lay before my readers.

Finally, I had abundant reason to congratulate myself on the success that crowned my steady efforts to obtain from Lord Palmerston, if not a distinct avowal of his secret motives, at all events such an honorable discharge from his employment as satisfied all my requirements. It was my determination to accomplish this from the outset, and for a novice I had no reason to blush for the result of my first "set to" with the Foreign Office, which is not in the habit of suffering defeat, if any means, however harsh, can avert it. I was so entirely content with the victory I had gained that I should have gone my way quietly, chanting *palmam qui meruit ferat*, and neither the noble Viscount or the world at large would ever likely have heard of me again.

A different fate, however, was reserved for me. An event, quite as unlooked for as my late diplomatic functions, befell me, affording the Foreign Office an occasion to pay me off for acts of presumptuous inquisitiveness, not easily forgotten, that was too tempting to resist; and I had reason to expiate at my leisure the folly of ever having risked its dread displeasure, and to bewail the cruel destiny that ever led me to offer my services to promote the "liberal, especially the pacific policy of Her Britannic Majesty's Government" in France and the United States. I reserve, for another chapter, the strange history to which I am alluding.

CHAPTER XVI.

A PRETEXT.

A volume entitled "My Courtship and its Consequences," which appeared in London in the spring of 1855, imparted to some portion of the reading public the details of a somewhat romantic story. The author, it was stated, had made the acquaintance, in May, 1835, of a lady, then a resident of Russell Square, London. The most cordial relations existed between them for a period of five years, when the parties lost sight of each other for an interval that extended up to April, 1851. Accident again brought them together, and their former intimacy was renewed. This time, however, the gentleman paid his addresses in due form, and, after sundry eccentricities of conduct on both sides, was received as a suitor, and, finally, rewarded by his *inamorata* with the solemn pledge of her hand, amid the usual tokens of a deep affection. The "course of true love never did run smooth;" and it so turned out upon this occasion, for the lady in question, upon some idle plea, suddenly resolved to postpone the marriage already agreed upon, and almost upon the day of her intended nuptials she left London for a winter's sojourn in Italy.

She soon, however, repented of her cruelty, and gave way to manfest signs of remorse, which were all duly conveyed to the victim of "hope deferred" by a sympathetic Figaro in the lady's train, and the joyful swain flew on the wings of love to overtake his fair tormentor, ready, in the overflowing of his fondness, to forget the past and to guarantee the future by their immediate union. Alas! the lady was still fitful, and his presence only fanned the flame of rebellion which broke out anew. The desperate lover sought to remonstrate, but the capricious dame refused him an interview, and in his extremity he resorted to the well-known expedient of a stratagem, and thus succeeded in beholding once more the cherished features of his Dulcinea.

By dint of protestation, entreaty, and *ruse*, the persevering Quixotte again carried his point, and the vanquished fair gave this time an earnest proof of her confiding fondness in according, by an unequivocal and decisive act, her prompt and generous forgiveness for his thoughtless but really flattering devotion.* "All's well that ends well," sang the exhilarated lover; but his cup of probation was not yet full. Sad to relate! his fickle betrothed again changed her mind, and by a series of acts, totally unpremeditated, she succeeded, finally, in lodging the victim of her inconstancy in the cheerless cell of an Italian prison, on the harsh accusation of "abduction."

She repented still more quickly than before, and all might yet have gone as merry "as a marriage bell" if a horrible dragon had not interposed, barbarously exacting that Juliet should still wear her spinster's costume, whilst poor Romeo should be consigned to the lingering horrors of fifteen months' imprisonment in a Genoese jail. "Can such things be and not excite our special wonder?" Though stranger than fiction, the story is true, for the heroine was Miss Jane C. Gamble, of Portland Place; the hero, the luckless individual now reciting his misfortunes; and the dragon,

---

* Vide page 196 of "My Courtship and its Consequences."

not an infuriated father, not a relentless guardian, but the identical Foreign Office that, since September, 1851, had played so prominent a part in the author's adventures.

Whoever will take the trouble to refer to the already quoted volume, "My Courtship and its Consequences,"* will see that I have told "a round, unvarnished tale;" and before I close this chapter I hope to adduce sufficient proof to show that I have all along dealt in sober fact, and not in the subtle weavings of an excited imagination.

Miss Gamble's motive in lodging a complaint against her lover's romantic folly, it is difficult to explain; but having determined on doing so, she sought the aid of the British Consul at Genoa. Though a native of the United States, she was domiciled in England, and this led her, no doubt, to give the preference to the latter rather than to her legitimate representative, the United States' Consul at that place. It so happened, to the misfortune of all parties, that Her Britannic Majesty's agent at Genoa, rejoicing in the euphonious appellation of Timothy Brown, was an eccentric compound of odd ingredients, in which, unluckily, humanity and common sense had no share whatever. No sooner had Miss Gamble laid her case before him than, without stopping a moment to verify it, he obtained a consular order of arrest, and, according to the custom of the country, threw me headlong into a filthy prison.

The intervention of a Bow Street Magistrate would have stayed uch a despotic use of consular authority; and I marvel that Sardinia, with her love of progress, has not transplanted so wholesome a protection to the liberty of the subject. The impetuous spring of

* Published in London in 1855.

the consular tiger on her quondam lamb naturally shocked Miss Gamble, and her gentle thought was now to rescue her late pet from his sorry plight. She appealed, at first, to the pity of the omnipotent Brown, but her delicate fingers failed to find the chord; whereon, rising from supplication, she cried—

"Beware! your intended victim is an agent of the Foreign Office, and a friend of Lord Palmerston."

This was, indeed, a startling announcement, and the terror-struck Timothy shivered for a moment at his rashness. Reflection intervened.

"What," he exclaimed, "a Yankee in our Foreign Office! Has the millennium come?—and do lions and nondescripts lay down together at last? Has John Bull so far forgot his self-respect? and is he so blind to his safety as to admit this new Trojan horse within his gates? The thing is impossible!"

"It is true," ejaculated Miss Gamble, dauntless in my defence.

"The proof," demanded my grim jailor, unwilling to yield his prize.

"Seek it yourself," was the reply.

I have briefly paraphrased the exciting scenes that rapidly followed my incarceration between Miss Gamble and the implacable Consul. Up to this moment my connection with Lord Palmerston had remained a profound secret to all save my affianced bride; and I had imparted it to her, as in duty bound, with every injunction of caution. It was only in her extremity that she revealed the fact, which I never, certainly, would have condescended to make known to a petty consular agent at Genoa.

An interregnum ensued. The strange news of the extraordinary capture he had made was instantly forwarded by the excited Brown to Her Majesty's Minister at Turin, Mr. James Hudson, who, in turn, was shaken from his propriety by the singular information that the alleged abductor of Miss Gamble was said to be in the employ of the Foreign Office. Proceedings were stayed till an investigation was made. Away flew the intelligence of my *mésaventure* from Turin to London, and Lord Palmerston, probably, never had a more agreeable surprise than when he discovered his 'tarnal Yankee *employé* so safely in his clutches.

It must have struck him as a special dispensation of Providence. His only anxiety for months past had been to get rid of me, and numberless expedients were tried, as I have recorded, for that end, when, a long-deferred act of civility had accomplished what diplomacy had failed to effect. Still, an apprehension must have lingered in his Lordship's mind, lest some day or other I might turn up again to discomfort him. The unlooked-for news from Turin offered a chance, at last, to clap an extinguisher on me that promised a final relief. Was ever anything so fortunate? Here was the object of his anxiety safe and sure in limbo, on a charge of "Abduction" in Genoa.

Was not Genoa in Sardinia? Was not Sardinia under the absolute control of H.B.M. Foreign Office? And what had its noble chief to do but whisper his wish to the Chevalier d'Azeglio (Prime Minister), who, surely, would not venture to refuse it. There is no denying that luck ran strong in favour of the Foreign Office, inasmuch as the *pretext* for carrying out its purpose was really most specious. Whilst affecting to protect a lady, it had a rare chance to dispose of one of its agents that had excited its suspicions, and might give annoyance hereafter. Whoever knows anything of the grim calculations that Foreign Offices occasionally indulge, from the days of the Genoese Oligarchy to the present, will not be surprised at the determination come to in Downing Street as to my unfortunate case.

It required five days for the despatch of the Minister at Turin to reach Lord Palmerston, and the same, of course, for his instructions to return. I remained all this interval safe under lock and key at Genoa. The United States' Consul meanwhile called frequently on his colleague, Brown, in the hope to appease his Olympian rage, but his reply was this :—

"I have forwarded the whole matter to Mr. Hudson, at Turin, and he has written to Lord Palmerston. I am instructed, meanwhile, to take no steps till an answer is received. On that will depend what is to be done."

This was plain enough, but my Consul persisted in his efforts to calm down the intemperate Brown, who yielded at length, and pledged himself to call and visit me in prison the next morning, November 30. Instead of this, however, he wrote next day to the United States' Consul the following letter, which sufficiently explains his change of intention :—

Palazzo Cambiaso, 30th November, 1851.

DEAR SIR—

From a note I received, yesterday evening, from Turin, after you had left my house, I am obliged decidedly to decline visiting Mr. Wikoff. *He will be left to be dealt with by the tribunals of this country* as the law directs.

The Chevalier d'Azeglio (the Prime Minister) had no further acquaintance with Wikoff than having seen him across a dinner-table, without knowing who or what he was.

Truly yours,

T. YEATES BROWN.

G. BAKER, Esq., United States Consul.

My Consul brought me this decisive document, and was kind enough to leave it with me as a souvenir. My fate was sealed for the Foreign Office had clearly launched its mandate to make the most of the occasion, and its agents at Turin and Genoa certainly displayed an excess of zeal that should recommend them for any similar job hereafter.

Brown, however, was, as I have intimated, an eccentric creature. He was regarded, as I learnt afterwards, by the people of the place as a very silly and offensive person, from his ridiculous airs of importance, as well as from his gruff manners. He was totally deficient in tact, and was so elated at the delicate diplomatic task assigned to him, which he thought would ensure promotion, that he could not contain himself. He declared openly to my Consul and everybody, that "he would send me to the galleys," and, to do him justice, he struggled hard to effect it.

A determined effort was made for several weeks to bury me alive for some ten years! in the galleys, and it was only the energy of my Consul that saved me. To be sure, I had committed no offence, but that is not at all necessary in Italy, even now-a-days, when you have got a puissant Foreign Office in pursuit of you, and a creature without soul or scruple, like Timothy Brown, to carry out its behests. Blessed are all they that live within sound of Bow bells; for they, at least, may sleep quietly in their beds without fear of galleys or prison, unless they have committed a crime to warrant it.

After strenuous exertions, my assailant had to content himself with bringing me, after three months' detention in a very nasty prison, before the Genoese Court of Common Pleas, when he endeavoured to obtain a sentence of five years against me; but his evidence broke down, and he was obliged to content himself with what he considered a pitiful condemnation to only one year's imprisonment, but which I found, God knows, tedious enough.

Let my sad fate be a warning to any aspiring countryman of mine, who might hereafter fall in the way of that Syren, the Foreign Office, and be offered a snug berth at £500 a-year. Let him beware! for with all his zeal, the utmost loyalty, and constant anxiety to do his best, he can never foretell what strange fate may be in reserve for him. He may fall as I did, and fall like Lucifer, too, by finding himself in a place nearer to a hell on earth than any other kind of conceivable abode.

Such were my doleful reflections at the time, and bitterly did I regret that I had ever listened to the voice of the charmer, and been lured from my own pleasant paths into the tortuous mazes of diplomacy, with mystery at one end, and a prison at the other.

Lest any of my readers may fancy that I am trifling with their credulity, and am only trying my hand at a work of fiction, I beg to refer them again for every detail and proof of what I have advanced to the published volume already alluded to, "My Courtship and Its Consequences."

He will see there, besides, that the agents of the Foreign Office at Genoa and Turin were not men to stick at trifles, and that they did not hesitate, even, to utter a flagrant untruth when it served their purpose. *O tempora, O mores!*

On page 264 they will find the following extract from the examination of the British Consul before the Court of Common Pleas at Genoa.

President—"Do you know whether Mr. Wikoff had any employment under the British Government?"

British Consul—"I do not *know*, but I *believe* not. I have, besides, spoken to the English Ambassador (Mr. Hudson) *who told me it was impossible.*"

The object of this disclaimer, it will be seen by reference to the aforesaid volume, was to make me appear in the light of a barefaced impostor; and the effect of this deliberate denunciation, on the part of the Consul and Ambassador of Her Britannic Majesty, convinced all who heard or read it that I must be a presumptuous vagabond, indeed, to prate of my relations with the English Government, when they were so peremptorily denied by its accredited agents.

This took place on the 10th of February, three months after my consignment to "durance vile," at Genoa; so it is plain enough that Messrs. Brown and Hudson had had time enough to ascertain the fact of my connection with the Foreign Office, or no. If it were not for fear of giving offence to these worthy gentlemen, I would not hesitate to assert, that they knew every particular of my employment at the Foreign Office at the very moment they proclaimed their disbelief of it. I hold ample proof of this, which only goes to prove that your Diplomatists are not the most scrupulous people in the world, after all!

After the farce of my trial was over, a strong movement was made to obtain my pardon from the Sardinian Government. The celebrated Count de Cavour was, then, the leading Minister of the Crown, and, from various considerations, he was most favorably disposed towards me. His estimable brother, the Marquis de Cavour, wrote to me in March, and bid me to forward my petition for pardon. It was now the turn of the higher functionary of the Foreign Office, Mr. Hudson, at Turin, who stepped forward, in the name of his Government, and protested vehemently against any act of clemency. This was sufficient to frustrate the humane intentions of the Count de Cavour, and I was forced to drag out fifteen weary months in a common gaol at Genoa.

Every one knows the power of Her Britannic Majesty's Government in Sardinia, which, at one moment, protected this gallant little State from Austria, and afterwards saved its credit by timely loans, and at all times exercises, through the Sardinian Cabinet, a salutary influence over Italy. This is well, but it was, in my view, a downright degradation of that majestic beast, the British lion, to make it sit on guard at the prison-door of a luckless lover till the very last hour of his infliction was over.

Should any be inclined to question the fact of Mr. Hudson's interference against my pardon at Turin, I beg to state the following: A distinguished friend of mine at Paris applied in the spring of '52, to the Count de Cavour, for my deliverance, who replied to him at the time evasively. On coming to Paris, a couple of months later, the Count called on my friend, and declared that "it was his fixed intention to pardon me, as he looked upon the whole thing as a farce; but that Mr. Hudson, the English Minister, opposed it on behalf of his Government, and that he was in consequence compelled to give way." I am ready, if challenged, to give names, which will put my assertion at once beyond all doubt.

On my return to London from this novel expedition, in the spring of '53, I was curious to know what was the actual humor of the Foreign Office towards me, and whether it was inclined to repent its unjustifiable prank at my expense. I felt sure there must be some uneasiness entertained at the course I might think myself entitled, after such huge provocation, to pursue. To ascertain all this the shortest way appeared to me was to address a letter to Mr. Addington, stating generally that I considered myself aggrieved by the conduct of Her Britannic Majesty's Consul at Genoa, in an affair that had occurred in Genoa in '51 and '52, and which I held myself ready to substantiate, if an occasion was afforded me. This was the likeliest mode to effect my object, and so I wrote instanter to Mr. Addington.

His reply was prompt, and to this purport :—

Foreign Office, March —, 1853.

SIR—

I have duly received your letter, in which you mention certain grounds of complaint, which you conceive yourself to have against Her Majesty's Consul at Genoa, for his conduct in a matter in which you were personally concerned, some time since.

I beg leave to request, that if you feel yourself aggrieved by the proceedings of Mr. Consul Brown, in a sufficient degree to justify an official representation, you will address such representation to Her Majesty's Secretary of State.

I am, Sir,

Your very obedient servant,

H. U. ADDINGTON.

HENRY WIKOFF, ESQ.

This sounded conciliatory, I thought, and tallied with my hopes that the Foreign Office would see the fitness of according me satisfaction for the outrage I had suffered at its hands, without compelling me to lay the whole case before the public. I felt great reluctance to do this, as it would oblige me not only to expose all the delicate details of my courtship, and renew the unenviable notoriety of Miss Gamble, but, further, to undergo another encounter with the Foreign Office, which dismayed me not a little. I had received so many severe proofs of its means of annoyance, and of the unscrupulous lengths to which it would go, that I was more inclined to take counsel of my discretion than of my wrongs.

Besides, I was not in a condition to appeal to public opinion against such formidable antagonists as I had to deal with; for my name and character had been studiously covered with obloquy by a series of ingenious attacks in the newspapers, in which calumny and misrepresentation were pitilessly employed. I considered it, then, far more judicious to parley pleasantly with the Foreign Office, and endeavour to get myself right again with its co-operation, rather than in spite of it, a disheartening task. It was not pecuniary compensation I meant to ask, but such reasonable concessions as would enable me to hold my head up again in society.

The best mode to effect this, that occurred to me, was a disvowal of Mr. Consul Brown's disreputable behaviour, but I was willing, of course, to leave my restitution to the superior wisdom of the authorities in Downing-street. I inferred my chances were all the better that Lord Palmerston, though a member of the Government, was no longer at the head of the Foreign Office. To be sure, his successor, Lord Clarendon, would take care not to compromise his noble colleague by taking any steps in my favour without consulting him, and it remained to be seen how far the latter would consent to repair the injuries I had endured. It is a rare thing for a great man in office to admit an error by doing an act of justice, not that he may lack magnanimity, but it would go to prove he had made a mistake, and we have the high authority of Talleyrand, "*q'une faute est pire q'un crime,*" (that an error is worse than a crime), not a very moral axiom, it is true, but in diplomacy the end invariably justifies the means.

The difficulty my case presented was how to satisfy my expectations without damaging the parties so active against me. One method had been hit upon which I had rejected. A pardon had been offered me whilst in prison, together with money, which Miss Gamble was ready to advance, *on condition that I should bind myself to leave Europe, and make no publication of all that had occurred.* I declined the bargain without a moment's hesitation.

The dilemma then remained how far it was possible to reinstate me without exposing the Foreign Office and its agents to the risk of being convicted, should the matter ever reach the public, of conduct towards an individual who had given no real cause of offence that was undignified, cruel, and pusillanimous.

I never doubted that the people of England and the United States would ope their eyes in some astonishment, should it ever transpire to what small uses a Foreign Office can be put, and that, besides its lofty functions of canvassing the affairs of States, it could also be as effectually employed in sating personal animosities, possessing all the versatile powers of the elephant, that can hurl dowr trees and pick up pins.

The letter of Mr. Addington adroitly suggested my drawing up a representation of my case, which would, of course, enable him to judge what facts I held that might be compromising to the Foreign Office, or its agents in Turin and Genoa. Much, I knew, would depend on this. Before gratifying his curiosity, however, I thought it would be as well to pay him a visit, and see what I could get out of him. My sensations were not as buoyant as of yore in recrossing the dismal precincts of the Foreign Office, and I almost feared to enter the gloomy old ante-chamber, lest the key might be turned upon me, and I should be kept on bread and water for the rest of my born days.

I had fallen into the most singular suspicions of diplomacy, and all its ways, and was disposed to regard its Ministers and Consuls as little better than so many well-dressed turnkeys.

I entered Mr. Addington's room *arrectis auribus*, eager for every word he might let drop. He received me most graciously but was on his guard, and not inclined to talk, for he pleaded pressure of business. I was just beginning a rather pathetic recital of all my troubles, when Mr. Addington interrupted me, by saying, in a hurried manner:—

"There, don't go into details; I know all about it."

He stopped abruptly, for he committed himself in making this avowal. It was no news to me, however, for I knew, first, that the south of Europe being under the special diplomatic surveillance of Mr. Addington, he must be aware of all that had occurred in Sardinia; and I was informed, in the second place, that after Lord Palmerston had left the Foreign Office, my affair at Genoa had devolved upon him as being familiar with it."

"Very well, Mr. Addington," I replied, "as you know it all it is unnecessary to go into details. But what do you counsel me to do?"

"Make out your case," he said, "and send it into me or Lord Clarendon."

"I will do so as soon as possible, and I hope that prejudice will not prevent its being favourably considered."

"You shall have *justice* done you," returned Mr. Addington, with some emphasis; when, seeing he was reluctant to prolong the interview, I took my leave.

The Foreign Office had taken its stand, and there was nothing left for me but "to make out my case." Unfortunately, I had a pair of cases to make out. The absurd conduct of the Foreign Office in throwing me into a prison under the silly pretext of abducting a lady already affianced to me; and, next, dragging me before a public tribunal to go through the mockery of a trial, in order merely to heap discredit on me, rendered it necessary that I should make out a case for the public as well as for the Foreign

Office. The broad fact of my condemnation to a year's imprisonment, coupled with the garbled statements which had appeared against me in the London newspapers, and which were copied into those of the United States, demanded I should give the facts to the public, in the hope of reversing the mistaken views entertained of the affair, if no middle course could be found to avoid it.

I shrank with natural repugnance from an *exposé* that would be offensive to Miss Gamble, and odious to myself; and I was equally solicitous not to be forced into a publication of my late connection with Lord Palmerston, which was of a confidential nature, and that I had many reasons not to reveal. Still the disgrace and suffering that had been inflicted on me simply because an occasion arose that tempted the Foreign Office into an effort to "get rid of me," left me no alternative. Either the Foreign Office must aid in reinstating me, or I must appeal to public opinion.

The better to prepare my case, I returned to the scene of my late disasters, Genoa, and gathered abundant evidence of the indiscretion of Consul Brown. I found that in more than one instance attempts were made to bribe certain witnesses by the solicitor of Miss Gamble, named Graziani, and who held out the patronage of the British Consul as a further inducement. This was done especially in the case of a landlord of a certain hotel, which is certified on page 393 of "My Courtship." I found, besides, that it was the fixed opinion of society in Genoa that my persecution by Her Britannic Majesty's Consul was in compliance with instructions from the Home Government, else he would never have presumed to carry his violence to such an indecent length, without any personal motive to stimulate him.

In August, '53, I sent my case into the Foreign Office, which I had drawn up with great simplicity, avoiding tedious details, that Mr. Addington declared were all familiar to him. A few days after I received the following reply from Lord Clarendon:—

Foreign Office, September 6th, 1853.

SIR—

I am directed by the Earl of Clarendon to acknowledge the receipt of your letters of the 28th and 30th ultimo, in the former of which you prefer a charge against Mr. Brown, Her Majesty's Consul at Genoa, and in the latter a charge against Mr. James Hudson, Her Majesty's Minister at Turin; both those charges having reference to the conduct of those gentlemen with regard to certain matters connected with a trial in the winter of 1852, in which you were concerned.

I am to observe to you that, as you are an United States' citizen' your complaint against a Diplomatic, or a Consular Officer of the British Crown ought to be preferred through your own Government, or, at least, through an Officer of your own Government.

I am, further, to observe that, on looking over the report of the trial in question, it appears to Lord Clarendon that the testimony given by Mr. Brown was given in his character of an individual summoned into court as a witness personally acquainted with you, and not in his character as British Consul.

I am, also, to state to you that Lord Clarendon can perceive nothing in Mr. Hudson's conduct in this matter which lays him open in any way to censure or disapprobation.

I am, Sir,

Your most obedient humble servant,

H. U. ADDINGTON.

HENRY WIKOFF, ESQ.

Sic volo, sic jubeo, sit pro ratione voluntas. This was the fiat of the Foreign Office. In plain English, a fig for your facts and your wrongs; it suits my purpose to ignore both, and my will is law.

I was a good deal surprised at the nature of the reply vouchsafed to me. The letter of Mr. Addington already given, dated in March, desired me, if I considered myself justified in making an official representation, to "address such representation to Her Majesty's Secretary of State." When I complied with this direction I am answered that I ought to prefer my complaint "through your own Government, or, at least, through an Officer of your own Government." Not very intelligible language, but plain enough to indicate that the Foreign Office, in bidding me do one thing one day and the opposite the next, simply meant to shuffle out of its responsibility. The deeper my insight into Diplomacy, the stronger my dislike was growing for it.

What a farce to set up a distinction between Timothy Brown, Consul, and Timothy Brown, an individual. Besides, facts were boldly misstated. The report of the trial, which Lord Clarendon "looked over," showed that Mr. Brown was allowed to give his evidence "on his honor, as British Consul;" and, furthermore, contrary to all usage, was not sworn. The suggestion that my ferocious assailant, Consul Brown, whom I knew nothing of whatever, was a "personal acquaintance of mine," struck me as something more than a quibble, and as nothing less than another joke of the Foreign Office.

As to Mr. Hudson's conduct, Lord Clarendon could "perceive nothing" in that which laid him open to censure, simply because he chose to regard it through his own diplomatic spectacles, and not through the medium of truth and impartiality. I did not omit to state the important fact already mentioned, that the Count de Cavour would have obtained my pardon immediately if Mr. Hudson had not interposed with energy to prevent it.

My appeal to the Foreign Office was thus repelled. It was

thought unlikely, no doubt, that I could ever interest the public in my case, even if I ventured to lay it before them; and, besides, what was a pigmy like myself to such a giant as the Foreign Office?

Denied redress in every quarter, I had to choose between my social ruin and an energetic effort at vindication. Armed with the justice of my cause, I set about it, and published the eventful history of "My Courtship" in England and the United States in the beginning of '55. Its success far transcended my most sanguine expectations, and the vast literary jury of both countries, which impartially reviewed the facts of the case, gave a verdict that completely set aside the shallow decision of one of those unscrupulous men, whose tribe the poet has justly satirized when he declares they will "hang the guiltless rather than eat their mutton cold."

Having set myself right in the misrepresented affair of Miss Gamble's abduction, I turned my attention once more to the Foreign Office, expecting to find it better disposed to accord me that "justice" (which Mr. Addington had once promised) from the fact of having re-established myself in public opinion. The Foreign Office usually takes a practical view of things, and without diving into the details of innocence or guilt, it only hears or repels those who can or cannot "make out a case." *Sequitur fortunam ut semper et odit damnatos.*

My former patron, the noble Viscount Palmerston, was now Prime Minister of England, and I lost no time, on returning thither, August, '55, in bringing my case under his consideration, rejoicing that he had such ample power to afford me that redress, which he, better than all men, knew me to be entitled to in equity. I was aware that my case was, really, a difficult one to manage, even for so dexterous a hand as his Lordship's is known to be.

If the Consul at Genoa, and the Minister at Turin, had acted under instructions, how could they, in fairness, be censured, and if that was denied me, then my claim to other redress must be considered, which it might not, however, be palatable to the Foreign Office to grant.

In spite of all my vexation and loss from ever having accepted the offers of the noble Viscount, yet such was my respect for his exalted position and character that I was most anxious to spare him the possible annoyance, as well as save myself the disagreeable task of laying my case before the public, if he would grant me such moderate concessions as the testimony I could bring to bear against his Consul at Genoa, and his Minister at Turin, fully entitled me to ask.

I stated this in the respectful appeal I addressed his Lordship on my return to London in August, '55, and received the following prompt reply :—

Downing-street, August 27th, 1855.

SIR—

I am directed by Lord Palmerston to acknowledge the receipt of your letter, dated 25th of August, and to inform you, in reply, that Lord Palmerston considers that you have no claim whatever on Her Majesty's Government, and that he must decline any further correspondence with you.

I am, Sir, your obedient servant,

CHARLES C. CLIFFORD.

HENRY WIKOFF, Esq.

Nothing could be more conclusive of his Lordship's final determination to uphold the irregular conduct of his agents at Genoa and Turin, and it remained for me to choose between quiet submission to so much wrong, or that legitimate satisfaction which, I trusted, the public would award me on perusing a simple and moderate statement of facts.

It will thus be seen that I have reluctantly been forced into the eventful history of my connection with the Foreign Office, after patiently abiding for upwards of three years to obtain that "justice" once pledged, and which the utmost effort had failed to secure.

Many may be surprised at the incontestible fact of my bitter persecution by Her Britannic Majesty's Consul at Genoa, as well as at the unseemly hostility of Her Britannic Majesty's Minister at Túrin, but be wholly incredulous as to the Foreign Office, in November, '51, taking any part in it. Whatever proofs I may have of this I will reserve, for it is not my purpose to draw up a bill of indictment against the Foreign Office or any one connected with it, past or present. It is sufficient, however, that Lord Clarendon, in August, '53, and that Lord Palmerston, in August, '55, indorsed the irregular and unjustifiable conduct of Consul Brown, and Minister Hudson, to justify me in saying that my imprisonment for fifteen months in a Genoese Jail was the act of Her Majesty's Government.

The motive for this novel exercise of diplomatic influence it is somewhat difficult to make apparent, but it arose partly from the conviction of Lord Palmerston that he had done a foolish thing in employing an American at the Foreign Office; and next, that he was disappointed at the result; and finally, that his Lordship was heartily anxious to "get rid of me," to borrow his own phrase to a Foreign Ambassador at the Court of St. James's.

Further, his Lordship may have apprehended annoyance from the publication some day of my relations with the Foreign Office, and the desire to conceal this fact is evident enough from the

British Consul at Genoa venturing, in his own name and that of the British Minister at Turin, to deny it in public court, though it was perfectly well known to them at the time. It was a "lost fear" on the part of the noble Secretary of State, for such was and is my profound respect for his brilliant abilities, eminent services, and remarkable career, that no morbid love of notoriety could ever have induced me to violate the tacit confidence reposed in my discretion.

My harmless freak at Genoa with a lady actually betrothed to me, afforded the Foreign Office an occasion for friendly interference on my behalf, which would have laid me under the obligation of a favour conferred; instead of which it laid hold of a miserable pretext to inflict on me, through its unscrupulons officials, not only extreme suffering, but such a weight of disgrace as to compel me, however reluctantly, to give this strange history to the English and American public.

In conclusion, I would not have it understood as my conviction that the Foreign Office ever contemplated the heinous act of immuring me alive for long years in the Genoese galleys. I attribute this odious attempt solely to its over-zealous agent, Consul Brown, whose callous cruelty libelled most foully that genuine humanity which is one of the noblest traits of the English nation.

CHAPTER XVII.

FOREIGN OFFICE VERSUS THE UNITED STATES.

It must be apparent from what I have previously related, that my first rupture with the Foreign Office grew out of the opinion I had formed of the true basis of a solid alliance between England and the United States, and which was so diametrically opposed to the traditions and actual convictions of that influential department as to expose me to the suspicion of either ignorance or disloyalty. I am not inclined to attribute to Lord Palmerston, when Secretary for Foreign Affairs, any sentiments of personal hostility to the United States. Nay, if he meant all he said as to his motive in employing me to carry out "a liberal, especially a pacific policy," it is pretty plain that his Lordship was really anxious to maintain the most friendly intercourse with the Union, rightly appreciating the vast interests, moral and material, dependent on it. My misunderstanding with the noble Lord, it appears, sprung only from the different views entertained as to how the same end was to be accomplished.

His Lordship clearly believed that the two countries might go on trading indefinitely, as well as augmenting in other respects their amicable relations with each other, whilst the Foreign Office continued to carry on its habitual policy of jealous interference and secret hostility to the territorial expansion of the United States.

I was much better informed than his Lordship on this vital

point, from understanding better the sentiments of my own country. I had long observed the profound dissatisfaction caused in the United States by the officious and ungracious intermeddling of the British Foreign Office with our "Colonial" policy, which had, at least, everything to justify it that could be alleged in the defence of the Colonial policy of the mother country. I remembered the surprise, naturally succeeded by anger, with which the Union beheld the English Government unite with that of France to throw every obstacle in the way of the annexation of Texas; next, the resistance it made to our advance in Oregon; and, finally, the earnest opposition attempted against our acquisition of California. The people of the United States, recollecting the spirit of conquest which for centuries had animated the English Government, and which had led to successive augmentations of their Empire in all parts of the world by force of arms, were astonished at the hardihood, and shocked at the hypocrisy of English Statesmen, who took exception to the territorial aggrandisement of the Union, by means both legitimate and honorable.

If anything could add to the offensiveness of this illogical and determined intervention in their affairs in the eyes of the American people, it was that they could find no motive for it in the interests of England, which were, in fact, benefitted instead of compromised, and they were obliged, therefore, to ascribe it either to the rancor of individual Statesmen, or to the political prejudices of an oligarchy. I was deeply convinced, when I entered the Foreign Office in 1851, that the period had arrived when it should lay aside its old aggressive policy towards the United States, as it had already done in the case of European States.

The foreign policy of England, under the influence of public opinion, had undergone a striking reform as regards Europe, and political sympathies, or aristocratic prejudices, were no longer allowed to decide grave questions of peace and war. A second French Republic, and a second Napoleon, had failed to create a second Pitt, but on the contrary, the wisdom of non-intervention in the affairs of other States, where English interests were not endangered, was imperiously dictated by the national voice. In Europe the mission of the Foreign Office was limited henceforth to cultivating alliances, and not to fomenting wars from political or selfish designs.

It was equally clear to me the moment had come when the Foreign Office must abandon, also, in the United States, in obedience to the public wish, its worn out and dangerous practices. I thought Lord Palmerston's singular sagacity had detected the bent of the national mind, and was solicitous to win the honor of inaugurating a new and wiser policy. It turned out I was mistaken, perhaps, as to his Lordship's purpose, but since then I have had abundant and triumphant proofs that England is determined to rectify the aberrations of its Foreign Office as regards the United States, and to put a timely stop to its ancient system of provocation and covert enmity.

It is important to notice these indications of popular opinion coming to the rescue of the national interests and the vindication of the national character. I quote the following from the *Times* newspaper, of April 26, '54:—

"Within living memories it has been thought our interest to "damage in succession almost every nation of the world. The re-"sult has shown that in every instance it has been our interest to "strengthen and conciliate them, if that could be done, and that, at "all events, they could not be ruined but to our own ultimate loss."

It were impossible, in fewer words, to pronounce a more crushing condemnation of the ignorant and pernicious policy of the Foreign Office, which for long years has provoked wars and committed acts of tyranny and injustice, rendering the English name odious in every quarter of the globe; and which, so far from benefitting the nation, has only saddled it with a gigantic debt, that preys daily on its industry and intelligence. Such testimony as to the misguided policy of the Foreign Office is valuable, indeed, coming from a journal that represents more faithfully than any other the opinions and interests of England.

Before passing on it may be as well, for the sake of my American readers, to say a word of this Leviathan of the Press. The daily circulation of the *Times* is the largest, and its influence, both at home and abroad, the greatest of any English journal, which, in part, is to be ascribed to its independent position, representing national rather than party interests, but, more still, to the singular ability displayed in its leading articles, as well as to the equally admirable skill exhibited in its management, down to the smallest details, and not less, perhaps, to the rare sagacity displayed in detecting the faintest vibrations of the public pulse. From these various causes it has gradually become the boldest expositor of the sentiments and the stoutest champion of the interests of the country against that class legislation and oligarchical policy which, since 1688 to within a few years, has treated England as little else than a vast preserve for the nourishment and recreation of a privileged class. The *Times* has, consequently, led the way, with equal force and address, in advocating those salutary measures of home policy, the Reform Bill, Repeal of the Corn Laws, Free Trade, Repeal of Navigation Laws, which since 20 years have greatly impaired the power and curtailed the resources of the aristocracy.

It will be seen from the paragraph quoted that the *Times* has turned its attention to the Foreign as well as to the Home policy of the Oligarchy, and it does no more in this instance than express, as in the others, the settled convictions of the public mind.

The policy of the Foreign Office in the past is now regarded in England as having merely ministered to the prejudices, or served the interests of the class that have hitherto controlled it; but it is evident that henceforth it must yield to national direction, and contribute to the national good. In Europe as in America, its crafty intrigues, its narrow jealousies, its presumptuous interference and insolent dictation, must be given up, for England sees her true policy in peace and its prolific gains, and her ruin in war with its intolerable burdens.

It is to be regretted that the *Times* newspaper considers it necessary to its prestige to keep up a semi-official connection with the Government of the day, which not unfrequently leads it away from its true mission and real instinct—the national cause. In '54, in deference to the views of Lord Aberdeen, then Prime Minister, it advocated concession to Russia, and compromised its popularity by pleading against the popular determination to resist the policy of the Colossus of the North. So far as the interests of peace were concerned, the *Times* performed a philanthropic duty, but the view every patriotic Englishman at that time took was simply this, that if Russian aggrandizement was not checked in Europe, the safety of England was endangered. Right or wrong this was the national sentiment, and Lord Aberdeen was, in consequence, obliged to retire from power, and the *Times* to change its tone.

The course of the *Times* since November, '55, on the American question, is equally equivocal and anti-national. It has chosen, with its accustomed ability, to support Lord Palmerston's irritating and hostile policy to the United States, and in so doing has thrown away its splendid *rôle* of sitting as umpire, in the name of England, upon the diplomatic feats of the Foreign Office, and the inevitable resistance of the American Government.

The sagacity of the *Times* must be at fault, indeed, not to know that the great industrial and trading classes, which now give law to England, are resolved against war with the United States as utter ruin to their interests.

It must, likewise, be deplorably ill-informed not to know that, in the United States, neither the views of any class, nor the sentiments of our public men are favourable to a war with England, which is universally regarded as not more unnatural than absurd. Yet the *Times* newspaper, for months past, has thought fit to encourage the wrangling spirit of the Foreign Office, for no other motive, apparently, than to be on terms of amity with the Government of the day, unless to this is added the journalistic necessity of writing piquant articles on an engrossing and prolific subject. Still, every friend of this great organ, the diurnal wonder of the century, must regret to see it, for one moment, abdicate its true functions, and neglect to express, with equal independence, impartiality, and fearlessness, the real opinions of England, or to sustain the cause of truth and justice everywhere.

From its lofty position it might exercise a vigilant and wholesome *surveillance* over the interests of both nations, kindred in language as blood, and its influence would be equally powerful in defeating the bellicose designs of an American politician, should such arise, as in checking the crafty machinations of the Foreign Office. In the paragraph quoted from its own columns, the *Times* declares that the policy of the Foreign Office in seeking to "damage nations instead of strengthening and conciliating them," is erroneous, which is profoundly true, as the policy of England is trade, and not conquest. Why, then, it may be inquired, has this journal not maintained its own doctrines in the recent differences between the Foreign Office and the American Government? I venture on these remarks with no small trepidation, for I am well aware that the *Times*, if it should condescend to notice me at all, can, by a single stroke of its ponderous pen, make me keenly repent of my temerity in presuming to question its eccentricity on any occasion; still I think it only right to utter this remonstance, and I must prepare myself to endure with exemplary meekness the probable penalty.

Another striking instance of the resolution of the commercial world of England to arrest that pragmatical spirit of the Foreign Office which threatens so much disaster, was given at the Lord Mayor's Dinner to the late American Minister at this Court, Mr. Buchanan. This gentleman, in the course of his reply to the Lord Mayor, made use of the following striking language:—

"There could be no political servitude where the English "language was the language of the country. It was impossible; "and so far from there being any jealousy either on the part of "England or the United States as to the honest and fair extension "of their borders, it ought to be considered a blessing to mankind "that they should extend them over all the unsettled parts of "the earth."

This candid avowal of the American Minister as to what he conceived to be the true policy of England and the United States, "the honest and fair extension of their borders," was received by the company assembled on that occasion, the *élite* of the industrial, financial, and commercial classes, with enthusiastic demonstrations of approval. Could anything better illustrate the settled convictions of these influential bodies, or convey a stronger rebuke to that querulous mismanagement of the Foreign Office, which not only undertakes to check the spread of civilization, but to throw obstacles in the way of the national prosperity.

The territorial extension of the United States, so far from being a cause of legitimate anxiety to England, is, on the contrary, an object that she must heartily desire, for the simple reason, that she must be the ultimate gainer. Every new town and harbour added to the American territory, as I have already observed, is only a new mart for her merchandize, and a new outlet for her navigation. If the question were decided, as it soon will be, by the commercial world of England, the addition of new territory to the United States, instead of being a ground of quarrel between the two countries as now, would be a source of mutual satisfaction.

The Foreign Office, that so recklessly risks the interests of England, and the peace of the world, in its churlish opposition to American annexation, against which it presumptuously seeks to draw the line of exclusion, "thus far shalt thou go, and no farther," happily entertains no such puerile scruples as to the extension of the English Empire in India. It was only the other day that we read the loud vauntings of the *Times*, and heard the triumphant rejoicings of the India House, over the splendid successes of the ex-Governor General, Lord Dalhousie. It is in these sonorous phrases that the *Times* records the prowess of the successor of Clive and Hastings:—

"It is enough to say that, with scarce a dissentient, he has "added four kingdoms, besides lesser territories, to our Indian "Empire; and meanwhile introduced and developed all the great "works of modern times, railways, electric telegraphs, canals, "irrigation, roads, manufacturing and agricultural improvements, "schools, scientific institutions, cheap uniform postage, and all the "public works necessary for the establishment of a civilized rule "in semi-barbarous countries."

The Chairman of the East India Company, in felicitating his fellow Directors on these solid achievements of Lord Dalhousie's genius, is less occupied with the interests of civilization, but naturally more engrossed by the mercantile result of these wholesale annexations. He describes the annual "nettings" of these civilising operations, as follows:—

The Punjaub	£1,500,000
Pegu	270,000
Nagpore, less Tribute	410,000
Oude	1,450,000
Sattarah	150,000
Shanshi	50,000
Hyderabad	500,000
	£4,330,000 per annum.

Sir James Hogg, the Chairman, in making this parade of figures, suddenly remembers that this purely financial view of annexation might possibly be considered by Foreign nations as somewhat sordid, so he falls back immediately on the old clap-trap phrases that have long appertained to the verbal armory of the India House. "The long continued cries of outraged humanity," says Sir James, with his hands piously uplifted, "have, at last, com- "pelled the removal of that disgrace which the guarantee to insure "good government has attached to the British name, in tolerating for "more than half a century a state of anarchy and misrule which "was fatal to the people and dangerous to us. Former Governors-

"General had given solemn but ineffectual warnings to the Rulers in "Oude, but Lord Dalhousie was the first to carry out the dictates of "*solid justice* and *sound policy!*" Right upon the heels of this high sounding period Sir James furnishes the pecuniary details above, which convey, in round numbers, his estimate of "solid justice and sound policy."

The *Times*, again, in pealing out its praises in anthem tones of Lord Dalhousie's glorious conquests, suddenly catches its breath, and is apparently seized with a secret misgiving that its "Trans-atlantic cousins" might, possibly, be struck with the inconsistency of the leading journal eulogising annexation in India, but de-nouncing it furiously in America. To relieve any unpleasant sus-picions of the sort, and to sooth American susceptibilities, the *Times* begins forthwith playing with this ugly word of "annexa-tion" pretty much as a Thimble-rigger does with a pea,—"now you see it and now you don't."

"We have said," the *Times* remarks, "that in this there are "happily wanting those drawbacks which the eulogist has usually "to endure or disguise; yet we are aware that 'annexation' in these "days is a word of reasonable suspicion, if not of just opprobrium. "Whether it be by peace or by arms, whether in the battle-field or "by diplomacy, it is equally ascribed to the lust of dominion and "the force of empire. As was truly observed the other day at "the India house, 'annexation' is a word of *various senses*, and "every one of these four instances (the four kingdoms in question) "requires a distinct consideration."

The *Times*, then, sets to work with exceeding ingenuity, art-fully drawing all its illustrations from the American continent, to prove how very justifiable "annexation" is in India, however abominable it may be in America. The *Times* might have spared itself this gratuitous display of dissimulation and dismissed its idle apprehensions of American criticism, for the United States entertain no pitiful jealousy at the extension of the British Empire in India, but rejoice to see British civilisation gradually extirpating anarchy and barbarism. To the suppression of the Juggernaut, and the abolition of the hideous immolation of the Indian widow, the Americans only regret that the British Government does not put an immediate stop to the horrible practice of *torture*, which its own agents actually and regularly employ to gather in the revenue. If such an atrocity as *torture* was employed in our Slave States, even, for the sake of revenue, what a hubbub the *Times* would raise, and most properly too; and above all, what a yell of horror would escape from Exeter Hall in the name of "British Humanity."

To come back to the Foreign Office, what would *it* say if the American Government should borrow the very phraseology of the Chairman of the East India Company, and justify the "annexation" of Mexico and Central America, on the ground of having "tolerated for near half a century the anarchy and misrule which was fatal to the people and dangerous to *us*." Would the Foreign Office accept our "guarantee to insure good Government," and like a well-behaved person leave us to attend to our business, and sensibly mind its own? It has refused to do so in the past, but from present symptoms it is likely it will be obliged to alter its conduct in the future.

In addition to the testimony already quoted of the revolution in the public mind of England, as to the policy of its Foreign Office, I would add another manifestation still more remarkable than the rest.

At the dinner given to the new American Minister, Mr. Dallas, by the Lord Mayor, in April last, that much respected oracle of the "City" thus expressed himself:—

"The Mansion-house had never pretended to be a diplomatic "corporation, but the authorities had endeavoured at all times to "be social and hospitable; and there were no people with whom "it was so especially necessary, or with whom it was so much our "duty to cultivate social and friendly intercourse, as with our "kindred friends of the United States. (Cheers.) Now, there "was no reason why we should be jealous of America. On the "contrary, there was every reason why we should be proud of our "connection with the United States. That mighty nation had "arisen from a colony of England, which had carried from the "Mother-country the seeds of civil and religious liberty; it was "there that a kindred soil was found, and the colony had since "become a great, a mighty, and an independent nation. We could "boast of being the only nation where such a case had arisen. "Other countries, such as Spain, &c., could only, comparatively "speaking, show stunted colonies; whereas, here we saw a vast and "powerful country, *which one day or other will span the whole of* "*that Continent.* All that was wished and desired by us was to "see the most intimate and cordial relations maintained between "the two great powers."

Could anything be plainer or more forcible than this language? One of the prominent members of that great mercantile body, which in reality govern England, here declares, with a Pharisaical sneer of something like contempt, that the "Mansion House," the City Palace, lays no claim to diplomatic *prestige;* but, in a tone of authority not to be mistaken, it makes known its utter scorn of the frivolous disputes of the Foreign Office about some obscure island, by making a present to the United States of the whole of the Continent, Islands, Mosquito Kings, Brazilian Emperors, and all, on the simple condition that England and the United States may remain "intimate and cordial friends."

Since the day that Alexander cut the Gordian knot, it is doubtful whether so many intricate difficulties were ever solved in a more imperial way than by this decisive *fiat* of the Mansion House. The Lord Mayor, with the clear-sightedness characteristic of the industrial and trading classes, sees that no greater good fortune could befall England than the United States taking possession, if such a thing were possible, of the whole American Continent, which would only increase to an incalculable extent the exports of Great Britain; but, meanwhile, to show to the United States, and the world, what the "City" thinks of the Foreign Office, that is playing skittles with its vast commercial and financial interests, it invites the American Minister to the "Mansion House," not merely to give him a dinner worthy of Lucullus, but to set before him, by way of dessert, a "sweet dish," such as he had never dreamt of before, much less been called on to digest, nothing else than what a French cook would style *un gros gateau à l'Americaine*, but which the Lord Mayor in plain English described as "the whole of the American Continent."

When he sat down on this occasion, the orchestra struck up "Yankee Doodle;" and to convince the astonished Minister of the United States that their worthy magistrate had not been uttering an idle compliment in the Spanish fashion, the assembled wealth and dignity of the "City," merchants, manufacturers, bankers—in short, the *élite* of the money-world—set to work with their knives and forks beating time to our national air, and with such downright earnestness, as to make the plates dance on the tables before them.

For one I appreciated the significance of this demonstration, and whilst my blood tingled at the extraordinary welcome given to the simple strains of our familiar ditty, as they rose high and clear above the din below, I could not help reflecting that the Foreign Office had been weighed in the balance and found wanting. I felt sure from that day that whoever was Prime Minister of England, he must give up skirmishing with the United States about her territorial expansion, or that he must give up his place.

Another incident occurred immediately afterwards on the same occasion that abundantly deserves record. No sooner did Mr. Dallas sit down—and his short, but impressive, address was listened to with reverent attention—than young Lord Stanley rose and uttered sentiments in the glowing language of eloquence that thrilled the auditory, and will leave an echo in history. But, first, a remark or two upon Lord Stanley, for he is of the new batch of Statesmen—the joint product of poor Sir Robert Peel and the spirit of the—age and between whom and the old school of English politicians there is really nothing in common.

He is the son and heir of the Earl of Derby, who, years agone, gave lustre by his talents to this same historic title of Stanley. In this instance it happens that the lord of hereditary acres has been fortunate enough to transmit not only title and wealth, but even more than paternal genius, for the son bids fair to outshine the brilliant reputation of his sire. Nothing could more briefly indicate the rapid march of democratic ideas in England than to measure the distance between the political tenets of the Earl of Derby at one period of his life and those now professed by his son.

The first, at one time, was an intense Tory, which is now so completely out of date that it would be hard to find in any receptacle of rubbish a specimen of the decayed creature left. What the son professes may be inferred directly from his own words. He is a member of the House of Commons, and about 35 years of age. For several years past he has taken a prominent part in Parliamentary debates, but he has attracted even more attention by his striking speeches out of doors.

The custom of public meetings on topics of popular interest is common enough amongst us; but in England, strange to say, we are completely outdone in this respect. It arises, in a measure, from the fact that numbers of aspiring men in the middle classes, who have no chance to figure in the Parliamentary arena, get up public meetings to let off their explosive eloquence, and attract a corresponding share of renown; but these constant gatherings have, also, another origin in the ten thousand societies, for every conceivable object, that are got up by shrewd calculators on the public sympathies, who constitute themselves perpetual secretaries, and get together annual subscriptions enough to provide comfortably for their families, if not for the ostensible charity in question.

At these assemblies it is sought to obtain the services of speakers of reputation; and the Aristocracy, to prevent the middle classes obtaining the lead in shaping public opinion in any matter, are in the habit of presiding and speaking on most of these occasions. Lord Stanley has availed himself liberally of all these opportunities of late to make his rare abilities known, and to conciliate popular opinion, and the more so, that in Parliament he is obliged to observe a certain restraint.

In fact, things have come to that point in the House of Commons when it may be said that there is neither a Government with a policy nor an Opposition to attack it. Stagnation has overtaken

English politics, which I shall have a good deal to say about at another time. Lord Stanley can't assail the Government in the House, and he is indisposed, for divers reasons, to support it. He has, therefore, been forced out the walls of St. Stephen's for a rostrum, and is frequently found speaking, during the "season," at the west end of the town, at the public meetings aforesaid; and during the recess, his fine swelling cadences come up to the readers of the *Times* from some one or other of the Provinces, where his name and talents have found a market.

His motive, therefore, in accepting the hospitality of the Lord Mayor is apparent enough; but it turned out, to the surprise of many besides myself, that he had another object in view than merely tacking his name to a showy discourse. He seized this occasion, and he could not have found a better, to enter his protest, with all the weight of his position, his talents, and his hopes, against the mischievous, if not bellicose, policy of the Foreign Office against the United States. The language he used showed at once that he was not bidding for the "sweet voices" of the citizens by specious and gaudy phrases, but that he was expressing settled convictions of what the policy of England required at the present juncture of her affairs.

The sentiments uttered would have sounded strange in the mouth of an English Radical, but coming from a feudal lord, a scion of one of the oldest houses, a representative of the territorial Aristocracy of England, they were really startling for their novelty, if for nought else. When he spoke the following words, Lord Stanley seemed fully to know their import. His manner was impassioned, his gesture ardent, and his voice vibrated:—

"On the cordial and united intercourse of Great Britain and the "United States must depend the hopes of mankind. In this

" question were identified the best interests of hundreds of millions " of the Anglo-Saxon race. It rests with England and the United " States to accomplish the mighty future. *He who sought to dis-" turb the good feeling between the two mighty nations, or to impede " the success of the one or the other, was an enemy to England.*" (Cheers.)

Not a hundred volumes could convey more positively than these stirring words the amazing revolution in the public mind, above all, in the Aristocratic mind, of England, that has occurred within a recent period respecting the United States. That the industrial and trading classes should discard prejudice and cling to their interests; that the middle class, in spite of their loyalty and dread of innovation, should yield, at times, to Democratic sympathies, and that both should extend the cordial hand of fellowship to the United States, is, after all, natural enough; but that a pillar of the Oligarchy itself, a champion of his order, the future defender of the Aristocratic creed, should turn towards the United States, not with the aversion of a natural antagonist, crying *procul, o procul este, profani*, but rather with the honest fervor of an enthusiast, declaring that man to be "an enemy of England" who would sow discord between the "two mighty nations"—all this partakes so largely of the marvellous as to excite wonder and inspire deep reflection.

What does it prove? Why, in a word, that the clear-eyed Aristocracy have perceived that the nation they govern, the bone and sinew of the nation, has made up its mind that, for divers reasons, it must be friends with the United States, and, consequently, that if they would continue to govern, they must think and act likewise. This is why young Lord Stanley, a Prime Minister in embryo, appeared at the "Mansion House" in April last, and in a strain of eloquence no report could portray, declared that the "mighty future" was in the hands of the Anglo-Saxon race.

This is why, too, that two months later, June 16, Mr. Disraeli rose in his place in the House of Commons, and recommended that an opportunity should be taken "of inquiring calmly what is the cause of these painful and frequently recurring misunderstandings with a country between which and ourselves there ought to be such constant sympathy and such cordial alliance."

From the grave rebuke administered on this occasion to the Foreign Office, it was evident that the decided language of the "City" had made its way to the "West-end," and Mr. Disraeli, with the readiness of a politician out of place, and with the astuteness and boldness characteristic of the man, seized upon it to read the Government a homily on its mistaken policy which is not likely to be forgotten.

Before quoting further from the novel and pungent remarks of Mr. Disraeli, it may be as well, for my American readers, to say a word of his actual position in the House of Commons. No one in the United States is likely to ask who is Disraeli, for his name, as identified with a *chef d'œuvre* of literary skill, is as familiar to the world of literature there as in his own country. The interest excited by his youthful prowess as a writer of romance has followed him in his political career, and his valiant struggles with the prejudices, piled mountain high, against his plebeian origin, have, perhaps, enlisted a certain democratic sympathy in his fortunes.

It was considered by us a triumph of genius, surpassing all former exploits, that from the despised of the "country party," the very essence of aristocratic intolerance, he should rise to be its leader and master in '52. Since then strange things have come to pass, and the "country party" has discovered that the surest way to prevent a popular assault upon the citadel of aristocratic monopoly is to throw down their arms and disband. The consequence is, that Mr. Disraeli finds himself in the anomalous position of a General without an army, and thus the talents of the most brilliant debater of the House of Commons, and, likely, as able a statesman as any, are obliged to go a-begging.

Disraeli, however, is not the man to rust away in sloth, and his powers of vaticination must be keen enough to convince him that the "Dead Sea" in English politics must soon be passed, and that stirring work awaits all those who may be found on the opposite shore. He keeps his armor on, therefore, and loses no fit occasion to break a lance with the champions of exploded ideas. Seeing that Lord Stanley had fearlessly taken the field against the Foreign Office, as related, he as resolutely followed his lead, and began his speech as quoted. What he further said was too new and striking not to be recorded, and I can well imagine the emotions of sorrow, if not of anger, awakened in the mind of the Prime Minister, as the warning words of the orator fell on his reluctant ears. Thus spoke Mr. Disraeli :—

"Sir, it is impossible to suppose that the recruiting, or the mode "in which it was conducted, especially after the apologies which were "offered by the Government, can really be the cause of the mis- "understanding which has unhappily occurred. I want to know "why the United States Government, even admitting their cause to "be a good one, is so prompt, if not eager, to insist upon immediate "reparation? It will be well if we take this opportunity—I do not "mean this evening, but before these great questions are settled— "of arriving at some definite result upon this point. It would be "wise if England would at last recognize that the United States, "like all the great countries of Europe, have a policy, and that "they have a right to have a policy. I observe in the papers which "have been laid upon the table of the House that the American "Minister who is here commenced his communications with Her "Majesty's Government by saying that he thought it right to "announce that the President had adopted the Monroe doctrine as "the foundation of his system of government. Now, Sir, the "Monroe doctrine is one which, with great respect to the Govern-"ment of the United States, is not, in my opinion, suited to the age "in which we live. The increase in the means of communication "between Europe and America have made one great family of the "Governments of the world, and that system of government which, "instead of enlarging, would restrict the diplomatic relations "between those two quarters of the globe is a system which is not "adapted to this age. In making that observation, however, I "would say that it *would be wise in England not to regard with the* "*extreme jealousy with which she has hitherto looked upon it any* "*extension of the territory of the United States beyond the bounds* "*which were originally fixed to it. I hold that that is not a good* "*policy which is founded on the idea that we should regard with* "*extreme jealousy the so-called 'aggressive' spirit of the United* "*States*. (Hear, hear.) I am of opinion that the treaty concluded "by Lord Ashburton was one of the wisest diplomatic acts that "has been performed in modern times, at least in this country "(hear, hear); that it was the indication of a sound and liberal "policy, and that those who oppose it are the supporters of a "policy which is regarded by the Government of the United "States as one hostile to the legitimate development of their power. "(Hear, hear.) *Moreover, I am persuaded that it is the belief* "*on the part of the United States that the British Government is* "*animated by such sentiments in their regard which has excited the* "*feeling that has seized upon the enlistment question as a means of* "*expressing their dissatisfaction and distrust*. (Hear, hear.) It is "through no desire to introduce controversial questions on the "present occasion that I venture to offer these remarks (hear, hear), "but simply because I wish to remind the House that such is the "feeling which prevails in America (hear); and that, if it is always "to be impressed upon England that she is to regard every expan-"sion of the United States as an act detrimental to her interests "and hostile to her power, we shall be pursuing a course which "will not prevent that expansion on the part of the States, but "which will involve this country in struggles that may prove of the "most disastrous character. (Hear, hear.) *I remember what* "*extreme jealousy existed a few years ago in this House in conse-*"*quence of the conquest of California by the United States. (Hear).* "*That was an event which was looked forward to with the gravest* "*alarm, and one from which the most calamitous results were antici-*"*pated. Have any of those gloomy forebodings been realized?* "*(Hear.) I would ask the House how far the balance of power has* "*been injured by the conquest of California by America (hear, hear),* "*and whether there is any event since the discovery of America* "*which has contributed more materially to the wealth, and, through the wealth, to the power of this country than the development of the rich resources of California by means of the United States? (Hear, hear.)* These things are worthy of consideration; for, believe me, sooner or later we shall have to adopt clear and definite opinions on this subject; and, indeed, I cannot hesitate to express my belief that if sounder views with respect to it had prevailed in this country, the Government might not have felt themselves justified in taking a course with regard to the Enlistment question which, whatever may be its immediate consequences, certainly has not terminated in a manner flattering to the honour of the nation or grateful to the feelings of any class of Her Majesty's subjects. (Hear, hear.) These are the two points to which the noble Lord, to whom we are indebted for this discussion, has particularly referred. *For my own part, I look on all that has happened with regard to the Enlistment question as indicative of the distrust which prevails in the United States, and which has its origin in the conviction that the policy of this country is hostile to the legitimate development of their power.* It is my opinion that all that America has fairly a right to expect she may obtain, without injury either to Europe in general or to England in particular (hear), *and that it is the business of a statesman to recognize the necessity of an increase in her power*, and at the same time to make her understand that she will most surely accomplish all the objects she proposes to herself by recognizing those principles of international law (hear) which in civilized communities have always been upheld (hear), and to impress upon her that, instead of vaunting that she will build her greatness on the Monroe doctrine, which is the doctrine of isolation, she should seek to attain it by deferring to the public law of Europe, and by allowing her destiny to be regulated by the same high principles of policy which all nations which have great destinies to accomplish have invariably recognized." (Cheers.)

It was like robbing a miser of his wealth, or, more appropriately, depriving a warrior of his arms, for Lord Palmerston thus to be solemnly told that he must henceforth give up his "extreme jealousy" of the territorial development of the United States. There is little doubt the illustrious Viscount has hitherto regarded America, in the spirit of a true diplomatic Nimrod, as the richest preserve a going for a good day's sport, when the dullness of European politics drove him across the Atlantic for the exercise of his skill. What must be his chagrin thus to be notified that he must abandon his favourite haunt for so many years past, and how deep his annoyance to see more than one candidate for his place map out the policy which the Foreign Office he has so long controlled must hereafter adopt.

May I be permitted to divine if in such an hour of retribution as this the remembrance of his luckless Yankee *protégé* crossed his mind, and whose only offence was the venial one of having sought to protect his patron from the mortification that has finally overtaken him? Whether the noble Premier has allowed a sigh of regret to escape him or not at the chance recollection of all the tribulations which he might so easily and magnanimously have averted from the head of the helpless victim of Timothy Brown, it is impossible, of course, to say; but I appeal to the most obdurate of my readers, and demand if I have not reason to congratulate myself on the triumphant vindication which fate has awarded me.

What had I not suffered for my conscientious scruples? What had I not sacrificed from a sense of duty? What martyrdom not undergone from a conviction of right? From dinners at Broadlands, and marked favour at the Foreign Office, I had fallen, first, under suspicion; thence descended into the chilly regions of "Coventry;" next, was called on to undergo a series of stunning rebuffs that were each expected to be mortal, and which it was my cruel destiny to survive only to be, finally, plunged into a diplomatic "*inferno*" from which Dante might have imbibed new inspirations, and lent new horror to the diabolical conceptions of his high-wrought fancy. More fortunate, however, than many better men who had preceded me, and thanks to the elasticity of a

Yankee disposition, which thrives on pressure, I have lived to see my merciless foe—the Foreign Office—brought to the bar of public opinion in its turn, emphatically accused of long and heavy dereliction, and formally condemned, on pain of utter demolition, "to go and sin no more."

Have I not reason, then, to rejoice, and could I in fairness be censured for a rude expression of feeling, were I to give utterance to my exuberant spirits in the boastful lines of the rhymster:—

"Oh, Victory! Joyful Victory!
Like love, thou bringest sorrow;
And, yet, for such an hour with thee,
Who would not die to-morrow?"

Still, I would not have it thought now, or hereafter, that I have anything in common with that vindictive spirit which, in my unhappy case, stimulated the Foreign Office and its well-chosen agents at Turin and Genoa to such discreditable acts; nor would I expose myself to the charge of an indecent display of facetiousness at the rare humiliation which has befallen an old antagonist. No; rather let me, oblivious of my own small crosses, and mindful only of the real gravity and dignity of the subject, rise to the magnitude of the consoling fact that, albeit the Foreign Office disdainfully spurned the services and advice of safe, though humble, guidance, it has at last been forced to listen to the stern voice of rebuke, and bid to mend its crotchetty ways and bend its perverse spirit to the exigencies of the epoch and the interests of the nation.

CHAPTER THE LAST.

THE LEX TALIONIS.

In the course of the present volume I have been obliged, by the harsh necessity of a false position, to carry on a sort of guerilla warfare with the ordinary standards of propriety in matters of private concern; and the result of a long continuance in sin has overtaken me in that recklessness which makes me not only indifferent to what may be thought of past offences, but hardens me for the commission of new and, perhaps, more flagrant ones. Before closing, I am vastly tempted to venture upon further revelations of diplomatic secrets; but this time, instead of diving again into the recesses of Downing-street, I am inclined to set off in quest of them to Washington. I feel far less dismayed at the consequences of such imprudence in that familiar latitude, for, accustomed as we Americans are to all forms and kinds of publicity, which, in fact, is the corner-stone of our system, I have little to fear from official frowns or social censure.

In England, some fifty years ago, *exclusiveness* was all the rage, and any publicity beyond the dry announcements of the *Court Circular*, or the stereotyped paragraphs of the *Morning Post*, was pronounced vulgar, and put under Aristocratic ban. But in these rough, practical, and Democratic times, *nous avons changé tout celà*, and little favor is now shown to canons of taste, or to fastidious notions of etiquette in matters where the public take an interest, and think it for their good to be informed. This, in my own eyes, is a safer refuge, if not a better excuse, for any unavoidable infractions of refined conventionalities I may have committed, than even the personal motives, however stringent, that led to the origin of this publication. I shall be gratified far beyond the utmost success which can attend "my case" against the Foreign Office, if in the course of this narrative I have succeeded in elucidating any points hitherto involved in doubt, in correcting any false views hitherto unsuspected, and in firmly establishing any truths hitherto contested. It is this modest hope which has chiefly stimulated me to undertake this volume, and which has sustained me in my unceremonious mode of dealing with the subject. It is, likewise, this which urges me to add another brief chapter to the adventures already recorded, and to incur the fearful risk of wearying my already sated reader.

Before saying anything of my short pilgrimage, nearly a year since, to our political Mecca, I must pause to remark on the singular chance that just at the moment I was busy collecting evidence of the past transgressions of that mischievous sprite, the Foreign Office, new events of great "pith and moment" should transpire to add to my list and swell the magnitude of its enormities. For several months past all England and the United States have been a prey to feverish apprehensions, and every day the chances of a fatal misunderstanding, ending in a calamitous war, seemed to grow more menacing. The subjects in dispute between the Governments appeared so frivolous that sensible people in England were quite at a loss to understand how it was possible to build up such a mountain of pother out of so contemptible a mole hill. Newspapers that were in the secret, and I may as well single out the *Times* at once, and newspapers that were not, accused the

American Government of a captious and quarrelsome disposition; and they went even farther, by charging upon the President an insane desire to provoke a war with England simply to favor his chances and bolster up his hopes of a re-election. The injustice of these surmises, and the absurdity of these diatribes, were palpable enough to Americans on both sides of the Atlantic, who regarded them with surprise and dissatisfaction, but they were received by the English public generally with unsuspecting good faith, and produced that discontent and irritation it was the purpose of their principal authors to foment.

It is extraordinary enough that, with a free Press as one of their boasted privileges, two nations should be gradually approaching the verge of war, not so much, perhaps, from the ignorance of their journalists as to facts, as from the deliberate misrepresentations of them through passion, or mistaken views of interest. That such an anomaly should ever occur is, no doubt, a profound consolation to sceptical Despots, but that the evil apparently aimed at did not ensue, is a proof that the instruction spread by a free Press is capable of curing its occasional excesses.

Now that the smoke of fiery discussion has cleared away, and the clash of diplomatic "passages at arms" has ceased, let us dispassionately look about, and find out the cause of all this disorder. Depend on it, where there has been so much difficulty and danger with no real reason for it, there has been some malignant spirit, some "damned Iago" secretly at work to compass its own ends to the ruin of everybody else's. When I gravely lift my finger and point to that *gazza ladra*, the Foreign Office, which is always trying to steal away the peace of nations, and roundly assert that it alone is at the bottom of all this rumpus, incredulous people will cry pshaw, and others will suspect I am only trying to pile

"Pelion on Ossa," in order to bring my former adversary more surely to the ground. In spite, however, of disbelief or insinuation I persist firmly in my allegation, and will endeavour to convince all sober people that I am not setting down "aught in malice."

I have already stated, what is worthy all credence, and which stands to reason, that the long course of adverse interference in American affairs on the part of the Foreign Office, first in Texas, Oregon, and California; next in Cuba, Central America, Dominica, and the Lord knows where beside, has engendered in the Government and people of the United States surprise, vexation, and, finally, a spirit of resistance. It was perfectly well known, as I have said, both to the American Government and people that neither the commercial classes nor people of England, had anything to do with this, and that it proceeded either from aristocratic jealousy or mistaken policy; but the necessity of resisting it, at all hazards, was manifest, tho' it may have been secretly hoped the good sense of England would interfere when the crisis became threatening.

In Texas and California the Foreign Office was resisted and defeated, but in Oregon, perhaps unfortunately, a compromise was agreed upon. The natural effect of this and other successes has been only to inflate its vanity and to encourage its pretensions, until, at last—what does the reader think—until, at last, the unhappy Secretary for American Foreign Affairs, Mr. Marcy, was just as good as locked up in his own office and the key put in the pocket of the representative at Washington of the Downing Street establishment, Mr. Crampton. This is figurative language, but the fact is not exaggerated. Mr. Crampton, backed by his sympathetic colleague, the Count Sartiges, Minister of France, kept up a *surveillance* so active, pertinacious and carping over the suspected, but unoffending, American Secretary, that if he had not been one of the most enduring and long-suffering Diplomatists in the world, would have led to dire disasters some time before they really came.

It will not do for me to venture helter-skelter upon staggering assertions about great personages like these, without laying down some positive proofs of my title to belief. I know it, and for this reason I will ask my readers to accompany me on a flying visit to Washington, and the last I will require them to make in my company.

I will say little, by way of introduction, of Mr. W. L. Marcy, Secretary of State for the Foreign "Department," as it is styled in the United States. At home everybody must recollect his career, and abroad no one would likely take much interest in it.

His political life has been a long one, and eminently successful, and he has reached the patriarchal age of three-score and ten, with a reputation for diplomatic adroitness that qualified him admirably to cope, not merely with Messrs. Crampton and Sartiges, at Washington, but with their far more formidable masters in Europe. It was well for the United States, and perhaps for other nations, that such a man as Mr. Marcy, so profoundly versed in the art—I will not say of chicanery—but of diplomacy, was at the helm of affairs at the critical period we have just passed through.

Mr. Marcy, when, in March, 1853, he took possession of the "State Department," knew the exact condition of the public mind of the country. Averse to war, above all other countries, with Great Britain, and by no means intoxicated on the point of foreign acquisitions, it was yet resolutely bent on exercising its own judgment in matters pertaining to its own welfare, without regard to the opinions of third parties. Now, had Mr. Marcy been an ambitious or a designing politician, he could hardly have desired a better occasion than this to carry out his purposes or to gratify a thirst for historical renown. It is strange, indeed, having achieved so much *éclat* as Secretary of War, under President Polk, in the campaign against Mexico, that he was not tempted to try his luck again on a grander scale of operations. That he has, on the contrary, resisted with unyielding firmness the enterprising spirit of the country, and borne with such praise-worthy composure the provocations heaped upon him by Her Britannic Majesty's Foreign Office, does equal credit to his patriotism and Statesmanship.

Anxious to comply with the wishes of the country by adding to our possessions the much-coveted prize of Cuba, he employed all his skill in seeking to obtain it by purchase, but the ubiquitous Foreign Office met him at Madrid and employed its superior influence to defeat him. Soaring aloft on his diplomatic wings, he fled to the uttermost parts of the earth and tried his luck in negotiation at the Sandwich Islands; but he was stealthily followed by that prying, inquisitive "detective," the Foreign Office, and forced to abandon commercial advantages to which he had the justest claim. Again, in Dominica, after securing, with much effort and no small skill, a Treaty favorable to our trading interests in that quarter, he was boldly robbed of it by the unceremonious interference of the British Consul, backed by his loving colleague of France, who without explanation or apology, peremptorily forbad the submissive Dominicans to comply with it.

All this was the more vexatious, not to say indecent, in that brazen-faced intermeddler, the Foreign Office, after the active and incessant exertions of Mr. Marcy to meet all the exactions of Her Britannic Majesty's Minister at Washington, by opposing and defeating, at the risk of his popularity and office, every attempt at "fillibustering" that had been detected. As is generally the case, every effort of the American Secretary to conciliate the agent of the Foreign Office at Washington only augmented his imperiousness, and all the sacrifices and unparalleled concessions of the badgered Mr. Marcy, failed utterly to lull the suspicions or subdue the hostility of the captious, cavilling, carping Mr. Crampton, who was obliged to obey instructions from Downing Street. How any mortal man could stand it, even a diplomatist, who is not a whit better Christian than other men, whatever his pretensions, I could not divine. It was just when Mr. Marcy's persecution had reached the culminating point that I made my way to Washington. I thought it would be just as well, perhaps, to take advantage of the savage ill-humour I expected to find him preyed upon, to "pour the leprous distilment into his ear" of my ill-treatment by the same indomitable foe to Yankee enterprise, whether in the east or the west.

I had heard much of Secretary Marcy's eccentric appearance, manners, and habits; and chained by the leg for the last two or three years, and worried and tormented, as he had been, by the unfeeling Ministers of England and France, I really feared to approach him till after applying every emollient within my reach. I had him written to by some of his best friends and nearest relatives. Provided, besides, with other resources of a soothing nature, I braced up my nerves for a visit to the "State Department," where I presented myself at two o'clock of a hot day in July, of last year, and sent in my card by the messenger in waiting. I was ushered in immediately, and augured well of this beginning. I found the object of so much misgiving on my part, whom I half expected to find frothing at the mouth, what with the heat, and the baiting he had previously undergone, quietly ensconced in a capacious arm-chair by a shady window, with his legs lazily stretched out, and his arms pleasantly folded—a perfect picture of contented repose. Reassured, but full of wonder at a sight in such pleasing contrast to all my anticipations, I readily obeyed his invitation to "take a chair."

At a glance I perceived I had to do with no ordinary man. His face revealed uncommon shrewdness, but there was an expression, besides, of bluntness and boldness that warned an experimentalist to beware. Though I had no intention of the sort, still I felt sure that "soft sawder" would be worse than wasted on Secretary Marcy—it might be thrown back in your own face. There was no pretension to official dignity, nor the least ostentation or semblance of ceremony, but on the contrary, a plain, off-hand manner that put you at ease without enticing familiarity. I observed this and more whilst remarking on the heat of the weather. Whether it was his beatified air of composure that had a sort of defiance about it—that piqued, though it subdued at the same time—I don't know, but I was seized with a reckless desire to give him a shake, in the mataphorical sense, and see what I could get out of him once excited. You can do nothing with a man, or I suppose with a woman either, until you get their blood circulating and their ideas flowing.

Everybody knows in the United States that Secretary Marcy has an affliction, to which the British Foreign Office would, in most people's consideration, be considered a trifle, in an editorial assailant, whose deadly aim makes the toughest politicians tremble at his darts. From some old feud or other the implacable Editor has for years past pursued the beleaguered Secretary through every phase of his official life, and neither his ingenuity nor his ill-will seemed to wear out in the least. I thought the bare mention of his name would infallibly convert the *sang-froid* of the self-possessed Secretary into a torrent of lava, so I resolved to use it, but in a way that would stir up emotion rather than fire indignation.

"If I had expected so pleasant a reception as this, Mr. Marcy," I began, after some desultory observations, "I should have brought you another letter of introduction tendered to me at New York."

"Who from?" demanded the Secretary in his laconic way.

"A former friend of yours," I returned, hesitating, and somewhat afraid of my own gun.

"Who's he?" enquired the unsuspecting Mr. Marcy.

"I dare say you will be surprised, but I hope not offended," I said, expecting to excite his curiosity.

"Ah," said the Secretary, gaping outright.

"Why, Mr. Bennett, of the *Herald*, offered me a letter to you, if I would venture to present it."

To my stupefaction, the Secretary, instead of bolting upright in his chair, his eyes flashing fire, quietly gaped again, and then asked,

"Well, why did you not bring it?"

"But what do you suppose its contents would have been?" I continued, making another desperate effort to rouse him. The Secretary crossed his legs leisurely, and left me to answer my own question.

"Why he meant to say that you had both been enemies long enough, and that he was willing to bury the tomahawk."

I plunged my glance into the Secretary's face, but there was no more commotion there than in a frozen lake. I fell back more than baulked, utterly humiliated. Without moving a muscle or disturbing his legs, the Secretary replied, and without mincing matters, in his way—

"Bennett's a simpleton. I am no enemy of his. I can't tell why he is always writing about me!" I remember that poor old Lear, in the play, was puzzled to know "the cause of thunder," but I was a deal more perplexed in conjecturing the cause of such profound placidity.

"Why, Bennett says," I continued, thoroughly subdued, "that you played him a trick once. That you made use of him when you ran for Governor of New York, and then repudiated him afterwards."

There was something like the shadow of a smile that flickered for a moment about a corner of the Secretary's dry mouth, but it vanished instantly, as if unacquainted with the neighbourhood.

"Bennett has always been under a false impression. I'll tell you how it was." Governor Marcy then related the amusing story which I had often heard from his antagonist, but the versions were, of course, different. I was glad, however, to detect the dissembling Secretary diplomatising with me, for he would never have wasted his time on this forgotten incident if he had not sought to ingratiate his formidable adversary by expecting me to repeat all he had said.

From this topic I went over directly to my own affairs. "One of my objects in visiting you, Mr. Marcy," I resumed, "was to ascertain if there was any remedy for my singular case, and to solicit the advantage of your intervention."

"What is it about?" demanded the Secretary in his curt manner.

"I have a complaint against the British Foreign Office."

At mention of this odious name, which appeared to touch him

more nearly than the one already used, the cautious Minister passed his hand slowly across his face, and finished by pinching his nose, which bit of pantomime conveyed, I suspected, his readiness to serve the Foreign Office in the same fashion if he could ever get his fingers near enough.

"What is it?" he enquired, after a pause.

I made then a brief statement of my case, which had already reached him through various channels. "I am the more emboldened," I concluded, "to appeal to you, as Lord Clarendon informs me that my claim for redress should come through my own Government."

"It is all nonsense," remarked Mr. Marcy, as if soliloquising, for it seemed from his countenance that he was deeply pondering over the matter.

"How so?" I exclaimed, in surprise.

"Why, if I undertake the matter," said the Secretary gravely, "it is the Sardinian Government I must call to account for allowing the British Minister and British Consul to interfere so grossly in an affair which in no wise concerned them. I don't see, though," and he stopped again to reflect—"No, I don't see any good *locus standi* against the British Foreign Office."

The tone of his voice, and, perhaps, something in his manner, gave me the impression that the clear-headed and sure-footed man presiding over the "State Department" felt quite as much regret as I did that he could discover no tangible mode of obtaining even a small victory over that plague of his official life, Her Britannic Majesty's Foreign Office, in atonement for the endless crosses it had occasioned him. His opinion was no great disappointment to me, however, for I had come long ago to pretty much the same conclusion.

"Well, then," I responded, "there is no other way left of winding up the affair to my own satisfaction than to lay the whole history before the world, and I am quite certain that the English public will form a judgment as impartial as our own, and that the Foreign Office will get the worst of it in the end, if my side is considered the best."

"That is your only alternative, as far as I can see," vouchsafed Mr. Marcy, who seemed in no way inclined to protect the Foreign Office from my shaft. "Now-a-days public opinion is your only final court of appeal, both in this country and elsewhere."

The Secretary uttered these words as though he honestly believed in them, which is not always the case with statesmen or diplomatists. By this time it was clear enough to me that the apparently impassive and hardened politician before me had one very tender spot, and I thought it might relieve him were I to probe it a little.

"Well, Mr. Marcy," I observed, in a careless sort of a way, "we have not got Cuba yet."

"No," he replied, rather grimly.

"I believe the country would like to have it, though I am not sure about the East."

"They would agree to purchase it," replied the Secretary, and, of course, he knew.

"And the South?" I queried.

"Would take it anyhow."

"Would the West oppose it, do you think?"

"I think *not*."

"What's the difficulty, then?"

For the first time Mr. Marcy turned round in his chair.

"The English Government," he said, without any sign of anger, but I was sure he was not as contented as he looked.

"What has England to fear?"

"That's what I can't make out," returned the Secretary, turning round again. "It would double her commerce there, at least."

"Well, it is hardly fair," I declared, sympathetically, "for you have gone very far, Mr. Marcy, everybody thinks, to sooth British apprehensions."

"There is no gratitude left in the world, I *do* believe," exclaimed the thwarted statesman, and he attempted to smile, but failed signally. "Why, would you believe it," he continued, getting quite restive, "they won't allow me to have even a coal-yard in Dominica!"

"How absurd," I responded; "they are as bad as the old Trojans with their *Timeo Danaos, et dona ferentes.*"

I don't know what there was in the allusion, but it pacified him almost instantly. Pulling down his waistcoat and smoothing away his old-fashioned ruffles, he remarked, in the spirit of a true philosopher—

"It requires an uncommon deal of forbearance to get along comfortably in this life."

"I wonder, Governor," I said, addressing him by his customary title, "that you don't give Mr. Crampton here a bit of your mind."

"For that matter, I do very often."

This made me very curious, and I bluntly asked, "Do you threaten him?"

"Oh no;" replied the discreet Officer of State, "I only tell him that he is a *most unreasonable* man."

This was the very language of our Prime Minister, and nothing could be more bland than his voice as he spoke; but whether there was something in the emphasis, or in the covert glance of his eye, I cannot tell, but I made up my mind on the spot that if ever Mr. Crampton let his diplomatic visor drop, his head would be in danger. My mind was gradually getting absorbed in meditations of the most engrossing character, and I rose to go. As I pulled on my gloves, I said in the way of a parting remark, "By the by, Governor, I had a chat with Mr. So-and-so lately" (naming a distinguished person), and he surprised me by pronouncing Lord Palmerston greatly overrated, and that "he looked upon him as little better than a blunderer and a sham."

"Mr. So-and-so is a donkey," asserted the plain-speaking Secretary, with what sounded like a growl of hearty contempt.

I was startled at so bold an epithet applied to so prominent a person, but I was glad, indeed, to see that the chief of the "State Department" was not labouring under any illusion as to the skilful adversary he had to deal with.

"However that may be," I answered, smiling, "I should say that Lord Palmerston certainly was rather an awkward customer to encounter in diplomacy or debate."

"Did you ever read his speech in defence of his policy in the summer of 1850?"

"Yes; and his Lordship presented me with a corrected copy."

"Well, then, I say," and the Secretary again appeared to put the utmost reliance on what he said, "that Lord Palmerston, or anybody else, who could make a speech like *that* must be a great man. Wonderful speech that!"

For a moment I allowed him to enjoy a deep conviction undisturbed, for it is rare, indeed, that a Diplomatist experiences a felicity of that sort; but as I retreated to the door the Secretary recovered from his momentary fit of admiration, and enquired after my stay in Washington, whilst tendering me the offer of his hospitality. I was obliged to leave the next morning, however, and saw him no more.

Now, I may have done very wrong, indeed, in violating in this outrageous manner the political sanctity of the "State Department," by relating as faithfully as I can recollect the rambling remarks of Secretary Marcy on matters of so much delicacy and moment. I don't know what the consequences may be; and I should not be astonished if my foot never crossed the threshold of the "State Department" again. But it is not such a fearful operation, after all, to sacrifice oneself for the good of mankind, and I will cheerfully submit to all the pains and penalties of "Coventry" hereafter, if my transgression should be found to have a saving moral and an application. The moral that might be deduced, methinks, from what I have reported is simply this. That a Secretary of State is, in fact, only a mortal like the rest; and that if a Foreign Office, British or otherwise, will be constantly tripping up his heels and obstructing his fairest intentions, it may be counted on as certain that he will, however patient and considerate, take the first chance to avenge the past and guarantee the future.

And now for the application. Need I point to the Enlistment question, which, after exposing England and the United States to the terrible contingencies of war, has, finally, ended with the expulsion of the representative of the Foreign Office at Washington, to say nothing of the Consuls at New York, Philadelphia, and Cincinnati.

Now, can it be seriously mooted, and will any sensible person believe it, that if Mr. Crampton had not acted in so "unreasonable" a manner, by catching maliciously hold of Secretary Marcy's coat-tail, and getting the French Minister, Count Sartiges, always to help him, even when the said Secretary was so innocently employed as to be only bargaining for "a coal-yard in Dominica," I ask, would Secretary Marcy, if he had been differently treated, ever have taken such cruel advantage of the peccadilloes of the said Crampton, when he was, at last, fairly caught and "cornered?" Most assuredly not; and this is just what Mr. Disraeli thought, and boldly declared in the House of Commons.

Is it not high time, therefore, for the people of England of all conditions to look to their Foreign Office? If it had not instructed its representative at Washington to act as he did, we should never have heard of the Enlistment question; and if it had not directed Messrs. Hudson and Brown to keep me locked up for fifteen months in a prison at Genoa, this book would never have been written. The first was near leading to a dreadful calamity; but, I trust, the latter will be infinitely more harmless in its effects.

APPENDIX.

FROM "*LA PRESSE*," OF NOVEMBER 20, 1849.

THE UNITED STATES.

TO M. EMILE DE GIRARDIN—

I have read with the liveliest sympathy the judicious articles you have recently published on the Constitution of the United States.

A stranger to France, the idea of mingling in this discussion would never have occurred to me, but for the reception given by the *Constitutionnel* to the letter of a countryman of mine, Mr. Harrington, of Ohio.

If I address myself to you, in preference, it is because of all the French journalists, you are the least biassed, apparently, by the conclusions you may have formed. It is not any favorite system you seek to establish, but rather the truth that you aim to discover. Disinterestedness like this is so rare, that you are exposed to the doubts of the timid and the sarcasms of the envious. The first shrink from your theories, the last accuse you of insincerity. But if your sacrifices and devotedness aid in resolving the problem of Government, you will be amply compensated, for the triumph of a just idea is the rarest and the purest of victories.

The question that I propose to treat is not merely as to the organization of the Executive power in the United States, or as to the manner it may be modelled in France. What I desire more is to explain the fundamental principles upon which repose the Constitution of the United States, and to which we are indebted for the *durable alliance of order with liberty*—that pretended chimera which for sixty years you have pursued in France, and which for sixty years has flourished with incontestable vigour amongst us.

In order that the merit of the American Constitution may be better appreciated, I will pass briefly in review what preceded it

When the North American Colonies declared their independence, and undertook to constitute a government for themselves, they deposited the supreme power in the hands of a Congress, consisting of a single Chamber only.

In the face of all the dangers of this epoch—anarchy within and invasion without—such was the want of harmony in this organisation, that the confederated States would have succumbed but for the extraordinary capacity of one man, General Washington.

The war finished and their independence established, the victorious States felt the imperious necessity of a better organisation, and the articles or bases of a new Confederation were drawn up and adopted. The Supreme Power, Legislative and Executive, continued to be confided to a single Chamber, which named three Ministers to the respective Departments of Foreign Affairs, War, and Finance. This second experiment at government was not more successful than the first, for after a short experience of six years, the necessity of indispensable modifications became more imperative than ever.

Two serious defects were found in this national government.

The first was the want of sufficient power in the Executive or Administrative Department. The American people were so jealous of their liberty, and so mistrustful of all power, that they refused to invest Congress with the power that was absolutely needed.

The second defect was more grave. The functions, so very distinct, of legislation and administration were exercised by the same body in a single Chamber. There can be no good administration without the complete *Unity* or independence of the Administrative Power. There can be no good laws if the two classes, upper and lower, of every country—in a word, of the Aristocracy and Democracy, do not unite in their creation.

The Confederated States admitted with unanimity that it was impossible to go on under these circumstances. This was the opinion of Washington, and of all the eminent men of the day. It was, also, the conviction of the people.

A Convention, composed of delegates from each State, then assembled, in order to make a third attempt at a Government that would be more practicable.

The existing Constitution is the result. On this occasion the Supreme Power was *divided.* The Executive Power was confided to one only. The Legislative Power was distributed between two Chambers, a Senate, and a House of Representatives. This national Government, in short, was only an imitation of the different State Governments, which were founded on the old English Constitution, where the authority was divided between the King, the Aristocracy, and the people; or, King, Lords, and Commons.

The Constitution had a complete success. It has lasted sixty years,* affording the utmost liberty, and securing the most perfect order.

What is the secret of this success? Does it belong to the Constitution itself, or has it to do with the character of the American people?

I will endeavour to prove that it is inherent in the Constitution. The Americans are not above the level of humanity. They are intelligent and patriotic; yes, but they are governed by the same passions, and influenced by the same interests as other nations.

To appreciate fully the excellence of this Constitution, let us stop for a moment to consider attentively the nature of society. A political system, which is opposed to the nature of man, cannot endure. How many Institutions in ruins encumber the path of history!

Every community contains these three principles—the Monarchical, the Aristocratic, the Democratic.

These principles represent the elements of which all society is composed.

Everywhere, in every country, there is some man who, by his intelligence and force of character, is the necessary chief of the country. He is the natural monarch—to exclude him from his share of power would be to arm him against it.†

In every country there is a select class, formed of all its notabilities, to whom their superiority assigns the first rank. This is the natural aristocracy. To exclude them from their share of power is, manifestly, impossible.

Finally, there is the multitude, and to exclude them from a participation in the Government is an error, nay, an injustice, which is avenged by their eventually overthrowing every Constitution which has overlooked them.

---

* Sixty years from the date of this letter, 1849.

† It may seem to my foreign readers a contradiction to my theory when I assert that in every country the "natural monarch" exists, and yet in my own that men of this class are, of late, excluded from the Executive chair. Such is the fact, and it may arise from the jealous apprehensions of the people. Whatever the cause of exclusion, the men of dominant intellect and will, that I speak of, exist, and it remains to be seen whether the people of the United States are capable of debarring them permanently from power, or whether it is wise to do so.

Therefore, a Constitution which admits these three elements, and isdtributes the supreme power between the Monarch, the Aristocracy, and the Democracy, combines all the conditions of a long duration.

The idea of this *Mixed Government* presented itself to the Legislators of Antiquity. Lycurgus, in his Constitution of Sparta, sought to combine these three principles, but he could not succeed in *balancing* them. He placed the Executive power in the hands of *two* kings. Here was a want of *Unity*. The error was fatal.

Romulus, the founder of Rome, adopted the same idea, and improved on the model traced by Lycurgus. He distributed the supreme power between the King, the Patricians, and the Plebians. The Executive Power had here the indispensable requisite of *unity*. But Romulus, like Lycurgus, failed to harmonise these three principles, which are naturally hostile. These principles cannot exist separately, and yet all the skill of the Ancients could not succeed in combining them harmoniously.

The merit of this solution was reserved for the founders of the Constitution of the United States.

It is evident that the idea of blending these three principles of every society is not new. The profoundest thinkers of the old world, Dionysius, Polybius, and Cicero, all declared that *this was the best of all the forms of Government.* The greatest Legislators, too, Lycurgus and Romulus, endeavoured to carry it into effect. In modern times, Montesquieu in France, and Brougham in England, have given their adhesion to this opinion. The only difficulty consisted in the necessity of finding an organisation such as would conciliate the antagonism of these principles, and so prevent the ruin of the Government. This obstacle must have been grave, indeed, to require so many centuries to surmount it.

What was the simplest means to put an end to this eternal struggle between these principles? Was it to weaken one and strengthen the others? No, for that was just the error of the Ancients. It was necessary, on the contrary, to *establish a perfect equality between them.* This was the precise aim of the American Legislators. How did they effect it? Why, by a simple system, or combination of checks and balances, perpetual and reciprocal. In this way these principles preserve the necessary freedom to their perfect action, whilst they are prevented from falling into those excesses which destroy that equality, ponderation, and independence, which are indispensable.

Let us look into this.

The Executive power, or Monarchical principle, of the American Constitution is confided to a single person called the President. The first great *check* applied to him is the limited time he holds office—that is fixed at four years. Again, he can do nothing without the concurrence of the other powers. He can make neither war nor peace. Even his nomination to places are of no weight until approved by the Senate. But, on the other hand, to make the Executive the slave of the other powers would be to violate the *balance* of the Constitution. To preserve his independence, therefore, the Executive is armed with a *veto*. Yet, this dangerous privilege is limited in its turn. The Executive has, also, the right to retain or dismiss his Ministers at his pleasure; no obstacle whatever interferes. Without entering into further details, it is seen that, in our Constitution, the Monarchical principle enjoys its greatest virtue, that of *Unity*, without which no Constitution can succeed.

The Aristocratic power, or principle, is represented by a body called the Senate, composed of the most eminent men of the country. The number is limited to two for each State, whether large or small. Thus, the States are equalised, whatever the difference of their population or wealth. This power has, in all times, exercised a preponderance by the superiority of its intelligence, but the American Constitution, whilst honoring it, has made no exception in its favor to its system of checks. In the first place, the duration of the Senatorial term is limited to six years, instead of for life. Again, it shares all its legislative functions with the second or Democratic power, and all its executive duties with the President, personifying the Monarchical principle. But although the privilege of independent action has not been conceded, yet this important power has not been rendered subordinate. Its independence has been carefully preserved, for it can refuse, on its own responsibility, to act with the other powers. The essential merit of this power or principle, which is that of *Conservatism*, has been displayed by many striking services to the country.

The Democratic power or principle is represented by a body called the House of Representatives. This power, also, has been regulated with the utmost nicety. It has no executive functions whatever, and its legislative acts are performed in common with the Senate. Still, its independence is guaranteed; for it alone has the right to originate any financial measure. It has, also, the privilege to *impeach* the President, but to the Senate is reserved the prerogative of sitting on his trial.

The wise founders of our Constitution foresaw the danger which would environ the Democratic principle if it were left alone to contend with its rival principles—the Monarchical and Aristocratic. Convinced that these would endeavour, as always, to control it or to corrupt it, they settled upon two years as the proper term for the delegates of the people, concluding that this short period would preserve them from any serious temptations. The Democratic principle possesses one immense excellence—that of the spirit of

Progress. For a Government to feel the salutary effect of this quality, however, it should be united always with the *Conservative* spirit—the essence of the Aristocratic principle—and the two cannot act efficaciously without that *Unity* which is the prime essential of the Monarchical principle.

The Ancients did not succeed, as we know, in reconciling these three principles. Wherefore? The cause of their failure is not to be explained by imputing the blame either to the Monarchical, Aristocratic, or Democratic principles. Each of these naturally obeys the known laws of human nature, and seizes upon the Sovereign Power whenever it can.

How to prevent one encroaching on the others was just the object at which the American Legislators aimed. Twice they broke down, but were triumphant in their third attempt, and the Constitution, of which I have given so imperfect an analysis, is the result.

This model Government has been everywhere adopted throughout the United States. Every town has its Mayor and two Councils, upper and lower; every State has its Governor and two Chambers, the Senate and House of Representatives.

For the three elements I have spoken of are found as well in the village as in the nation; and the first condition for a regular and tranquil Government is to secure a legal orbit for the fundamental principles which represent them.

By way of comparison, this *Mixed Government* may be said to resemble the mechanism which indicates the passage of time. The nature of the Democratic principle, *Progress*, may be likened to the mainspring, which is incessantly at work; whilst *Conservatism*, the attribute of the Aristocratic principle, is represented by the wheel-work; and *Unity*, the essence of the Monarchical principle, is the regulator, which gives steadiness to the whole.

As long as the balance, established with so much felicity by our great Legislators, is scrupulously maintained, the Constitution of the United States will endure unshaken.

I will explain how this exact counterpoise might be disturbed in commenting on the Constitution of another country. This investigation, however, I shall reserve for a second letter.

HENRY WIKOFF,

of New York.

From "*LA PRESSE*," of December 12, 1849.

ENGLAND.

To Emile de Girardin

In my last letter I proposed to show how a Constitution founded on the three principles in question, the Monarchical, Aristocratic, and Democratic, may yet be overthrown. I said I should take, for an example, the Constitution of another country. That country is England, and the Constitution so violated is the famous British Constitution. In undertaking this serious examination, I beg to submit certain personal reflections.

To treat a political question connected with my own country was comparatively easy. The subject was familiar, and I had no fear, above all, of wounding any prejudices. But how many irritated feelings will rise against me on venturing to touch on European politics? An American who speaks of Europe is always under the apprehension of falling into one of two errors—either of giving way to enthusiasm or yielding to a spirit of injustice. A plain Republican, the splendour of her opulence dazzles him, and the *prestige* of her renown overwhelm him. A severe Democrat, the inequality of ranks offend him, and the misery of the populations shock him.

In endeavouring to guard against weakness on one hand, and prejudice on the other, I hope to show myself more sensible of the honor, Sir, you have done me, as well as more worthy of the confidence of my readers.

The English cannot deny me the privilege of discussing their Constitution, for they have carried, even to abuse, the common right of investigation, in attacking with virulence, not merely the institutions of my country, but likewise its society. I will avoid imitating such an example, but will endeavour rather to treat the buestion in a philosophical spirit, and with all the consideration that becomes a descendant of the mother country. In fine, I will seek to be moderate in order to be just.

There are some striking contrasts that offer, at once, between the Constitutions of England and the United States. The one dates from yesterday; the other from many centuries. The one is traditional; the other is written. But for all the rest the resemblance is easy to explain, for one is the product of the other.

The three great fundamental principles, Monarchical, Aristocratic, and Democratic, were borne across the sea by those independent and resolute Puritans, who preferred the pain of exile to the chagrin of seeing the equilibrium of a *Mixed Government* destroyed. They were wedded to the belief that it was the only form of government which guaranteed the liberty of each with the security of all. They carried with them, also, imbedded in their very natures, those inestimable institutions *Trial by Jury*, and the act of *Habeas Corpus*, which soon took root in a soil dedicated to the growth of liberty.

The English boast of their ancient Constitution, and they have great reason to do so, since it affords for the security of person and property such guarantees as do not exist, and never have existed, elsewhere in Europe.

From whence comes this glorious distinction? Their history explains it.

After the Conquest, in 1066, by the Normans, King William and his warrior-barons found themselves in a country conquered but still hostile. Exposed to the same dangers, and impelled by the same voracity for the common prey, they lived for a time in amity.

But, as in all times and all countries, the natural jealousy between the Monarchy and the Aristocracy broke out, and a struggle of interest, coupled with ambition, began. The English people, profoundly indifferent to the aims of either, looked only to what concerned themselves; and during several centuries they gave their support at one time to the King, and at another to the Barons, on condition of certain privileges which they exacted. In this way was brought forth the *Magna Charta*; from hence sprung the act of *Habeas Corpus*; hence, also, the right of the Commons to share with the Barons (the Lords) in Parliament the legislation of the country; hence, finally, by degrees, the division of the Supreme Power between the King, the Barons, and the people—King, Lords, and Commons.

Carried away by its jealous hatred, and by the fears which the Royal prerogatives inspired, the Aristocracy always rallied to the side of the Democracy in its attacks upon the common enemy, until the downfall, at last, of the Royalty decapitated.

Under Cromwell, the Monarchy disappeared, but the Aristocracy was, also, levelled, and thus the *old Constitution was violated.*

Up to that epoch the *Mixed Government*, Monarchical, Aristocratic, and Democratic, existed. Its attributes, it is true, were badly assorted; the necessary limits were not defined; but, although the indispensable balance was not attained, an approximation towards it was made.

The Aristocracy soon saw the error they had committed, and they set to work to repair it. By their efforts the Monarchy was restored, and, then, the struggle between the rival principles recommenced.

Once more the Monarchy sought to wield its prerogatives, and again the Aristocracy opposed it, but this time with greater moderation. The people, as usual, joined readily in the conflict. James II refused to reign without governing, and rather than yield, he abandoned the country.

The Sovereign power then fell into the hands, jointly, of the Aristocracy and Democracy. The first was ready for the crisis; the latter found itself without a leader, but both were unanimous in their hatred of absolute Monarchy. William III accepted the part allotted to the new Royalty, and agreed to give up the exercise of the executive power.*

This was the result of the Revolution of 1688.

The ancient British Constitution, which distributed the supreme authority between the three great elements of the State, ceased to exist. The *Mixed Government,* which had grown out of the Norman conquest, which was better organised, and longer established than anywhere else in the world, was destroyed a second time, in 1688, by the abolition of the Monarchical principle. The shadow of this principle has always survived, but the shadow only.

The Aristocratic and Democratic principles then remained standing face to face. As it was impossible to establish any *balance* between them, it was necessary for the tranquillity of the country that one or the other should abandon its pretensions to power.

The Aristocracy had on its side all the superior intellect as well as the wealth of the country; but neither one nor the other of the rival principles had any force at its command. Intelligence and skill naturally triumphed, and since 161 years the Aristocratic principle has wielded the Government in England.

The Aristocracy, by the simplest manœuvres, has entirely succeeded, up to the present time, in paralysing its rival principles.

At the beginning the usage was established that Ministers should retire after a hostile vote of *Parliament.* The Executive thus fell into insignificance the moment it had no longer the right to retain its Ministers, who depended, as is seen, on the good will of Parliament. Monarchy in England thus became a mere form. In fact, it has preserved neither power nor independence.

The Democratic principle was not long in disappearing from the House of Commons, for its members, being elected by the middle class, and holding their seats for seven years, have always fallen

* He said to the deputation from Parliament, that "he would always ask the advice of Parliament, and that he would ever trust to its judgment rather than his own." History of England, by Macaulay, vol. 1, page 524.

under the control of the Aristocracy, who retain in their hands not only all the honors, but, also, all the resources of the State. Since 1688 the masses have never, by any constitutional means, exercised their legitimate influence over the legislation of the country. The suffrage is so limited,* and elections are made so expensive in England, that the people are obliged to have recourse to threats and to tumultuous assemblages in order to be heard. It is thus apparent how two of those three elementary principles of all governments have been suppressed in England. We may be surprised that they should have submitted for so long a time to the deprivation of their just share in the division of power, but we are forced to admire the art, both ingenious and profound, with which the Aristocratic principle has contrived to maintain its ascendancy.

To understand this more fully, it will be necessary to establish the existence of four great influences in every society, founded on the strongest passions of the human heart. These four influences are the love of religion, of war, of knowledge, and of gain. These predominating influences are represented, or, as one might say, put to profit, by four powerful classes—the Priest, the Soldier, the Thinker, and the Capitalist.

The endless struggle between these influences to subjugate society to their will is the secret of all those convulsions which make the history of the world. The better to succeed they ally themselves invariably to one or the other of the constituent principles of the government. At one time they abandon the Monarchical principle for the Aristocratic, and, at others, divided between themselves, they sustain one principle against the other. In the United States these influences have occasionally striven to acquire an ascendancy over one or all of these elementary principles. The Religious,† the Military,‡ and the Literary influences have failed, but the Financial influence succeeded in establishing a connection with the Government, from which sprung Protective laws and a National Bank. Hence arose our political dissensions.

The Democratic principle perceiving, at last, that this influence was disposed, from its nature, to aid in the undue development of its rival principles, struggled hard to break off the tie. In consequence the National Bank was overthrown, and the Protective laws are fast giving way. The tranquillity of the country will be

---

* The electors for Great Britain and Ireland do not much exceed one million, for a population of near 30 millions.

† Such is the state of religious tolerance amongst us, that sects are innumerable, and their mutual jealousy entirely prevents any connection between them and Government.

It may be said we have no Army, so limited is its numbers.

more firmly established when once the influence of the Financial class no longer weighs upon any of these principles—that is to say, upon the Government.

Let us return to England!

How acted the Aristocratic principle in 1688, in the presence of these four influences exercising great sway in the midst of an advanced civilisation? Intoxicated with its power, did it blindly make war on them? Did it enrage the Religious class by seizing on the rich revenues of the English Church? Did it refuse honors and wealth to the Military class? Did it irritate the Financial class by not promulgating any law which increased its gains? Did it turn the pen of the Thinkers against itself by refusing to them either places or pensions. No! The Aristocratic principle, enlightened by experience, understood its interests far better.

A sagacity beyond all precedent has brilliantly distinguished this principle in England. Instead of wrangling or displaying any sordidness with these powerful classes, it accorded liberally all that was exacted. To the Church, it left its revenues. To the Army, it gave nobility and wealth. To the Capitalists, it granted a National Bank* and Protective Laws. To the Thinkers, it awarded pensions and lucrative sinecures. Thus strengthened and supported, the Aristocratic Government of England has lasted 161 years. It has been pretty rudely shaken now and then; as, for example, in 1832, when it had the air of yielding to the Democratic principle its proper share in the representation, but escaped that emergency by its ingenious *Reform Bill,* which enacted that henceforth every town should have *two* representatives or members in the House of Commons. It followed, therefore, that twenty-four small towns, under Aristocratic domination, with a population of 132,000 inhabitants, were represented in Parliament by 48 members, whilst the democratic town of Manchester, with a population of 240,000, had no more than 2 members.

More recently, in 1845, the Democratic principle accomplished, it is true, a decisive victory in abolishing the *Corn Laws.*

Before pronouncing any judgment upon this Aristocratic Government, there are two important enquiries to be made.

First, has it contributed to the welfare of society, or only promoted the interests of the classes that support it?

Next, what is the probable duration of this Government under such circumstances?

To demonstrate how much the great majority of the community suffers, it is only necessary to cite the facts that daily arise, and

* The Bank of England was founded in 1694.

which are found thrillingly arrayed in the speeches of Lord Ashley,* as well as in Parliamentary reports. A still stronger proof of the excess of poverty is shown in the necessity of creating a system of laws (Poor Laws), for the special purpose of relieving it.

For conclusive evidence, on the other hand, of the benefits conferred on the ruling classes, is it requisite to point to the tax of 38 millions sterling laid upon articles of consumption, which necessarily weigh upon the people, or to the revenues of the Church, some eight millions sterling,† and chiefly borne by the people. Whereas the land-tax in England, mostly contributed by the Aristocracy, does not much exceed one million sterling. The Income-tax, which produces near five millions sterling,‡ falls indirectly on the working classes, for the rich economise in their expenses the sum which the tax yields.

Now for the second inquiry.

The sway of the Aristocratic principle over the Government in England, supported *unanimously* by the influences indicated, would have no other limit than in the patience of the people. Finding the yoke, at last, insupportable, the masses everywhere would imitate the unhappy Romans, and like them, would withdraw to another *Mons Sacer*, until, finally, driven to despair, and overpowered by suffering, they would give themselves up cheerfully to the first invaders.

This monopoly of power, however, by a single principle, is destined in England to another fate. It will fall by the desertion of those very influences which have so long and so skilfully upheld it. Already a branch of the Financial class, the manufacturers, are contending against it at the head of the Democratic principle, and, as I have stated, it was defeated, in 1845, under Cobden and Bright. A portion of the Literary class, headed by such as Carlyle, and the writers in the *Times*, are beginning to assail it with vigorous blows.

It may, then, be considered as inevitable the downfall of the usurpation of the Aristocratic principle in England, and the resurrection of its ancient *Mixed Government*—the one which contains those three elementary principles that contribute to the preservation of Liberty and the maintenance of Order.

I come, finally, to the consideration of the Constitution of France, that noble nation which has done so much for the destruction of

---

* Now Lord Shaftesbury.

† The Church has skilfully managed to set Statistics at defiance by concealing the exact amount it annually extracts from the country, but Mr. John MacGregor, M.P. for Glasgow, and the first Statistician of England, recently remarked to me, that it was considerably above the sum I have stated.

‡ This tax was doubled during the late war, and now produces nearly ten millions.

false dogmas, and for the emancipation of mankind. Her sacrifices and her heroism, through long centuries, render her eminently worthy the gratitude of the civilised world. In my next and last letter may a stranger be permitted to speak of a country which, next to his own, he loves and respects the most.

HENRY WIKOFF,
of New York.

From "*La Presse*," of January 2, 1850.

FRANCE.

To Emile de Girardin—

In my first letter I stated that in every society there existed three political principles—the Monarchical, Aristocratic, and Democratic, which, by their skilful combination, could alone form an indestructible Government, that would guarantee liberty, whilst it maintained order. I adduced, as an example, the Constitution of the United States—the only one in the world where these three principles are found in full play and in perfect harmony.

In my second letter I followed the vicissitudes these principles underwent through the history of England. I showed how, in the beginning, they existed together, but in a state of discord; how, in 1640, the Democratic principle, under Cromwell, vanquished the two other principles; again, how, in 1688, the Aristocratic principle, usurping in its turn, and supported by the four dominant influences of every society, has succeeded in maintaining up to our day its unjust ascendancy.

Now, in my last letter, to prove that I am not amusing myself with vain theories, but that I am treating of the science of Government, I propose to investigate the history of France, which, better than the history of all the other nations of Europe, furnishes a striking demonstration of this truth—viz., that neither of the three principles can permanently govern alone.

Will you allow me to make a single reflection? I have often heard, in foreign countries, the French reproached with the fickleness of their character; but I have always attributed this accusation to ignorance or to calumny. Strange to say, however, I have heard the same thing repeated by the French of themselves.

I invite them to read over again their own history, and they will find themselves forced to the same conclusion as myself, that, instead of being capricious, they are a people as logical as courageous. This is what I shall undertake to prove.

The fall of the Roman Empire is the preface to French history. Historians have given a thousand different explanations of this grand event, but there is only one. It was the new religion, Christianity, which brought it about; for when it proclaimed the equality of all men before God, the Roman people began to understand the injustice of their slavery, and repudiated Paganism. At last, instead of continuing to bear the terrible yoke of despotism, they preferred yielding to the Barbarians, far less to be dreaded than their own tyrants.

The first Governmental principle which reappeared after this moral inundation was the Monarchical. At this epoch of transition and confusion the vital want was *Unity*, and that was just the essence of that principle, as I have explained. For several centuries Monarchy sought to govern society, and with the aid of the Religious influence, at that time all-powerful.

It is proper to observe that Christianity, at its advent, sustained the Democratic principle against Paganism, which was allied to the rival principles. After the downfall of Paganism, however, Christianity went astray by identifying itself with Monarchy, instead of seeking to exercise a beneficent influence over all these Governmental principles alike.

Finally, in the 10th century, the Monarchical principle was overthrown, and the Aristocracy, with the support of the Democracy, seized upon Power, and began to govern by organising the *Feudal System*. During this epoch the Military influence was the strongest, but the Religious influence, also, lent its protection to the Aristocratic Government. It was these two influences that originated the *Crusades*. After the lapse of several ages it became evident that the Aristocratic principle had done nothing but imitate the Monarchical, that is, govern for its own interests. The Democratic principle, disowned and oppressed, abandoned in its turn the Aristocratic principle, and, under Richelieu, the Monarchy once more recovered power. The Aristocratic principle was now entirely excluded from Government; but the Democratic principle was not admitted. It was thus proved that in lending itself first to the Monarchical, and afterwards to the Aristocratic, principle, that it had gained nothing in either case. It was different in England, as I have shown; for after the Norman Conquest the English people, before granting their support to one or the other of these rival principles, demanded certain concessions, such as *Magna Charta* and the *Habeas Corpus* Act.

Under this second restoration of the Monarchy the other two social influences I have named—viz., the Literary and Financial influences—attained their highest development. They allied themselves with the Democratic principle, which, no longer putting faith in the Monarchical or Aristocratic principles, only thought now of grasping at power for itself. The 18th century beheld the spectacle of an ardent contest between the Monarchical principle, supported by the Religious and Military classes, on one side, and the Democratic principle, defended by the Literary and Financial classes, on the other.

The first revolution, in 1789, witnessed the advent to Power of the Democratic principle, which, first, avenged itself for the centuries of suffering it had undergone, and, next, set to work throwing off all those burdens which had been heaped upon it by the rival principles to their own exclusive benefit. Its mission being thus accomplished, it would have done better to have taken for its model the Constitution of the United States in dividing the power with the Monarchical and Aristocratic principles, which are, likewise, imperishable, and possess qualities equally precious.

By not acting in this manner, whether from ignorance or from mistrust, it lost itself. In fact, the necessity of *Unity* became so imperative, in consequence, even, of the useful *Progress* made by the Democratic principle, that the Monarchical principle, under Napoleon, forced itself, for the third time, back into power. It happened then what was sure to follow, for the laws of human nature are there to prove, that when there is no *check* to its will it is certain to run into abuse.

The Monarchical principle entered upon the Government without conditions, and naturally governed for its own advantage. The ingenious example set by the Aristocratic Government of England was followed in France, and the Monarchy sought the support of the social influences. The Religious, Military, and Financial classes rallied to its maintenance, with a view to stability; but the Literary class, in great part, refused to accept its recompenses, or to yield to its menaces. During this epoch the same scheme was carried out as in England—the Clergy were endowed by the State; the Army was honored and enriched; and the Capitalists favored by Protective laws and a National Bank.*

On the fall of the Monarchy, in 1815, the Aristocratic principle returned to power, but disguised in a Constitutional form. Aware that force could avail no longer against its rival principles, as in the middle ages, it transplanted to the French soil the Constitution successfully established in England. For the first time a Parliamentary Government, with Monarchical prerogative limited, and the Democratic principle excluded, was essayed in France. The Monarchy, however, refused its assent to the new organisation, and, stimulated by the Religious influence, attempted resistance, whereupon the Aristocratic principle, allying itself with the Democratic, and reinforced by the Literary and Financial classes, overthrew it in 1830.

A second experiment was made of Parliamentary Government, and this time the Monarchy, mindful of the past, united with the Aristocratic element, and together directed the Government.

* Founded in 1810.

The Democratic principle was, in reality, excluded from power, for the suffrage was limited to 173,000 electors for a population of 35 millions.* The two principles, Monarchical and Aristocratic, being so strong, and the Democratic principle so weak, the same results were reproduced after the same laws, and the interests of the greatest number were sacrificed for the benefit of the few who held the power.

It was unlikely that a people so intelligent and resolute as the French, and who had twice vanquished the rival principles, would long resign itself to its defeat. After manifestations sufficiently significant, the Democratic principle, sustained, in great part, by the Literary class, again revolted in 1848, and again with the same success.

Once more absolute master of power it exhibited the most incontestable moderation. A new Constitution was ordained, but instead of seeking to exclude the rival principles from power, the Democratic principle merely sought to protect itself against their encroachments, in subjecting them to certain restraints, and by assuring to itself broad and solid guarantees. Universal suffrage was proclaimed, and by this means alone the Democratic principle can always exercise a salutary control over the rival principles. In addition, it applied the same check to the Monarchical principle that exists in the Constitution of the United States by limiting its duration to four years.

The Democratic principle was carried too far, however, by its natural apprehensions, and it fell into some grave errors. For example, in refusing a veto to the Executive power it rendered its constitutional independence impossible, and thus the necessary balance between the three Powers could not exist. Also, in refusing re-eligibility, it in no wise encouraged the Monarchical principle to deserve well of the country. The French Constitution, in adopting these precautions, has gone beyond the American Constitution, and so long as they exist an exact counterpoise is impossible. Serious faults have, also, been committed as regards the Aristocratic principle. With a view to check its excesses, the Democratic principle has, with too much temerity, shut itself up in the same chamber with its rival, which derives its value always from its superior intelligence. Aristocracy simply means the intellectual force of any country, which makes it, at the same time, valuable and dangerous. Honors and wealth are the natural and just product of its intelligence; but leaving it the power to monopolise all,

* To be an Elector it was necessary to pay 200 francs of direct taxes, which is equivalent to an income of 1,250 francs.

the masses are deprived of their rights, which are as well founded, and not less sacred.

How can restrictions sufficiently stringent be applied to the Aristocratic principle without injuring its vital independence? This is just the problem the American Constitution has perfectly solved. By giving to it a Chamber apart, and submitting it to the restraints already explained, the Aristocratic principle, whilst it balances the other principles, fulfils its Conservative office.

It follows, therefore, that in the French Constitution are found the three political principles, which history and logic demonstrate are indispensable to a stable and tranquil Government. But in consequence of the apprehensions already alluded to, and which are perfectly natural, the balance necessary to the harmonious action of the three elemental principles does not exist. That is all. It is a state of things, at this moment, preferable to any existing elsewhere in Europe.

In England the Aristocratic principle monopolises the Government, and before the three principles that constitute the basis of its ancient Constitution are restored, that country will have many trials to undergo.

In nearly all the rest of Europe it is the Monarchical principle which governs. As civilisation advances, and I mean by that the union of the three political principles, Europe will be forced to go through the phases of many struggles and revolutions that the United States have already undergone, and to the end of which France seems to be approaching.

There is one remark that it is proper to add. The legislation of France, for the last fifty years, has been the exclusive work of the Monarchical and Aristocratic principles, and engrossed by their own interests, for such is human nature, they have neglected the interests of the Democracy. Whenever, therefore, the present Constitution shall be so improved as to establish the necessary balance between the three Powers, there will still be nothing to apprehend from the ardent activity of the Democratic principle, which, obeying its *Progressive* impulse, will still have much to do in raising its condition to that of its rivals.

In closing the sketch I have just drawn of the brilliant future that awaits France, I do not wish to shut my eyes on the dark cloud that throws its shade over the picture. A senseless struggle is at this moment going on between the three principles that the Constitution recognises. The Aristocratic principle will not yield its just share of power to the Democratic principle, whilst the Monarchical principle, hampered as it is by the restraints of the Constitution, is compelled to fluctuate undecided between them. I cannot help indulging here in a reflection that savours of a reproach to the Democracy. If it does not exercise its legitimate influence over the legislation of the country, of which it has reason to complain, whose fault is it? The Constitution was its own work, and in seeking to surround itself with too many precautions, it has only exposed itself the more to the two hostile principles.

Still it ought to show itself patient, and the more so, that the period of trial is limited. The Democratic principle well knows its force, and it is hardly to be feared that when the final moment arrives that the Monarchical and Aristocratic principles will exhibit so much injustice and thoughtlessness as to insist on the retention of their privileges, and thus risk plunging this great and noble country once more into all the miseries of 1789. Let what will happen, there is but one solution—a *Mixed Government.*

After a whole century of catastrophes there would be found at the end but one remedy—the system of *checks* and *balances* of the Constitution of the United States.

To recapitulate.

There are three political principles which represent the three elements of every human society, viz., Monarchy, Aristocracy, and Democracy.

A Government is only just and durable when these three principles possess an equal share of power and independence, but under such a system of *check* and *balance* that their special virtues of *Unity*, *Conservatism*, and *Progress* may exercise their individual influence upon the laws which govern society.

This Government is designated a *Mixed Government.*

There exist, also, four great social influences, which must be carefully taken into account—the Religious, Military, Literary, and Financial influences, that are represented by four classes, the Priest, the Soldier, the Thinker, and the Capitalist.

The history of all nations show that these four classes invariably seek, with a view to their own interests, to connect themselves with Government in order to sway it.

It follows from these premises, that a *Mixed Government,* free from all alliance with clerical, military, literary, or financial institutions, is the only one which presents the certainty of duration and tranquillity, because, then, *liberty* is united with *order*.

The Government of the United States approaches the nearest to this perfection; but still its alliance with any financial influence has yet to be dissolved. Amongst other nations, the Government of France resembles most the American Government; nevertheless, the three principles which its Constitution recognises have yet to be regulated, and the connection kept up alternately with the classes above-mentioned ought to disappear. It must be admitted, however, that an immense advance towards this consummation has been made within these last sixty years.

I have been too impartial, I fear, not to have offended all parties. My sole object has been to speak the truth. This justice, I trust, the French Press will not refuse me, if it is thought useful or timely to discuss the ideas which I have submitted to its appreciation.

HENRY WIKOFF,
of New York.

Since the appearance of these letters in Paris, in 1849, the "dark cloud" I alluded to has burst. The "senseless struggle" between parties that I spoke of, terminated in December, 1851, and as might have been foreseen. I stated that the Aristocratic principle would not yield its just share of power to the Democratic principle, whilst the Monarchical principle, hampered by Constitutional restraints, was forced into a state of inaction. Such a condition of things could only lead to a catastrophe, and the Aristocratic principle has paid the penalty of its third attempt to erect in France the Parliamentary Government of England.

At the close of '51, the Monarchical principle united with the Democratic, and, supported by the Religious and Military influences, took possession of the State. A Constitution was adopted, which was the necessary consequence of preceding events. The three fundamental principles were admitted, but no effort was made to balance them. The Monarchical principle reserved for itself the largest share of power, but the Democratic principle was guaranteed its independence, under certain well-devised restraints. The Aristocratic principle, however, was reduced to well-nigh a nullity.

So long as harmony exists between the Monarchical and Democratic principles, this Constitution will endure, and the Democratic principle cannot fail to derive important advantages, not only from its joint share of power, but from the identity of interests that constitute the basis of its present alliance.

It is not to be supposed, however, that the Aristocratic principle, which, as I have said, is the intellectual force of the country, will ubmit to its subordinate position longer than it can avoid.

It has fallen through its own excesses, and its actual degradation is a just punishment, and may be a profitable lesson. Sooner or later it must recover its legitimate influence, but there is little to fear from its acquiring again an undue ascendancy.

The history of the last sixty-seven years in France, plainly demonstrates that under a *Mixed Government* only, with a nice adjustment of *check* and *balance*, can *Liberty* and *Order* be permanently consolidated.

SARATOGA.

A Story of 1787.

NEW YORK:
W P. FETRIDGE & CO., PUBLISHERS,
FRANKLIN SQUARE.
BOSTON:
WILLIAMS & CO., 100 WASHINGTON ST.
1856.

THE

OLD VICARAGE.

A NOVEL.

BY MRS. HUBBACK,

AUTHORESS OF

"THE WIFE'S SISTER," "MAY AND DECEMBER,"

ETC. ETC.

NEW YORK:

W. P. FETRIDGE & CO., PUBLISHERS,

FRANKLIN SQUARE.

MY FIRST SEASON.

BY

BEATRICE REYNOLDS.

EDITED BY THE AUTHOR OF

"COUNTERPARTS," AND "CHARLES AUCHESTER."

NEW YORK:
W. P. FETRIDGE & CO., FRANKLIN SQUARE.

www.ingramcontent.com/pod-product-compliance
Lightning Source LLC
LaVergne TN
LVHW020209110826
845151LV00003B/658
* 9 7 8 1 4 2 5 5 3 4 9 2 9 *